THE IMMIGRANT HERITAGE OF AMERICA SERIES

Cecyle S. Neidle, Editor

Great Immigrants

by

Cecyle S. Neidle

Twayne Publishers, Inc.   ::   New York

This book is dedicated
to the memory of
Marks Neidle

FOREWORD

General readers and scholars alike should welcome *Great Immigrants*, the most recent volume from Mrs. Neidle's spirited pen. For here she presents a group of twelve outstanding but too-little-known Americans of foreign birth—sketches their backgrounds, impersonal as well as personal; describes conditions in America at the time of their arrival; analyzes specific reasons for migrating; and then gets on with the main business of revealing how the lives of the immigrants became intertwined with the growth and development of the United States. In her biographies, brief but comprehensive, she presents a record of Old-World frustrations and barriers, New-World opportunities and challenges, ultimate success and notable contributions by individuals who overcame both the handicap of feeling inadequate and the debilitating effects of poverty. All this she does with great competence—at times with brilliance—as well as with an almost limitless store of understanding and sympathy.

This is no record of easy success. The emphasis is on the hunger and search for freedom—freedom from distinctions of religion, race, and class, freedom to live out the dream of fully realizing one's potential and to provide opportunity for one's children. The immigration story as a whole is the story of this search for freedom—but of freedom bought at a price—and Mrs. Neidle never lets one forget it. The immigrant found that he was not quite at home in the New World, and that success—that will-o'-the-wisp—called for an effort on his part greater than was demanded of the American of older stock. If his education, social status, and experience of life in the homeland tended to equalize the struggle somewhat, so much the better, but he quickly learned that he was a "stranger in a strange land" and that he must struggle hard for acceptance against the barriers of prejudice and language.

It is interesting to note that Mrs. Neidle has selected as the subjects of her study people who might be regarded as "typical" immigrants, avoiding the temptation—in an effort to reveal America's debt to the newcomer—of selecting well-known persons like Alexander Hamilton, Carl Schurz, and Albert Einstein. Similarly, she has resisted the tendency to emphasize the refugees from persecution of the period following Hitler's rise to power. And with good reason, as her purpose in large measure has been to focus on persons "who are no longer accurately recollected or recollected at all," and to direct attention to some who have died recently, or who are still alive and have remained almost unknown—individuals who, if they have received much in the New World, have also given manifold in return.

The appearance of *Great Immigrants* can only please those who have given years to the study of immigration. Although there is some tendency in the academic profession to recognize the part played by the immigrant in America, as a nation we have yet to attain to that maturity of mind which draws no unnatural distinction between citizens because of their country of origin or time of arrival. Despite a considerable body of material put together by men trained for research and exacting in their standards, some scholars brand as "filiopietistic" the most careful studies of migration and immigrant life. In fact, it is still possible, in a serious reading of the history of the United States, to find little enlightenment concerning the immigrant except as a hewer of wood and a drawer of water, whose fortune it was to supplement the labor force that exploited American resources and turned the wheels of an expanding industry. A look at the careers of men like Gallatin, Altgeld, Roebling, Carlson, Godkin, Tesla, Waksman, and others should go a long way toward correcting such a distortion.

It is encouraging, too, that Mrs. Neidle has included among her twelve immigrants not only politicians, scientists, a physician, and a labor leader, but also a man like Rölvaag, who sought to provide an attitude toward Old-World cultures and an interpretation of the word *American* that would do justice to a great nation and at the same time prove the truthfulness of early immigrant statements about American courtesy and hospitality. Herman Badillo, speaking as a Puerto Rican, is quite right in stressing that until we discard our indifference to Puerto Rico and to Puerto Ricans and other disadvantaged peoples—foreign-born and natives of the United States—there is little hope of our understanding or of our being understood by the minority groups in this country and the many peoples of this world. Just as we leave a treasure-trove of sources for our natural history buried in the files of foreign-language newspapers and correspondence, so we also fail to draw on our varied and almost inexhaustible human resources in meeting the domestic and foreign problems of our day.

Students of American history have often observed that the victims of nineteenth-century "Know-Nothingism" were themselves inclined at a later date to look condescendingly on recently arrived immigrants. Thus, the Germans and the Irish regarded the Italians, Greeks, and Slavs with disfavor. The latter, in turn, have been anything but friendly to Mexican Americans and Puerto Ricans. The prejudice and bigotry shown the Chinese and Japanese are reflected again and again in the immigrant press. And most Americans of European origin have been consistently hostile and arrogant in their dealings with Blacks. Though present from Colonial days, the Blacks, too, have been strangers in America, their contributions largely ignored or overlooked. They are the exception to a general truth proclaimed by the author: "natives in the grip of poverty could at least feel they belonged."

One of the tragedies of the American epic lies in the fact that immigrant leaders generally have been either indifferent to ethnic groups other than their own or too preoccupied with the problem of being favorably accepted by older Americans to sense the interrelatedness of the problems confronting the immigrants.

All too often they have sought to win esteem by downgrading other groups. Frequently they have worked mainly for their own interests.

Not Mr. Badillo. Toward the conclusion of her absorbing study of *Great Immigrants* Mrs. Neidle wisely quotes a statement by this lawmaker that in his "Urban Strategy" "the voices of Irish, Italians, Greeks, Blacks, and Puerto Ricans would be heeded." We can safely assume that he would be willing to include "the voices" of any other native or immigrant group.

Kenneth O. Bjork
Northfield, Minnesota

Professor of History at Saint Olaf College
Editor Norwegian-American Historical Association

PREFACE

Darwin tells us that all life is struggle. The principle underlying Natural Selection is that all life—animal and vegetable—must continuously exert itself to survive, or suffer extinction. An extension of the struggle deriving from Natural Selection is the effort to go beyond surviving to surpassing. Probably it is because of man's "noble qualities . . . his god-like intellect," which Darwin recognized in the closing paragraph of his *Descent of Man,* that humans are driven to make the additional effort to secure some of that recognition which lifts an individual above the mass of his fellow beings. To win, to triumph over one's difficulties, is one of man's instinctual drives.

This book concerns itself with a specific group of individuals and their conquest of obstacles, severe enough to require more than the average endowment of courage and perseverance. The men whose life stories follow were at one time all aliens in our land. Consequently, in order to make a mark on their society more effort was required of them than of those who were brought up from birth in the American way of life. Yet it can be said of all included herein but one, that in some way they surpassed many of their contemporaries, foreign-born or native.

One of the burdens afflicting newly arrived immigrants was that the effect of transplantation made them susceptible to an "occupational disease," as it were, which showed itself in a loss of self-confidence, followed by a crippling feeling of inadequacy. The handicap of being shut off from communication—an inability which characterized all but English-speaking immigrants—isolated them and deepened their sense of inferiority.

An additional stumbling block was that most of them had to cope with economic insecurity, if not with grinding poverty. Though indigence is not limited to immigrants, natives in the grip of poverty could at least feel they belonged. It was their

America; they had a place in it from which they could not be ousted. They could demand change and sometimes they took action, as the did under the leadership of Jacob S. Coxey and others, when they organized a march on Washington to present "a living petition to Congress." Among the suppliants there were workmen of foreign birth, but the leadership was in the hands of natives.* They did not gain their purpose, but they succeeded in calling attention to their plight. However, aliens could not criticize freely, for they ran the risk of being silenced by the pointed question: "Who sent you an invitation to come here? Go home if you don't like it!" The recognition that as immigrants they had no standing was instantaneous. They knew themselves to be scorned, disparaged; frequently they were threatened. Even the educated and the skilled, who brought gifts of special training urgently needed by a developing society, did not always receive cordial treatment. A sense of inferiority was the inevitable corollary of their status as immigrants.

Yet countless numbers of them overcame all handicaps and succeeded magnificently. Why?

Some had had very good educational preparation of the kind that was marketable, ultimately if not immediately. Others had good reason to hope that they could continue their education as soon as they had mastered the language. For them it was comparatively easy to forge ahead. But for many the impetus to overcome the onus of their situation arose out of the immigrant experience itself. It did not take long to realize that the individual who did not want to remain forever a robot who worked to live and lived to work must strain as never before to make something of himself, whether as an agricultural settler, industrial worker, or in any of the professional or intellectual endeavors. The challenge, then, was embedded in their

---

* In 1894 several attempts were made to lead armies of the unemployed in a march on Washington to agitate for the adoption of work programs. The locus of protest was in the Midwest and Northwest—"Populist country." See Donald L. McMurray, *Coxey's Army* (Boston, 1929), pp. 130-72, *passim.*

situation. America helped in furthering ambition, not by easing the way, but by not placing in their paths the kind of barriers that had been hindrances in Europe since time immemorial—such as distinctions of class and racial or religious discrimination.

Not until the period dominated by Hitler were immigrants given any kind of *direct* official aid, or favored treatment, by the American authorities, and even then the considerations they received extended only to some and did not go beyond the easing of entrance requirements. The rule was: "Hands off." Those who succeeded in distinguishing themselves did it by their own efforts. The much vaunted American "opportunity" lay in the fact that the road to success was as open to the foreign-born as to anyone else. Uncle Sam never interfered with attempts by anyone to distinguish himself; he was blessedly impartial.

It was no small task of elimination to choose twelve out of a multitude who found in the American environment an overflowing measure of fulfillment. How and why were these twelve selected? Why they and not others?

The author admits that any number of individuals might have been chosen who are equally deserving of being pointed to as outstanding. Space is always a compelling reason for limitation. Another is fallibility of judgment. One method that was *not* followed was to select the dramatis personae on the basis of national origin, that is, under the restriction of: no more than one from any national group, or one from every national group. Thus, four Germans are included while many ethnic groups are unrepresented. However, the inference that some ethnic groups have been omitted because there are no worthy representatives among them is unwarranted; each nationality can rightfully boast of its share of individuals who made their mark in American society. Nor were they chosen on the basis of specific types of accomplishment: one from each of the various fields of endeavor—the areas of public service, business, the professions. Nor were they chosen on the basis of specific criteria—as one might characterize Andrew Carnegie as being the wealthiest and Albert Einstein the brainiest among the foreign-born. The only yardstick was: Do or did their accomplishments in American life entitle them to being considered outstanding?

The author observed one restriction: to let those who are so well known that they have not been forgotten rest in their well-deserved glory. This explains why such illustrious men as Carl Schurz, Andrew Carnegie, Samuel Gompers, Felix Frankfurter, and others of their ilk are absent from these pages. Instead, it seemed the better part of wisdom to concentrate on those who are no longer accurately recollected or recollected at all. More than half fall into the category of being remembered only if the memory is joggled, although their roles in American life would be recalled without too much prodding. Too many have remained much more obscure than their accomplishments warrant; three are alive and only two among them would be easily identified.

The question might well be raised why no women were included in this volume. They were deliberately omitted because a special volume by the same author on outstanding women immigrants is in preparation.

One more explanation seems to be called for. It concerns the specific format of the book which includes two historical essays for each individual whose life and activities on the American scene are set forth herein. One essay deals with the European scene the immigrant has left behind, which has caused him and others like him to break the ties with his homeland; the other depicts the situation in America which he and other immigrants encountered at that particular time in our history. In certain instances, as for example with medicine and science it seemed desirable to trace the history of those subjects from the beginning of the American experience.

The author claims impartiality toward all and sympathy for the black sheep who appears as a pitiful victim of malevolent fate. As these characters are presented in their strengths and weaknesses, playing out their lives in the American world, the reader is welcome to bestow or withhold his sympathy, admiration, or scorn.

ACKNOWLEDGMENTS

To offer one's thanks to those who have helped in the creation of a book is a happy task. My first obligation is to Professor Kenneth O. Bjork, Professor of History at Saint Olaf College and Editor for the Norwegian-American Historical Association, who counseled, then read the whole manuscript and kindly wrote a Foreword to the whole endeavor. I also owe no less of a debt to Professor Sigmund Diamond of Columbia Univeristy, who read the manuscript through and offered valuable comments.

The manuscript was read in part by the following experts in the various fields of the history of immigration: Professor Arlow Andersen of Michigan State University, who generously offered material from his own files; Professor Clifford A. Hauberg of Saint Olaf College, who shared with me his knowledge about Spanish-speaking minorities; Professor Gerald Govorchin of the University of Miami, who advanced pertinent suggestions; Professor Leo Schelbert of the University of Illinois, who called attention to material with which he was familiar. I also offer my sincere appreciation to Mr. Leon Stein, editor of the labor newspaper "Justice" who made himself available for consultation; to Mrs. Louisa Quintero, newspaperwoman, who contributed many facts about Puerto Rican life; and to Congressman Herman Badillo, who despite the pressures on his time permitted himself to be interviewed time and again. Lastly, I thank Mr. Jacob Steinberg, publisher, who cut through and disposed of a morass of details.

But even a large number of well-meaning counselors cannot always eliminate errors of fact and conception. For these I assume complete responsibility.

Cecyle S. Neidle

CONTENTS

Nothing great was ever achieved without enthusiasm.

Ralph Waldo Emerson

ALBERT GALLATIN
1761-1849

Servant of the Country

The constitution had barely gone into effect when this young, well-educated Swiss started his political career. He advanced rapidly from the legislature of the state of Pennsylvania to Congress, where the soundness of his fiscal views earned him the appointment as secretary of the Treasury under Presidents Jefferson and Madison.

He financed the Louisiana Purchase under President Jefferson; he struggled to find the funds for the successful prosecution of the War of 1812 under President Madison. Another noteworthy achievement was his role as one of the peace commissioners who helped to arrange peace terms between Great Britain and the United States at the conclusion of the War of 1812.

Geneva in the Late Eighteenth Century

Long before the founding of the North American colonies, there existed a small republic on the shores of Lac Leman. It was the city state of Geneva. In 1536, while the Reformation was sweeping Germany, the Genevese deposed their feudal lord, a prince bishop (with the help of a Gallatin[1]) and adopted Protestantism. At the same time Jean Calvin, a fugitive from France who had been living in Basel, appeared in Geneva. Calvin reinforced the teachings of the native Genevese, Guillaume Farel, by imposing a theocratic government on Geneva, thus turning the city into a bastion of "Calvinism."

[1]

Geneva was no true republic, for, like Venice (a republic since the Middle Ages), it was ruled by an oligarchy. Even during the boyhood of Albert Gallatin, more than two hundred years after Calvin, no more than one-twelfth of the male population was enfranchised.[2] Those who could vote elected the chief officers of the city at a meeting at St. Pierre's Cathedral, whose lofty spire dominates the skyline of Geneva to this day. The legal machinery that was in force during the late eighteenth century resembled the voting system of the Puritans in seventeenth-century Boston, who were Calvin's direct spiritual descendants. In the Massachusetts Bay Colony only church members could vote and no one not specifically declared one of the "Elect" was permitted to be a church member. In Geneva authority was exercised by two councils, whose members, said to have been eleven,[3] came from a group of highly placed families of French or Italian descent. In these councils Gallatins were frequently prominent. Public offices were likely to be handed down from father to son or heir. Though by the eighteenth century the moral climate had become more lenient than during Calvin's lifetime, the injunction against ostentation in dress, jewels, carriages, and other symptoms of luxurious living was strictly maintained. Anything even faintly suggestive of moral taint was condemned. Bankruptcy was interpreted as a sign of moral turpitude, for the children of bankrupts could not hold public office.[4] This might explain why Johann August Sutter, finding himself bankrupt in 1834, preferred escape to America to facing the consequences in Switzerland. While members of the middle class possessed the vote, they were politically impotent. This condition caused periodic unrest, even clashes between the aristocratic faction and the disadvantaged. A tradition of resentment against the rich and the powerful lingered, for long after Switzerland had received a liberal constitution, the watchmakers of the Swiss Jura could be depended upon to give their support to radicals of all hues.[5]

A more beneficial aspect of Calvin's system was to encourage the spread of education and knowledge among the people (for the reason that Calvin subscribed to the idea that in the primitive church one man was the equal of another). The children of citizens could obtain free of charge a complete education from the primary grades through professional school. Albert

Gallatin was a beneficiary of this system and the advantages of free public education so impressed him that throughout his lifetime he remained devoted to the idea of promoting education in America.

However, opportunities in Geneva for educated young men were strictly limited. Consequently, Switzerland became an exporter of young men of training and ambition.[6] Among the talented sons of Geneva who developed notable careers outside their birthplace was Jacques Necker, who, as finance minister to Louis XVI, preached thrift and efficiency to the French court. Had his advice been heeded, the American colonies might not have secured France's financial support for the War of Independence. Albert Gallatin also distinguished himself in the field of finance, thus earning the epithet, "another Necker." But at the same time Geneva was also the refuge of such religious and social rebels as Calvin and John Knox, Voltaire and Rousseau. After 1850, when Russia and Germany became hives of revolutionaries, Geneva became a center to which radicals fled. It was the first stop of Mikhail Bakunin, Sergei Nechaev, Johann Most, Enrico Malatesta, Elisée Reclus, and others.[7]

The ferment following the French Revolution brought many popular reforms to Switzerland. In 1848 a new constitution was established that guaranteed democratic principles. Thus, Switzerland became one of the more liberal states of Europe. With slight changes this constitution is still in effect.

America during the Post-Revolutionary Period

Until the battle of Yorktown in August of 1782, when the British General Cornwallis surrendered, American energies were concentrated on the winning of the Revolution. Yorktown was a decisive defeat for Great Britain, yet the British continued to hold New York, Charleston, and Savannah. Though Britain indicated that she recognized the independence of the "Thirteen United States of North America," as she looked upon the victorious colonies, there was reason for worry. Would the Mississippi form the western boundary? Would the West beyond

the Appalachians remain in American hands, or would the
northern half be kept by Britain? Would Britain retain Florida,
or would it be ceded to Spain?—which, indeed, did happen.

Negotiations began in Paris in the spring of 1782, and, sur-
prisingly, England, wishing to remain on friendly terms with
her former dependents, was willing to grant the new sovereign
state a favorable treaty. Congress under the Confederation
ratified it with twenty-three members present. But Great Britain
continued to hold the military forts of the Northwest for the
protection of Canadian fur traders, thus encouraging the Indian
tribes to resist the expansion of the frontier. Great Britain did
not agree to withdraw from the western forts until Jay's Treaty
of 1794, which was debated in Congress when Albert Gallatin
was serving his first term as a representative of the state of
Pennsylvania.

Though under the Articles of Confederation a new and revolutionary government had been brought into existence even
before the actual outbreak of war and radical governments were
established in many of the thirteen states, universal manhood
suffrage was still several decades away. Property qualifications
were retained in every state, except in Vermont, where the right
to vote was given to all men over twenty-one. (Vermont did
not become a state until 1791.) In some states a man had to
be a landholder to be eligible to vote; in addition, higher property qualifications were required of office holders. When voting
qualifications were finally removed in the older states, it was
due to the example of the new "western" states. This did not
occur until the nineteenth century was well under way.[8]

The new nation had gained the Mississippi boundary, but
title to some of the western lands were held by six eastern and
southern states under original grants from the British crown.
These were slowly ceded to the central government; not until
Georgia surrendered her claim in 1802 was the cession of the
western territories to Congress completed.

Settlement beyond the Appalachians was intensely desired
by pioneers in search of land and opportunities in new territories and by the national government, to whom sales of land
represented a source of revenue which was urgently needed.
Government under the Confederation lasted until 1789, when
government under the Constitution took over. Impotent in many

ways, the old Congress did its best work in organizing the West. To Thomas Jefferson belongs the credit for the Ordinances of 1784 and 1785, which set up the rules by which the western territories were to be divided into states, and which also provided the plan of government until they could be admitted to statehood.

From 1785 activity in the purchase of western lands was greatly stepped up. Companies were organized, notably "the Ohio Company of Associates" and "the Scioto Company," which acquired options to millions of acres along the Ohio River at two-thirds of a dollar an acre. These land speculators proved overoptimistic, and some of their holdings had to be dropped. The price of land fluctuated. In 1796, it was two dollars an acre, but by 1804 it had dropped to a minimum price of $1.64 an acre and later to $1.25. Agitation for lower land prices, even to make land free, was constant, until, in 1862, in the midst of the Civil War, the Homestead Act was put into effect. Under this legislation natives and foreigners (provided the latter declared their intention of becoming American citizens) received 160 acres free. After living on the land and making necessary improvements, the individual became its exclusive owner.

Between the pioneers and the settled East there existed a lively antagonism. Easterners considered the rifle-toting pioneer brash and uncouth. To the westerners, the East was composed of enclaves of privilege. To the easterners, the new settlers constituted a potential menace in drawing off labor, in their clamorous assertions of democratic principles, and in their unceasing demands for internal improvements. From the point of view of Rousseau and his disciples, the men and women dwelling in the forests and on the prairie were uncorrupted children of nature—"noble savages"—but few easterners saw much that was noble in them.[9] The Constitution had not yet gone into effect when, in 1790, Albert Gallatin settled among the pioneers of Pennsylvania and began a political career.

I

It was in the year 1780, when the Revolution was in full swing, that a nineteen-year-old Genevan decided on a bold move—to go to America and to make an appraisal of his chances of success.

A tall, gangling, sharp-featured youth with dark hair and piercing eyes, he was not prepossessing in appearance; but he was bright, well educated, and very good at mathematics. His intention was to remain in the New World if he met with encouragement; if not, to return to Geneva.

Like many an immigrant before and after him, he must have spent many hours on the sailing vessel dreaming of the future in a new country and wondering what was in store for him. In those days any young man of good health and spirits had reason to hope that with luck he would meet with success, unless, like Gallatin's childhood friend, who was accompanying him, he were to sicken and die young. No sober young man would have dared to imagine that within two decades he would become one of the important men in the government of the new nation. Gallatin's success exceeded anything he could have expected. Only one other newcomer was slated to play as important a role in American political life as Gallatin. He was Carl Schurz, who came to America seventy years later. One who had made a very good start earlier than Gallatin was Thomas Paine, but he did not retain the esteem of Americans for a long time. As for Schurz, his political career was by comparison with Gallatin's of short duration. While Schurz was compelled to leave Germany as a consequence of his involvement in the Revolution of 1848, Gallatin came in search of opportunity and adventure. But essentially the quest of the two was the same: to find a niche that would provide an outlet for their abilities in freedom and honor.

In 1780 the political future of the colonies was still uncertain. Gallatin drifted into politics by accident; Schurz passionately hoped for the opportunity to enter the political arena and, as he reveals,[10] in his thoughts he was preparing himself for it as he was deciding to leave England, his first place of exile, for America. By the time Schurz arrived in 1851, Gallatin was dead two years after a long and fruitful life, during which he had been instrumental in saving the young nation from many financial and political pitfalls. Gallatin's contribution was in the field of finance and diplomacy; Schurz's was that of an idealistic political servant, newspaperman, and reformer.

Though Gallatin's work demanded a practical point of view, he was at the same time idealistic. In his aversion for slavery he anticipated the reaction of European immigrants of the nineteenth century. Though he showed his opposition to slavery in specific actions, the challenge to take an active part against it did not come in his lifetime. To fight for abolition was Schurz's opportunity. Schurz was the first German-born senator (for a short period only) and cabinet member (under President Hayes), but it was Gallatin who was the first foreign-born senator and cabinet member. While Schurz is held to be the best known and the most venerated of all the foreign-born, Gallatin never received the recognition due him for his able and devoted service to the welfare of the nation.

One measure of the respect Gallatin inspired in those who knew of his work, is to be found in Henry Adams' estimate of him. Adams, the grandson and great-grandson of two presidents, was an acerb as well as a shrewd observer of men and events. Adams declared that within twenty years of his arrival in America Gallatin appeared to him to be

perhaps the best informed man in the country; for his laborious mind had studied America with infinite care and he retained so much knowledge of European affairs as to fit him equally for the State Department or the Treasury.[11]

Even when evaluating Gallatin alongside of his grandfather, John Quincy Adams, sixth president of the United States, when Gallatin and Adams were peace commissioners following the War of 1812, Henry Adams states: "...he [Gallatin] was properly head of the mission," and declares that "only the authority and skill of Gallatin saved the treaty."[12] It was a meaningful admission for someone who was known to venerate his family and particularly the achievements of his two progenitors who had served as chief executives of the nation.

II

Albert Gallatin was the son of a distinguished family who had belonged to the minor nobility of Savoy and had settled in Geneva in the sixteenth century. In his biography of Gallatin Henry Adams mentions that the Gallatin family, then known as "Gallatini," may have descended from a Roman consul in the year 494. The family had the right to use the "de" in front of their name, a prerogative they rarely exercised. Having lost both parents by the time he was nine, his upbringing was entrusted to a distant female relative whom his mother had held in high regard. At twelve he entered the College of Geneva, and at fifteen, the Academy of Geneva, an always superior institution to which, a hundred years later, the celebrated Harvard philosopher, William James, would send his son. Today, a visitor sitting on a bench in the ancient quadrangle facing the university buildings will encounter students of all races, speaking a variety of languages.

When the young man graduated at nineteen, he received several prizes, including one in mathematics. But he was undecided as to what course to pursue. He was not interested in law, the ministry, commerce, or in entering the army of a neighboring prince. Geneva offered no other outlets to an educated young man of good family.

During his boyhood and youth Jean-Jacques Rousseau, then living as an exile in Geneva, provided a powerful intellectual stimulus to young people who rejected the indiscriminate acceptance of standards current in the Old World. The new experiment that was being put to the test on the American continent held out a strong promise to a young man in quest of experience. The young university student had a smattering of English. He and a similarly minded young friend made their plans to leave Geneva by stealth, for both knew their families would object. They had the equivalent of four hundred dollars. While they waited for their ship to sail they purchased a cargo of tea, for which they hoped to find a good market in the American colonies. Even then Gallatin seemed to have had good business sense.

They landed in Massachusetts and found Boston a busy seaport that bore little resemblance to an unspoiled Arcadian spot, as the young romantics had envisaged it. Their first reaction, like that of millions of later immigrants, was one of homesickness and of disappointment by the difficulties with which immigrants were confronted. Yearning for bucolic simplicity, they betook themselves with some goods they hoped to be able to sell to the Maine frontier, where a small American garrison was stationed. They sold them four hundred dollars' worth of goods and received a warrant on the Treasury, but Treasury notes were hard to cash and they were forced to accept one hundred dollars in cash. This severe loss made their financial position precarious.

Upon returning to Boston, they found that friends of Gallatin's guardian in Geneva had alerted someone to help them. The outcome was that the young men were offered positions as tutors of French at Harvard College. The tuition was paid directly to the tutors by the parents of the students who wanted to be instructed in the French language. Among Gallatin's students were the sons of some of the most prominent New England families, soon to be identified as Federalists (advocates of a federal union between the states, and the adoption of the Constitution). One of his students was Harrison Gray Otis, who became the foremost leader of the Federalists and a champion of the Hartford Convention.[13] When Gallatin was in Congress, Otis was to refer to him contemptuously as "a foreigner who had come to this Country without a second shirt to his back," a remark as invidious as it was untrue, for which Otis later apologized. But Henry Adams, whose fitness to act as social arbiter cannot be questioned, declared: "Gallatin was an aristocrat . . . born and bred a gentleman."

The two young men remained at Harvard for two winters, but their ambitions did not lie in the field of teaching French to young men who considered themselves superior to foreigners and looked down upon them. For this they had not come to America. After securing a recommendation from the authorities at Harvard testifying to his "unblemished character," Gallatin decided to proceed south. He was accompanied by a new acquaintance, his childhood friend having decided to try his luck in Jamaica, where he soon died.

Philadelphia enchanted the young Genevan as it was to enchant Johann August Roebling,[14] an immigrant from Germany, half a century later. By then Gallatin had come to be convinced that America was "the freest country in the universe." With restored enthusiasm, the young man entered into a partnership to buy a tract of one hundred and twenty thousand acres in western Virginia, for which his new friend advanced the money. It was an out-and-out speculation as popular then as investments in the stock market are today. Later, when he received an inheritance from the estate of his grandfather, he added to his holdings and bought a farm in Pennsylvania on the Mononga-hela River, which he named "Friendship Hill." Among the tracts of land he owned, one became the seat of a glass factory. In time it became successful, but he never made any money on his investments in land. In the 1830's he sold all his holdings at a sacrifice.[15]

Continuing to travel farther south, he became acquainted in Richmond with a young girl, Sophie Allegre, the daughter of a respectable boardinghouse keeper. A gentle, well-raised girl, she charmed the young man. Despite the objections of her mother, who had expected her daughter to make a more pros-perous marriage, they were married and Gallatin took her to live at "Friendship Hill." But good fortune was not in store for her, for she died within five months.

Before his marriage Gallatin had had a taste of politics at a state-wide meeting at Harrisburg that had been called to pro-pose amendments to the Constitution. To the men on the frontier, whose characteristics were independence and a fierce individ-ualism, some of the features of the Constitution appeared to be restrictive of liberties they had come to take for granted. To argue, to protest, and to call for rectification was an American custom that antedated the Revolution and that frontier life encouraged. The speeches Gallatin made at the meeting, in a conspicuous accent, to be sure, stamped him as a moderate. He agreed that a more efficient government than that under the Articles of Confederation was needed, but he suggested several amendments that were later included in the Bill of Rights. His convictions marked him as unsympathetic to the Eastern elements, most of whom were enthusiastic Federalists, and placed him among those who were to find their leader in Thomas Jefferson. Both groups became aware that he was a young man to watch.

III

The death of his young wife upset him so much that Gallatin considered returning to Geneva and calling the American experi-ment a failure. But before her death he had been elected a delegate to the convention that was to create a new constitution for the state of Pennsylvania. His newfound interest in politics prevailed. He went to the meeting, where his "democratic bias" came out clearly. Among the measures he favored was the proposition to give the franchise to all males over twenty-one, whether or not they paid taxes (a truly revolutionary idea for those days), and a lower house in which all parts of the state were to be equally represented. He opposed the suggestion that state senators be elected by the lower house instead of by the electorate and ranged himself with those who favored that printers and journalists accused of libel be assured trial by jury. That, too, indicated a liberal point of view. The state constitution that emerged from this meeting was to serve Pennsylvania for forty-seven years.[16]

Gallatin also emerged as the spokesman for free education in Pennsylvania, but for this eighteenth-century America was not ready.[17] However, if he could not achieve this radical innovation, he succeeded in persuading the legislature to grant aid to the two colleges in the state—the Academy in Philadelphia and Dickinson College in Carlisle. He never outgrew his interest in promoting education. When Ohio applied for statehood in 1802 while he was secretary of the Treasury, he was instrumental in having a clause inserted that one section of each township be set aside for the use of schools.[18] Even in his old age he responded to the call to take part in a meeting at which plans to found New York University were discussed. He was then close to seventy.

The next political office to which Gallatin was elected was that of senator. By then he had met the girl who would become his second wife. She was Hannah Nicholson, the daughter of a socially prominent family. Her father was a naval captain who had distinguished himself in the Revolution and was the leader of the anti-Federalists in New York. Hannah Nicholson was an intelligent young woman and politically sophisticated. That Gallatin had respect for her acumen is reflected in his letters to her,[19] in which he constantly mentions matters that the average woman of any period would consider boring. Her interest in politics was recognized and commented upon by friends and visitors in their home. To her husband she was "a tolerable democrat and at the same time a moderate one." That is to be taken as an encomium, because moderation was to him a most desirable trait, though he seems at times to have been immoderate in his unrelenting dislike for some opponents. His marriage was to prove a good and enduring one; in addition, it brought him valuable connections. But disappointment lay ahead, for in this, his first attempt to serve on the national scene, he was checkmated.

His enemies among the Federalists, anxious to reduce the number of opponents, succeeded in disqualifying Gallatin on the basis that he had not been a citizen for nine years as required by the Constitution. But he occupied his Senate seat for two months and he used the time to launch an attack on the "loose" fiscal policies of the secretary of the Treasury, Alexander Hamilton, which infuriated the Federalists further. He called on the secretary of the Treasury to furnish a statement on the domestic as well as on the foreign debt, and an accounting of receipts for each year since 1789 (the beginning of constitutional government), which the Treasury had hitherto failed to provide. The Senate passed these resolutions, but Hamilton was spared the embarrassment of having to comply, because Gallatin was unseated by a vote of 14-12 against him.

Another excuse for the attack on Gallatin was the attitude he had displayed during the Whiskey Rebellion, which began in 1791 and by 1794 had grown into open insubordination against the government. An excise tax of seven cents per gallon (a Hamiltonian measure) on every gallon of distilled liquor had been imposed. It caused an uproar among frontiersmen. People living in the back country were resentful because the difficulty of transporting their grain to market made it practicable to convert it into liquor. As cash was always scarce on the frontier, the penalties were bound to be considered oppressive. Gallatin was implicated because he had acted as clerk at a meeting called by his disgruntled constituents and had acquiesced to the adoption of a set of resolutions that were violent and inflammatory. But he soon realized his indiscretion in lending his name to a document which advocated resistance to the government and acknowledged it as "my only political sin." Though in the end the insurrection was quickly quelled, partly because he counseled submission, his enemies would not let him forget that he had acted unwisely. Years later, they still referred to him as the "whiskey patriot."

Gallatin was also disliked because of his sympathy for the French republic, which was proclaimed in 1792. Like so many republican young men, he saw the aims of the French Revolution as representative of "mankind against tyrants." Though he was outspokenly critical of the excesses that followed the execution of Louis XVI in 1793, and fully approved of President Washington's Proclamation of Neutrality, the fact that he kept cautioning against war with France caused him to be labeled a "pro-French revolutionary."

IV

Gallatin was barred from political life only for a short period. In 1795 he was reelected to the Assembly of the state of Pennsylvania and on the same day he learned that an adjacent congressional district had unexpectedly elected him to Congress. He was to remain in Congress for six years, until 1801, when he was named secretary of the Treasury by the newly elected President Jefferson. Henry Adams expatiates in these words on Gallatin's fiscal views, which brought him, as if predestined, to the management of the finances of the young republic for twelve consecutive years:

To Mr. Gallatin finance was an instinct. He knew well, as Mr. Hamilton had equally clearly understood before him, that the heart of the government was the Treasury; . . . he had one great advantage over most Americans of his time, even over Mr. Hamilton and Mr. Jefferson; he was an economist as well as a statesman; he was exact not merely in details but in the morality of affairs; he held debt in horror; punctilious exactness in avoiding debt was his final axiom in finance; the discharge of debt was his first principle in statesmanship; searching and rigid economy was his invariable demand whether in or out of office, and he made this demand imperative upon himself as upon others.[20]

Hamilton had retired to be succeeded by a much weaker and a more colorless man than his predecessor. Gallatin's suggestion that a committee be appointed to look into finances was the origin of the standing Committee of Ways and Means.[21] Both Madison and Gallatin were appointed to this committee and Gallatin served on it as long as he remained in Congress.

While in Congress he continued to play the same tune as in the Pennsylvania Assembly, except that he elaborated upon it and added variations. Like the Roman Cato known as the Censor, who always returned to the theme that Carthage must be destroyed (*Carthago delenda est*), Gallatin continued to stress that the public debt (which had increased by five million dollars since 1789),[22] must be diminished. Consequently, he recommended economies in the military establishment and the foreign service, and additional taxes. The suggestion of increased taxes was no less unpopular then than it is today. Equally resented, though not by the same group, was his insistence on the need for reducing defense expenditures, for throughout the decade of the 1790's war with France was a constant threat. Even the members of his own party, the Democrat-Republicans, as the partisans of Jefferson were called, were loath to support him in this.

In Gallatin's opinion France posed no threat to the United States. Hence, he argued, elaborate defense preparations were a waste of the people's resources—useless gestures intended to threaten potential adversaries. It was the reason why he refused to support proposals by the Federalists for a "provisional" army, an expanded navy, and, in particular, the creation of a separate Department of the Navy. The navy was his especial *bête noire* and the thought suggests itself that he might have been prejudiced because Switzerland had never had a navy. His philippics attracted the attention of Jefferson, who suggested that he draw up a statement on the financing of the government. The "sketch" he presented contained two hundred pages. In it he accused Hamilton of having "wasted" about eleven million dollars (scaled down in a future edition to ten million) by the hasty and careless operation of the debt-assumption program.[23] But because he approved of the function of banks, he would not attack the Bank of the United States, another of Hamilton's creations.

V

As secretary of the Treasury he continued his theme song with even greater insistence. Besides harping on the need to reduce the public debt, he added the stipulation that appropriations be earmarked for specific purposes only and that a scrupulous accounting of the authorized amounts be made mandatory. When he announced his plan to reduce the public debt at a rate that would extinguish it within sixteen years,[24] even his opponents were sufficiently cowed to permit the slashing of military appropriations, the threat of war with France having temporarily been lifted. Everyone was impressed. John Randolph from Virginia, a leading member of Congress who was related to Jefferson, pronounced Gallatin's plan a "substantial reform."

In the twentieth century when the prescription for economic well-being is frequently apt to be more and more pump priming, Gallatin's insistence on a balanced budget and strict economies seems reactionary. Throughout the nineteenth century the promise of a balanced budget was an important campaign issue. Even when Franklin Roosevelt conducted his first campaign, one of his important points was that he would cut expenditures and balance the budget. Gallatin's view may have been influenced by his own inclination to parsimoniousness, for he was always concerned about not exceeding his salary of five thousand dollars per annum. But, at that particular time, a stringent financial policy seemed very desirable for the good of the nation. When so much needed to be done in the way of internal improvements, the theory of spend-less-than-you-receive-so-you-may-accumulate-a-surplus appealed tremendously to the people, to the congressional members of Jefferson's party, and to Jefferson himself. Interest charges on debts that had to be met were looked upon as a good reason why desperately needed improvements, such as an expanded communications system, lower land rates, and elimination of certain taxes, could not be authorized. The issue of eliminating internal debts and the interest rates on them was considered so important that Gallatin felt he had been called into office specifically to reduce the public debt and to make money available for other purposes.

His plan worked so well that when the Louisiana Purchase was consummated in 1803 at the price of fifteen million dollars, the Treasury had a surplus and was able to pay more than a quarter of the purchase price without resorting to additional taxes.[25] Even when the United States became involved in a "Captain Kidd" kind of war with the Barbary States (Tunis,

Tripoli, Algiers, and Morocco), Gallatin was able to supply the needed naval appropriations by increasing import duties instead of floating a loan which would have increased the national debt. It was the first "little war" that was fought in unaccustomed waters far from home.

Gallatin proved himself a farsighted statesman. Like Jefferson, he was a Nationalist. He approved fully of extending the western boundaries through the Louisiana Purchase and would have been delighted to see the nation provided with an expanded communications system. The Cumberland Road, the first major link between East and West, was first proposed under Jefferson. By 1808 the public debt was sufficiently diminished for the secretary of the Treasury to outline a plan for internal improvements to cost twenty million dollars, to be carried out over ten years on yearly appropriations of two million; but Congress refused to adopt it. That Gallatin's careful husbanding of funds was based on his desire to accumulate a surplus with which to make needed improvements possible was recognized by Adams, who explained: "If Gallatin wished to . . . cut down expenditures to nothing, he aimed not so much at saving money, as at using it with the most certain effect."[26]

He was also a man of a pronounced moral stance. In condemning slavery, he was a forerunner of later immigrants who regarded the custom of treating human beings as slaves as a moral evil. He had joined the Pennsylvania Society for the Abolition of Slavery while he was in the legislature, and as secretary of the Treasury he resolutely enforced the law against importation of slaves when Louisiana passed to the United States. Had he lived in the middle of the nineteenth century he would most likely have been an active abolitionist.

VI

It is a safe statement that Gallatin's handling of the Treasury contributed to Jefferson's overwhelming victory in 1808, when he won more than twice the number of electoral votes he had received in 1804. The influence of the secretary of the Treasury was so strong as to cause Henry Adams to declare: "During the eight years the country was governed by these three men:

Jefferson, Madison and Gallatin."[27] That this was no isolated opinion can be inferred from a speech by Josiah Quincy, a prominent Federalist, who remarked: "For these twelve years the affairs of this country have been managed . . . by two Virginians and a foreigner."[28]

The years of Jefferson's administration were halcyon years. The danger of involvement in the Napoleonic Wars had receded and the country was prosperous. But during the second term new dangers of war with Great Britain, then in crucial opposition to Napoleon, confronted the nation. The situation exploded in 1807 when Britain seized the United States frigate "Chesapeake" in American waters to conduct a search for British deserters. It was then that Gallatin reversed himself, recommending a declaration of war against Britain. It was not because he had caught the war fever, but because he was convinced war could not be avoided and he felt it would be more advantageous to declare war when the Treasury was in good shape than to postpone it for later. He outlined a definite scheme for raising the needed war costs, but Jefferson preferred peace at any price.

The president proposed an embargo instead, prohibiting all shipping, American or foreign, from entering or leaving American ports. It was a disastrous decision, but Jefferson hoped to compel both belligerents, Great Britain and France, to recognize that they could not get along without American exports. In addition, Congress authorized a large increase for defense, almost one-half for enlarging the "mosquito fleet," which Gallatin disliked particularly. Though he was fully aware of the dangers inherent in an embargo, he agreed to support the president in carrying out his program.

Thus far, Gallatin's effectiveness as secretary of the Treasury had been partially due to the support he received in Congress from the members of his own party. He had a loyal backer in the chairman of the House Ways and Means Committee, the erratic John Randolph of Virginia. Another ally was the second ranking member of the committee, Joseph Hopper Nicholson, his wife's cousin. But Gallatin was one of Milton's "sad friends of truth," and consequently not without powerful opponents. One was Samuel Smith from Maryland, whom he had antagonized by hampering his preparedness program and his recommendations for an enlarged navy. Smith had wangled the job of secretary of the Navy for his brother, Robert, in the face of Gallatin's outspoken opposition to the job as well as to the man. Furthermore, in his constant hunt for extravagance, Gallatin had connected Smith's firm with peculations he had uncovered, but from which Smith was cleared. The result was that Smith became an implacable enemy.

The enforcement of the embargo lay mostly with the employees of the Treasury—the customs collectors, weighers, gaugers, etc., employed at the ports. The law proved so ruinous to the country that it was openly flouted. The tobacco crop of Virginia remained unsold and shipping ceased. The effect on the Treasury was so devastating that it was clear that for the first time since Gallatin assumed charge of fiscal affairs there would be a deficit. Nevertheless the secretary of the Treasury not only enforced the law with all the resolution of which he was capable, but drafted a bill that would close all the loopholes that made evasion easy. Congress, torn between loyalty to the country's interests and loyalty to the president, who refused to have the law repealed, seethed with resentment. But Gallatin remained loyal to the president. As Adams says: "He accepted the responsibility and kept silence." A letter he wrote to ex-President Jefferson during Madison's first term, when the war hawks were accusing him of being more interested in keeping the public debt down than in providing defense, reveals most clearly the view he had of his function as secretary of the Treasury:

The reduction of the public debt was certainly the principal object in bringing me into office; and our success in that respect has been due both to joint and continued efforts of the several branches of government and to the prosperous condition of the country. . . . If the United States shall be forced into an actual state of war, all the resources of the country must certainly be called forth to make it efficient, and new loans would undoubtedly be wanted. . . . I do not ask that in the present situation of our foreign relations the debt be reduced, but only that it shall not be encreased as long as we are not at war. . . . I cannot, my dear Sir, consent to act the part of a mere financier, to become a contriver of taxes, a dealer of loans, a seeker of resources for the purpose of supporting useless baubles, of increasing the number of idle and dissipated members of the community, of fattening contractors, pursers and agents.[29]

VII

Jefferson left his office a beaten man. During the months preceding the takeover by the new president, hostility to the embargo reached such a point that insurrection was openly discussed. Instead of repealing the law, Jefferson left it to Madison to do so. On the day on which Jefferson was to retire, Congress terminated the embargo and replaced it with a Non-Importation Act, which permitted American ships to trade with all nations, except Great Britain and France. It was a slap at the president who had brought the country to a sorry state. Even members of Jefferson's own party voted for this act, which they knew was intended to humiliate the president.

As for Gallatin, the coalition against him had hardened. Much of the resentment against the embargo had transferred itself to the secretary of the treasury whose duty it was to implement the law. Besides, he had lost some of his most influential adherents. Nicholson, his wife's cousin, had retired and Randolph had broken with Jefferson, which had forced Gallatin to drop Randolph, though he was personally fond of him. In addition to Samuel Smith, Gallatin had other determined foes in several Pennsylvanians to whom he had refused patronage. (The bestowal of patronage in Pennsylvania had been his privilege.) Now all those who bore grudges against Gallatin combined with the Smith faction against him. "A small knot of men in the Senate," remarked Henry Adams, "were more powerful than the President himself."[30] They were preparing to let the ax fall, not once, but again and again until he would be driven from his post. Even then they would not cease to embarrass him.

Even before Madison assumed office Gallatin knew he was in serious difficulties. He had been slated to become Madison's secretary of state. "Hit fitness for the job was so evident," thought Henry Adams, "as to make his appointment the best that could be suggested."[31] Nevertheless, his opponents banded together to block his appointment in the Senate. Upon being assured that Gallatin would not be confirmed, Madison was forced to offer the State Department to Robert Smith, brother of the ringleader to block Gallatin. Thus, he added another incompetent to his cabinet, which was already overburdened with mediocre men. Gallatin agreed to remain as secretary of the Treasury out of loyalty to Jefferson and Madison, whom the outgoing president had chosen as his successor. But he was so unhappy that he was considering retirement from public life. The desire to be secretary of state may have been his bid for immortality. He might have known intuitively that secretaries of state have a better chance of being honored by posterity than secretaries of the treasury.

The next serious blow came in 1811 over the recharter of the Bank of the United States. Gallatin's prestige was at stake, for he had recommended it. He knew he needed the bank. But the bill for recharter was killed by one vote, with Henry Clay, Speaker of the House, voting against it. The negative vote was a terrible defeat, for it was not only a repudiation of him, but he was aware he would have difficulty in securing loans for the treasury. The fact that Robert Smith, to whom he had lost the State Department, had joined his enemies in defeating the measure drove him to take the most assertive step of his career. He presented the president with an ultimatum: either he or Robert Smith would have to leave the cabinet. Of this act Adams comments:

Gallatin never used the knife except when every other means had been tried; but when he did so, his act was proof that no other outlet could be opened by the clearest head and the most patient temper of his time.[32]

Madison upheld Gallatin and James Monroe became secretary of state.

With the outbreak of War in 1812, Gallatin entered upon the most difficult period of his career. Congress authorized the funds, but in the absence of support from the official government bank, loans were hard to secure. New England was particularly averse to giving financial help to the government. When the Treasury was almost empty, the secretary found himself compelled to secure a sixteen-million-dollar loan though the help of a syndicate composed of three foreign-born citizens: John Jacob Astor and David Parish, both born in Germany, and Stephen Girard, of French birth. Thus was the United States government saved from bankruptcy. It was the most difficult deal Gallatin had ever arranged and one by which the three bankers, Astor, Parish, and Girard, increased their fortunes tremendously.

By then Gallatin had no longer the wish to remain at the head of the Treasury. An unforseen turn of events provided him with the opportunity to escape without loss of pride. The Czar of Russia had offered (for reasons of his own) to mediate the conflict between Great Britain and her erstwhile colonies. Madison accepted the offer and upon Gallatin's request appointed him one of the peace commissioners. When Gallatin arrived in Russia, he learned that his enemies had struck at him again by blocking his nomination by one vote. Also, Britain rejected the good offices of the Czar. However, she soon proposed direct negotiations, Madison again appointed Gallatin, and this time he was left unmolested. Carl Schurz, as balanced and as perspicacious an observer as ever there was, comments that but for the "conspicuous ability, the exquisite tact, the constant good nature . . . and the inexhaustable patience," of Gallatin, the peace treaty might not have been as favorable to the United States as it was, inasmuch as everything was left as it had been before the war. In his judgment, Gallatin's eminence has never been appreciated as it deserves.

VIII

Thus, Gallatin entered a new phase, in which he was to prove his skill in several diplomatic assignments. When the secretary of the Treasury resigned, he was again offered the post, but he rejected it, preferring the post as minister to France. He remained there seven years. During his stay he negotiated an important treaty with the Netherlands and two with England that laid the groundwork for the improvement in British-American relations.

In the election of 1824 Gallatin was considered as vice-president on the ticket with William Crawford of Georgia,[33] but nothing came of it. At the age of seventy he was not yet ready to retire to obscurity. He accepted the offer of his friend, John Jacob Astor, to become the president of the National Bank of New York (now part of the Hanover Bank), which Astor was backing, and remained in his post until he was succeeded by his son. In that capacity he performed a great feat of persuasion in 1838. The country was suffering from the effects of one of the most severe of the early depressions. As a result of the panic of 1837, the banks had suspended specie payments. But Gallatin was able to persuade them to resume payment in specie within the year, thus bearing out his conviction that the function of banks was to promote, not to hinder, the financial health of the country. In addition, he was publishing articles on banking and currency. He had also become interested in the Indians and produced two treatises on the North American Indian and the tribes of Mexico and Central America. Even in his eighty-fourth year he was asked by President Tyler to serve again as secretary of the Treasury. He declined because of his age.

When his life came to an end in August of 1849—in his eighty-ninth year—he had served the United States for forty years, seventeen in diplomacy. He had lived seventy years in America and had labored assiduously in behalf of his adopted country. His reward is a place in the history books, in having one of the forks of the Missouri River named after him by Lewis and Clark, as well as the entrance to Yellowstone Park—the "Gallatin Gateway." Also, there is a statue of him at the north side of the Treasury Building in recognition of his having earned an honored place in the pantheon of America's devoted public servants.

JOHANN AUGUST ROEBLING
1806-1869

Bridge Builder

A pioneer in the construction of suspension bridges, he was one of the most important builders of our country. He built the first suspension bridge over the Niagara, the bridge across the Ohio at Cincinnati, and the Brooklyn Bridge connecting Brooklyn with Manhattan. One of the most graceful spans in the world, the Brooklyn Bridge is a lasting monument to him and to his son, who brought the bridge to completion from the plans of his father after the latter's death, caused by an accident at the site of the project.

He was also the founder of the firm of John Augustus Roebling's Sons of Trenton, New Jersey, manufacturers of wire rope, who have played a role of continuous importance in industry and during wars, in the furtherance of the national interest.

The Effects of the Uprisings of 1830

After Napoleon's abdication in 1814 the Congress of Vienna attempted to repress the revolutionary hopes he had aroused in the peoples of Europe. The overriding concern of the powers that had defeated Napoleon—Austria, Russia, and Prussia—was to restore the principle of legitimacy and to reestablish the status quo ante that had existed prior to 1789. The monarchical elements, the clergy, and the nobility were returned to power by the two chief architects of the Congress: Count Metternich of Austria and Alexander I of Russia. But the effect on the middle classes was to intensify the desire for such reforms as equality before the law and sovereignty of the people. The police methods of Metternich and the hypocritical ideals incorporated into the Holy Alliance by the Czar were intended to keep the middle classes down, but the expectations aroused by the French Revolution could not be extinguished.

In France the uneasy peace imposed by the Congress of Vienna lasted until 1830, when the French people turned against the reactionary politics of the Bourbon king, Charles X. Three days of bloody street fighting followed, during which workmen shouted, "Down with the Bourbons!" The government was handed to another, an "illegitimate Bourbon," Louis-Philippe, who was head of the younger branch of the family. In 1792 he had served as a volunteer in the revolutionary army, which served to remove the onus of being considered a royalist. One significant reform with which he rewarded the middle classes who supported him was an extension of the franchise. His reign, which lasted until 1848, was known as "the reign of the bourgeoisie." He was called *"le roi bourgeois."*

The French uprising in 1830 was a signal for other outbreaks. There were clashes in the German states, in Warsaw, in Belgium, and in the Papal States. The Austrians suppressed the rebellion in the Papal States; the Poles, successful at first, were brutally overwhelmed by the brother of Alexander I, who had succeeded him. Belgium was the only country to achieve a significant success, in being separated from Holland and becoming an independent nation.

The revolts in the German states were of a scattered nature, like lightning seen in various places. German unity was nonexistent. There were thirty-eight sovereign German states, including Austria, that were loosely held together in a Germanic Confederation, a "Bund," and that shared a Diet which was impotent and reactionary. (Austria had entered the Bund in in 1815.) Absolutism was in the saddle, and liberal opinion in the press and in the universities was severely repressed. The German uprising achieved no significant results, because the two strongest states, Prussia and Austria, remained uncompromisingly conservative. In Germany, the Revolution of 1830 had liberal rather than national aims. The lack of a strong middle class made the failure of the insurrection inevitable. The fabric that Metternich and Alexander I had woven was unraveling, but it would hold together. Even the Revolution of 1848 would not rend it asunder beyond repair.

The young liberals who had actively participated in the fighting and saw their efforts fail were forced to flee for their lives. Others, not personally threatened, decided it was time to break with the pattern of the past. One of those was Johann August Roebling. Many of those who forsook their homelands came to America. In this way America received the first group of intellectual Germans. They became known among their own people as *"Die Dreissiger."*

The American Setting

In the late 1820's America, too, was in such a state of ferment that the period has been designated as "The Revolution of 1828." The Revolution of 1776 was fought to free the colonies from England's rule, but the people had not been freed from the rule of "their betters," those who possessed wealth, education, and influence. By the 1820's a mood was abroad that demanded "popular rule," an opportunity for the common people to participate in the affairs of government. Whereas the president and his advisers had been chosen from the old aristocracy —the scions of wealth and tradition—the new spirit called for more democracy. The admission of ten new states between 1792 and 1820[1] had strengthened the spirit of independence and "frontier democracy." Why not, demanded the men of the frontier states, choose a president and the officials of the government from among these new elements? The plain people, they averred, were as fit to exercise authority as those who considered themselves superior by virtue of their background and education. "The Revolution of 1828" was successfully carried out when the aristocratic John Quincy Adams was replaced by Andrew Jackson, frontiersman, representative of the plain people, and the "anti-establishment man" of the period.

Jackson was the son of immigrants from Northern Ireland who had settled, as many of the Scotch-Irish did, in the back country of the Carolinas. He was a boy in his late teens when he volunteered for service at the very end of the Revolution. From then on he was to revert at intervals to his role of frontier warrior against the Indians and the English (whom he hated).

He defeated an English force at the Battle of New Orleans, a short time after the War of 1812 was officially over. In between his military exploits he pursued a political career which he began as a frontier lawyer in Tennessee and continued in the Tennessee Supreme Court and later in the Senate of the United States. It was as senator from Tennessee that he made his first attempt to gain the presidency in 1824, to be defeated in a four-cornered election by John Quincy Adams. It was the second and last election to be thrown into the House of Representatives. Adams' election, Jackson's supporters claimed, had been arranged through a corrupt bargain between Adams and Henry Clay. But in 1828 Jackson was overwhelmingly elected by the West, the South, and the farmer and labor elements of the Northeast.

This "revolution"was accompanied by an enormous extension of the suffrage. Whereas the original thirteen states had limited the franchise to those who could meet property qualifications, the ten new states entered the Union with state constitutions that granted universal manhood suffrage or lowered qualifications for voting so drastically that they could not be considered a serious barrier. This assault on the privileges of wealth forced the older states to drop their restrictions against universal manhood suffrage. During the presidency of Andrew Jackson (1828-1836) the barriers against full voting privileges were removed in most eastern states.

The "Jacksonian Era," so called because of the imprint upon it of Jackson's influence, lasted through the forties and fifties. Due to a high birthrate and an enormous acceleration in immigration, the country was growing by leaps and bounds. It was a period of unrestrained optimism. Speaking of our "boundless resources," Emerson, the most respected spokesman of the era and one of its most influential orators, reminded an audience in Boston in 1884: "The bountiful continent is ours, state on state, and territory on territory, to the waves of the Pacific sea;" and quoted, "Our garden is the immeasurable earth."[2]

It was an exuberant age, and people had good reason to let their chests swell with pride and hope. The doctrine that it was "the Manifest Destiny" of the United States to reach the Pacific was an exhilarating prospect. It was the belief in "Manifest Destiny" that led to the annexation of Texas in 1845 and subsequently to the war with Mexico. Many people realized that the danger of a collision between North and South was made more real through the acquisition of territory into which slavery might spread, but their counsel did not prevail. The conflict was only postponed.

Consonant with the optimism that was in the air, local, state, and federal government enthusiastically supported the spread of a communications system. After the opening of the Erie Canal in 1825, a rash of canal building ensued. At the same time the Cumberland Road, which had been meandering westward since the second decade of the nineteenth century, received continuing assistance through more liberal appropriations by Congress. Steamboats on the rivers, which had also begun to appear early in the century, added a strong impetus to travel and commerce. But the greatest consideration was reserved for the railroads. After the Baltimore and Ohio made its appearance in 1830, dozens of short and disconnected lines were built to provide connections with the principal cities. To promote efficient and quick railroad transportation bridges across the rivers became a necessity. The spanning of some of our rivers was Johann August Roebling's contribution to the enormous growth of the United States during the first half of the nineteenth century.

I

Though Johann August Roebling had not actively participated in the uprising of 1830, he was one of those who had hoped for its success. He was bitterly disappointed over its failure. Born in 1806 in Mühlhausen, Thuringia, he was the son of a tobacconist and the youngest of five children. His father, staid and phlegmatic, reflected the atmosphere of Mühlhausen. An old medieval town, it was more justified in its pride of the past than for its accomplishments in the present. The Peasant Revolt of 1525 had swept over Mühlhausen and its environs and it was there the fanatic Thomas Münzer had attempted to impose a millenarian regime, with the result that peasants and clergy were drowned in blood. One cause for pride was the twelfth-century Gothic church of St. Blasius, where Johann Sebastian

Bach had played the church organ. In his own time, the boy Johann played on the same church organ. Later, the town would be proud that it was Roebling's birthplace. Whereas the father was content with what life had brought him, his mother was not. An ambitious, driving woman, she hoped that her children would not become tradesmen like their father. But only her youngest son showed promise. She herself taught him the piano. He also learned to play the flute, on an instrument he had inherited from his maternal grandfather. Frau Roebling scrimped and saved to assure her youngest son the kind of education necessary to provide an entrance into a larger world where it would be possible to achieve success and distinction.

A bright boy, Roebling reacted sensitively to his surroundings. During his childhood he witnessed the advance and retreat through his town of Napoleon's armies and those of his adversaries, as they fled from Napoleon's soldiers or pursued them. The stir and excitement that accompanied the presence of French and Cossack soldiers stirred his imagination and made him conscious of the outside world. At the town gymnasium he distinguished himself in mathematics and architectural drawing. At seventeen he decided to study engineering. His mother produced the necessary means to enable him to enroll at the Royal Polytechnic in Berlin, then the foremost engineering school in Europe.

At the Polytechnic he studied not only engineering, architecture, hydraulics, and bridge building, but also philosophy under Georg Friedrich Hegel, whose favorite student he became. Hegel, then approaching sixty, had accepted the authoritarian Prussian government, but in his youth, he had defended the French Revolution. He told the young student he considered America "a land of hope for all who are wearied of the historic armory of old Europe." It was bound to make a strong impression on a young idealist to whom life seemed restricted and authoritarian.

Bridge construction was his favorite study. During his student days a small suspension bridge was built over one of the smaller rivers in Germany. He went to see it and was so thrilled at the sight of it, that as he stood gazing at it, he saw his lifework ahead of him. In his mind's eye he might have envisioned graceful structures, larger and stronger than the one he was viewing, glinting in the sun. Having begun to think of America, he might have visualized its rivers, as large and untamed as America itself was reputed to be, which he would span with suspension bridges as beautiful as they would be utilitarian.

But Roebling was not yet ready for emigration. Armed with his new degree, the twenty-year-old civil engineer entered the employ of the Prussian government as assistant engineer on road and bridge building projects. After three years he would be eligible for a permanent government appointment. During these three years he discovered how irksome it was to work under a bureaucratic regime. Circumvented in his attempts to put his ideas into operation, and hampered by regimentation, red tape, and official delays, he felt bound and gagged. An observation he made upon arriving in America indicates how much he must have resented the bureaucratic delays of the German system. Acidly he remarked:

Let one inquire about the gigantic construction of the New York canal (Erie Canal), the Ohio canal, the multitude of smaller canals, roads and railways, and the German wonders how all this could have been accomplished without first having had an army of governmental councillors, ministers and other functionaries deliberating about it for ten years, make numerous expensive journeys by post, and write so many reports about it that for the amount expended for all this, reckoning compound interest for ten years the work could have been completed.[3]

When the Revolution broke out Roebling was encouraged to hope that it would result in a freer atmosphere which would permit him to pursue his career in his native land. Instead, it failed, and the government increased its repressive measures. It was then that he made up his mind to leave his place of birth and start anew in America. With his brother he began in stealth to organize a group of emigrants. When they had assembled forty-four men, women, and children, they were ready to depart. The townsfolk, his mother included (whom he was never to see again), accompanied them as far as the outskirts of the town. He had three thousand dollars, he was twenty-five, and the year was 1831. That the conditions in his native country had driven him out emerges from a diary he kept during the two and a half months voyage, in which he stated:

It is not contempt for our Fatherland that causes us to leave it, but an inclination and an ardent desire that our circumstances may be bettered and that they may have a decidedly human aspect. May Fate soon grant to Germany that to which her educated populace can lay claim with most well-founded right, and which has been so long unjustly withheld from her. You know what I mean.[4]

A cautious statement with a clear implication: "You know what I mean." His disappointment had caused him to abandon an assured position in his native land for an uncertain future among strangers.

II

Landing in Philadelphia, Roebling received a favorable first impression of the city and its people. Americans struck him as clean, neatly dressed, and polite. They did not appear "to seek to cheat any more than the inhabitants of the German commercial towns." He declared Philadelphia to be "the most beautiful city in the world." Berlin, he stated, "offered no comparison and seems to be a city of poor oppressed people." He observed that "nowhere does one see a person in rags; all, even the common workmen, go very cleanly and neatly dressed." The resentment over conditions he had left behind was still fresh, for he declared: "What a contrast to the oppressed German population." The only adverse criticism he offered, was the existence of slavery, a reaction he shared with many Germans. Although some Germans settled in the South, specifically in Texas (and later supported the Confederacy), a large number would not consider living in the South because they were repelled by its slave system. He perceived that the existence of slavery "contrasts too greatly with the rest of their political and civic institutions." He was prophetic in declaring that the situation in the South was "the greatest cancerous affliction from which the United States is suffering."[5]

The possibility of settling in the South was immediately ruled out. The emigrant group shrank considerably, many having decided to go their separate ways. Roebling and his party set out for Pittsburgh, three hundred miles from Philadelphia. It was an arduous journey, over the partially completed Pennsylvania

Canal to Harrisburg, and finally by wagon for another hundred and twenty miles. The journey took four weeks.

In Butler County, twenty-five miles from Pittsburgh, they purchased a three-thousand-acre tract on which a farmhouse had been erected but which was otherwise undeveloped. The price was $1.37 an acre. The original owner, Robert Morris, who had had charge of finances during the Revolution, had paid ten cents an acre to the federal government.[6] Roebling settled down to coaxing a living from the soil and to attracting other German settlers to the colony.

For a year he led an unrelieved pioneer existence, which meant hard and unaccustomed work and isolation. It was not long before he knew he did not like farming. The colony, first called "Germania," was rechristened "Saxonburg." At home entertainments and dances he played the piano and the flute. He would remain an enthusiastic musician until his hand became maimed by an accident. Though the soil was poor and the climate trying—very hot in the summer and bitterly cold during the winter, the settlement grew. The daughter of one of the newcomers, who was a tailor by trade, became Roebling's wife. In Europe it would have been unthinkable for an engineer to marry the daughter of a tailor, but in the new surroundings class distinctions did not matter.

In 1837 his son was born. The father was so committed to his new life that he named him Washington Augustus Roebling. In the same year John Roebling, as he now called himself, became a citizen of the United States. By then the direction of the colony could be entrusted to others. It released him from much of the onerous work of farming and enabled him to follow his own bent. He began with a series of mechanical inventions, some of which he patented. Later his invention of wire rope would turn Saxonburg into a busy commercial hamlet and would bring a measure of prosperity to all his neighbors. After he moved his business to Trenton, oil and gas were discovered in Saxonburg.[7]

Until the Panic of 1837 broke the upward spiral of prosperity, all Americans expected that the extension of internal improvements, about which they were wildly enthusiastic, would continue. In 1830, for instance, ninety-six million dollars, a prodigious sum for these days, was allocated by the federal government for roads, canals, and other means of communication.[8] In addition, the states strove mightily to keep pace with the building program of the federal government. The Erie Canal, completed in 1825, which seemed to have contributed tremendously to the prosperity of the State of New York, inspired many of the seaboard as well as some of the western states to follow the example of Governor Clinton of New York. To emulate him, most states went into debt to foreign investors, which they repudiated when panic and depression followed. The state of Pennsylvania had built an elaborate network of canals to connect Philadelphia with Pittsburgh and beyond, and was planning a railroad through central Pennsylvania. Roebling, who had come to realize that he could not be happy unless he could work as an engineer, was fretting over how to fulfill his ambition, when he received a letter from a former schoolmate, asking him if he would care to join the engineering staff engaged in the construction of the Sandy and Beaver canals. His friend's communication seemed an answer to a prayer. Leaving the care of the farm to his wife, he departed for Harrisburg.

III

He was back before long, for the Panic of 1837 interrupted the work on the canal. But within a year he was recalled to work on a project for a feeder canal that would bring water from the Allegheny River to the project. When this job was finished, Roebling was asked by the state to make a survey for a railroad route to connect Harrisburg with Pittsburgh. It was demanding and difficult work, for it took him from home and family and imposed serious hardships on him. But he was happy to be employed at his profession. Mapping out routes reawakened his old ambition to build bridges. His trained eye saw the need for spanning rivers, where communications between both banks was limited to boats and rafts. His tenacity, determination, and power of will came out clearly during these early years when he strove to gain a foothold in his profession. He became a hard, driving, intensely ambitious man who was willing to impose the harshest discipline on himself and his family. Though they saw one another rarely, he brooked no complaints.[9] It was a lucky break that brought him back to his profession, but his success was due to an iron determination to let nothing stop him, regardless of the cost. He scrimped, lived without comforts in rooming houses, and devoted his leisure hours to plans and calculations. He expected the same sacrifices from his family. His wife took charge of the farm, and when he began producing wire rope on his property in Saxonburg she cooked for the men who worked for him. He did not see her and children for long periods. While building the bridge over Niagara Falls, it was the superintendent in charge of the wire plant who informed him of the birth of another child. Roebling had seven children, of whom the first was to follow his profession. His second and third sons developed the wire business he had started. During the Civil War, when his reputation as a bridge builder was firmly established, he heard from his superintendent that his wife was gravely ill. He did not go home, but returned for her funeral.[10]

IV

At the time when John Roebling was making his start as an engineer, the construction of bridges was entrusted to carpenters and builders. Only one individual was known as a professional bridge pioneer—Charles Ellet, a native American. He had received his degree from the Ecole Polytechnique in Paris and had added to his technical training by traveling through England, France, and Germany for the purpose of studying the design of existing bridges. He, too, was enthusiastic about suspension bridges. As an adroit politician, he was Roebling's most serious rival.

In 1844 Ellet and a local contractor who intended to employ Roebling competed for a contract to build a suspension bridge across the Schuylkill at Fairmont in Philadelphia. Ellet won the contract through his political connections. Roebling could not fail to be aware that the future of suspension bridges in America depended on how the Fairmont bridge would turn out. He realized that if Ellet were to be successful, his reputation as the leading bridge engineer would be assured. If Ellet failed, the future of suspension bridges would be seriously jeopardized and he himself would never get a chance. It was therefore intensely to be desired that the results should not be disappointing.

It was while working as an engineer for the state of Pennsylvania that Roebling's inventive mind seized upon the idea that was to prove of pivotal significance to the fortunes of the Roebling family and the future of suspension bridges. This idea was to replace the six- and nine-inch hempen hawsers used to haul passengers and vehicles up steep inclines with ropes made of wire. Because hemp ropes frayed and broke easily, they were more expensive, less durable, and more hazardous. The wire rope Roebling invented laid the foundation for the business that would eventually become the world's largest producer of wires and cables. Throughout his life he retained a lively interest in the progress of his business. He worried about orders, payments, the efficiency of his workmen; and when away on engineering jobs he sent detailed instructions to the plant superintendent, whom he trusted implicitly. The first elevator rope was produced in his shop in 1862. During World War I the company supplied submarine nets to the Navy for the purpose of entangling and thus destroying enemy submarines. The first wire ropes were produced by a hand-operated twisting machine that was worked by neighbors and friends in Saxonburg. Later, he changed the method of making cables by placing the wires parallel to one another and wrapping the whole with wire. By then he had moved his business to Trenton on the suggestion of Peter Cooper, who had established an iron business there.

It was not easy to overcome the resistance of politicians and manufacturers of hemp rope, whose hostility to the idea of having their product replaced by another was to be expected. At the first test demonstration an attempt at sabotage was uncovered. Someone had been hired to cut the wire ropes in order to discredit their use. But before long Roebling's product was specified for use on canals, portage railways, and for a variety of commercial purposes. Wire ropes proved particularly important in the building of bridges, for they were essential in creating stronger and longer spans.

The breakthrough in Roebling's career occurred when he received a contract to build a suspended aqueduct across the Allegheny River at Pittsburgh. He was then thirty-eight and had been in the United States for thirteen years. Built during the bitterest winter weather, the bridge was finished in nine months, as specified in his contract. The cost was sixty-two thousand dollars and his profit for a year's work was thirty-five hundred dollars. The completion of the aqueduct marked the beginning of his reputation. The bridge he replaced had been in use for seven years. While some bridges had to be replaced for reasons of safety, the bridges he would erect withstood the effects of time and weather. This first bridge of his making was to last from 1844 to 1861, when the canal was abandoned.

V

Within a year he was at work on his second assignment—to replace a bridge destroyed by fire over the Monongahela River. It was his first suspension bridge. Built at a cost of fifty-five thousand dollars without profit to its engineer, it was one of the most economical structures on record.[11] It was also one of the most solidly constructed bridges. Again the work went on in freezing temperatures. Finished in eight months, it lasted until 1883, when it was taken down, not because it was unsafe, but because traffic conditions required it. Built to last, it outlasted its builder by fourteen years.

The next six years, during which he erected six more bridges— five canal aqueducts and one for highway traffic—were a preparation for a more significant undertaking—the suspension bridge over Niagara Falls, the first bridge intended for railroad traffic. The contract had originally gone to his chief competitor, Charles Ellet. Ellet had proceeded no further than erecting a footbridge when he gave up his project—"threw it away for some immediate profit or pique."[12] Roebling was not one to indulge in pique, though there might have been some justification for it, because his original bid had been turned down in favor of Ellet. But when a contract was offered to him after Ellet stepped down, he accepted the challenge.

Engineers all over the world, including Robert Stephenson of England, warned that a suspension bridge could not be built to sustain a railroad, but nothing could deter John Roebling. He knew it could. Begun in 1851, the bridge was completed in 1855 at a cost of less than four hundred thousand dollars.[13] Trains

made thirty crossings on an average per day, creating a minimum of vibration. How had Roebling achieved it? By rein-
forcing the structure with *Girders, Trusses* and *Stays* to give it
the necessary stiffness. During the four years he was occupied
at Niagara he sacrificed all of his interests to this project. He
managed his business by correspondence with the plant superintendent, indicating by the contents that he worried about
recessions, slow payment, and other business conditions. He
seemed to have been so short of time that frequently he instructed
the superintendent to read his letters to Mrs. Roebling.[14]

Fear for the bridge's safety troubled many minds even when
it was completed. A year before a bridge built by Charles Ellet
over the Ohio at Wheeling had collapsed. The troubling question
was—were cable bridges safe? Would the Niagara bridge prove
vulnerable to the storms of Canadian winters? To calm the
apprehensions of the company responsible for the undertaking,
Roebling released in a statement the exact measures he had
taken to give the bridge the stiffness and rigidity he considered
necessary. He explained that he had based the strength of the
cables on the following calculations: weight of the train plus
weight of the structure; also the weight of a number of teams
which might be on the bridge at the same time. including a
foot of snow. Then, he allowed no less than five times the
strength of wire.[15] His bridge, he asserted, was intended to be
"proof against a hurricane."

And so it proved. Other bridges were swept out of existence
by storms or floods; Roebling's endured. For forty-two years the
Niagara bridge sustained trains and highway traffic, and its
lofty span delighted the eye. In 1897 it was replaced, not because
of faults in its construction, but because it became necessary
to have a two-track bridge to accommodate increased rail traffic
and to provide for an electric trolley line.

VI

In 1857, Washington Augustus Roebling, John Roebling's
eldest son, graduated as a civil engineer from the Rensselaer
Polytechnic Institute at Troy. The Institute was to train three
generations of Roeblings for the engineering profession. The
year after Washington Roebling's graduation, his father received

the commission to replace a wooden bridge over the Allegheny at Pittsburgh, which was no longer deemed safe. For the first time he worked with his son at his side. The work had just begun when a contract materialized that had been pending for ten years for a bridge at Cincinnati between Ohio and Kentucky. John Roebling left his son in charge of the Allegheny bridge and started on the new project in Cincinnati. The Allegheny bridge, finished shortly before the Civil War, was judged an "artistic gem," and was said to possess "a peculiar beauty of its own."

When the Civil War broke out, Washington Roebling was tempted to enlist as a private soldier. The story was that he was wondering how to inform his parents of his intentions when a jeering remark by the elder Roebling on his son's prolonged dependence drove him to do so the very next day.[16] His letters home were addresssed to his mother and to the plant superintendent who was held in great affection by all the members of his family. In 1862 the young soldier was transferred to the engineering department, where he was assigned to the task of building and repairing suspension bridges. It was not until father and son met at the funeral of Mrs. Roebling that there was a silent reconciliation between them. By the time the young man was mustered out in 1865, he had attained the rank of colonel and was married to the daughter of his commanding general. He joined his father in Cincinnati after his father had asked for his help in completing the bridge.

The Cincinnati project was finished in 1867 after being under construction for more than ten years. The delay was due to an unusual string of difficulties: nature's caprices, financial troubles, and the Civil War. A dry river bed, floods, and weather that caused the Ohio to freeze over were barely overcome when the Panic of 1857 and the recession that followed exhausted funds. Financial difficulties were not an unusual occurrence, for construction was generally started as soon as an initial sum was pledged. (In 1878 work on the Brooklyn Bridge had to be suspended for six months for lack of money.)[17] As for the Civil War, its effect was bound to be felt in an area that divided North from South. In 1862 a Confederate army moved into Kentucky, and the danger to Cincinnati was only narrowly averted. After work was resumed in 1863, the bridge company was plagued by financial problems due to a steep rise in prices and a scarcity of trained workmen. But from then on the work moved forward. Opened in 1867, Roebling's bridge was destined to become the main artery leading to the states beyond the Ohio. It justified itself during several floods that occurred periodically throughout the rest of the nineteenth century. During the catastrophic flood of 1937 it was the only crossing open on the Ohio River over which food and needed supplies could be sent to stricken cities in Kentucky.

VII

While the Cincinnati bridge was nearing completion, Roebling admitted to being tired and hoping for a rest. But one wonders how much he really desired a rest, for in 1865, at the height of his preoccupation with the Cincinnati bridge, he drew up plans for the erection of a bridge over the East River and submitted them to some of Brooklyn's civic leaders. Brooklyn was still an independent municipality and would not become one of New York City's five boroughs until 1898. The vision of a great span connecting Brooklyn with its enormous neighbor had captured his imagination even earlier, while his attention was engaged by the Niagara bridge. It was then that he suggested the idea to Abram D. Hewitt, one of New York's civic leaders, later a member of Congress. For the next two years, while Brooklyn kept growing rapidly, its people depended on ferry service to take them to work in Manhattan and to bring them home in the evening.

The idea of a bridge had occurred to forward-looking residents of Brooklyn since the early nineteenth century. But many influential people were doubtful about the success of such an undertaking. The bridge would have to have a longer span than any yet constructed. Roebling assured them it could be done. The trust he inspired was such that when a prominent engineer was questioned about the safety of such a bridge, he is said to have replied: "I believe it, because Roebling says so."[18]

What finally activated the project was the severe winter of 1866-67. As the ferry struggled day after day with gales and chunks of ice that obstructed its passage, people began to demand a less difficult mode of transportation. At last, several prominent citizens of Brooklyn decided to take the initiative by prevailing upon State Senator Murphy, a former mayor of Brooklyn, to draft an enabling bill for the construction of a bridge and to submit it to the legislature. It was passed early in the spring, and the call came to Roebling to undertake the new project as chief engineer at a salary of eight thousand dollars per annum. Again he and his son would work as a team. He was then sixty-one and his son was thirty. It was as if he felt time's winged chariot drawing near, or, as if in the words of Housman he was prodding himself: "Up lad: When the journey's over, there'll be time enough to sleep."

This undertaking was to form the apogee in the careers of both father and son, and it was to be one of the grandest engineering triumphs anywhere in the world. Roebling however, was destined to be the first of the project's many victims. His son was to be another, although his life would be spared. He would see the bridge finished, albeit through binoculars from his home in Brooklyn. The bridge was destined to become not only a showpiece of utility, but also of beauty in an age that was to be distinguished for imitativeness in architecture. To Lewis Mumford, who regarded the last quarter of the nineteenth century as "the Brown Decades"—not a term of admiration—the bridge was "not merely one of the best pieces of engineering the nineteenth century can show anywhere, but perhaps the most completely satisfactory structure of any kind that had appeared in America, ... in every way a classic." He offers this judgment:

in its absence of ornament, its refusal to permit the steel to be other than its unadorned reality, the Brooklyn Bridge pointed to the logic and aesthetics of the machine and it did this far more rigorously than its later rival, the Eiffel Tower in Paris, with its early Art Nouveau treatment of the base. Finally, the bridge existed in its own right, independent of its influences and potentialities as a work of art, a delight to the artist and the poet, but equally well appreciated by the man in the street.[19]

Before he started on the actual work, Roebling dispatched his son to Europe to study English, German, and French methods of bridge construction, particularly the new French method of sinking caisson foundations. He occupied himself with making surveys and design studies and drawing up estimate costs. He innovated the use of steel wires instead of iron. Later, his son would specify that the cable material be galvanized to prevent rusting.[20] There was to be a promenade for strollers, a feature which has not fallen into a state of desuetude to this day.

In order to make the bridge more resistant to vibration and the force of the wind, Roebling proposed the use of iron trusses and "inclined stays" from the top of the towers to the floor. But it did not keep people, including Horace Greeley of the *New York Tribune*, from voicing fears that the enormous length of a span of 1,600 feet—fifty percent longer than the Cincinnati bridge—would be unsafe. The bridge was designed to carry a a load of 18,700 tons. In order to quiet the doubts of the public, Roebling suggested that a board of consultants composed of the most eminent members of the engineering profession be called in to study the plans. His calculations were unanimously confirmed.

Construction had not even begun when Roebling was felled by a freak accident. He was making a survey of where the Brooklyn tower was to be placed and was standing on a timber pile, when a ferry turned to enter its berth. It lurched against the spot where he was standing and his foot was caught and crushed. His toes had to be amputated, and lockjaw set in. He had always believed in a water cure and refused to submit to conventional treatment. He died after two weeks of intense suffering. It was July, 1869, and he was sixty-three.

VIII

A month later his son, Washington Augustus Roebling, was officially appointed to succeed his father as chief engineer. His task was to be marred by deaths and injuries of the men beside whom he worked. Nor was he himself spared. During the first three years he shared the most difficult assignments with his men, including the work in a pneumatic caisson for creating a foundation of concrete beneath the river bed to hold the masonry above it. He was one of those who were stricken with caisson disease—"the bends"—which turned him into a permanent invalid.

The sinking of a pneumatic caisson was a new technique, and "the bends" was a new disease about which little was known. It affected the "sandhogs" upon emerging from an atmosphere of compressed air into the ordinary atmosphere. Later, it was found that the reduction of pressure liberated nitrogen bubbles from the blood and tissues, which caused cramps, vertigo, and paralysis. The bridge claimed one hundred and ten cases of "the bends," three of whom died.[21] In 1872 Colonel Roebling was brought out of the caisson unconscious. In a few days he was thought to be sufficiently improved to return to work. But he collapsed again, and this time he remained paralyzed below the waist. It was three years after the death of his father and he was thirty-five.

Nevertheless, he would not give up. Continuing to direct the work from his sickroom, he spent a whole winter drawing up plans and writing instructions for making the cables and creating the superstructure. The heroine of the project was his wife, Emily Warren Roebling. In order to be able to assume the role of her husband's contact with the men, she studied higher mathematics with him and visited the bridge daily to bring his instructions and to report the day-to-day progress to him. After twelve years, only nine months before the bridge was completed, an effort was made to displace Washington Roebling from his job as chief engineer and to appoint the first assistant engineer to the post. It was then that Emily Warren Roebling appeared before the American Society of Civil Engineers with a statement from her husband, appealing to the engineering profession for their support to prevent him from being supplanted.

In May of 1883, after sixteen years of unceasing work and worry and the loss of twenty lives, including that of the chief engineer, the completed bridge glistened in the sunshine of a beautiful spring day, its wire cables hanging like necklaces from the towers. Washington Roebling could not attend the opening ceremonies. He watched them through field glasses from a window of his home in Brooklyn Heights. Later, the president, Chester A. Arthur, the governor of the state of New York, and the trustees of the project came to his home to pay him homage.

The names of the two heroes and one heroine are indissolubly linked to the bridge—the man who had envisioned it, laid the plans, and lost his life in the effort to transform dream into reality; his son, Colonel Washington Roebling, who accomplished what his father had begun despite his infirmity; and Emily Warren Roebling, through whom the stricken man kept in touch with the construction from his sickbed. In 1908 the people of Trenton raised the cost of a monument in bronze to the memory of John Roebling. In 1951 the Brooklyn Engineers Club subscribed to erect a memorial tablet to Emily Warren Roebling, Colonel Washington Augustus Roebling, and John Augustus Roebling, in this order, to be placed on the bridge. The tablet bears the following inscription:

THE BUILDERS OF THE BRIDGE

Dedicated to the memory of

EMILY WARREN ROEBLING
(1843-1903)

With faith and courage, she helped her stricken husband

COL. WASHINGTON A. ROEBLING, C.E.
(1837-1926)

to complete the construction of this Bridge
from the plans of his father

JOHN A. ROEBLING, C.E.
(1806-1869)

who gave his life to this Bridge

"Back of every great work we can find the
self-sacrificing devotion of a woman."

———

This tablet is erected in 1951 by

THE BROOKLYN ENGINEERS CLUB

with funds raised by popular subscription.

New York, 1950.   D. B. Steinman.

The tablet catches the eye of strollers coming from Manhattan to Brooklyn.

From Germany:

JOHN PETER ALTGELD
1847-1902

Man of Conscience

A fighter for justice, he reached one of the highest positions to which one who was not a native could aspire—the governorship of the state of Illinois. Two of his actions as governor assure him a permanent place in the history of the nation: his pardon in 1892 of the anarchists serving prison sentences as the result of "the Haymarket Affair," which took place in Chicago in 1886, and his opposition to President Cleveland's action in dispatching federal troops to quell the Pullman Strike of 1894.

Though condemned and abused as few men were, he was to many a hero. To the poet Vachel Lindsay he was "Eagle Forgotten"; Howard Fast wrote of him who was foreign-born as "The American."

Economic Dislocation in the German States

The Napoleonic Wars left to the German-speaking people a legacy of profound discontent that affected all classes of German society. While the ruling cliques strove to maintain the status quo ante, the intellectuals, chafing under the restrictive climate, yearned for revolution. The middle and lower classes were suffering from enonomic and social changes of such significance that slow stagnation and even starvation seemed ineluctable. The effects of the Industrial Revolution, with its introduction of the factory system and labor-saving devices, were ruining the cottage industries, particularly producers of linen. Thrown out of work, people found themselves unemployable.

The rural population was not exempt. Crop failures were filling them with despair. Others were alarmed over the introduction of compulsory military training, a lesson of the French Revolution the German princes had accepted with unanimous enthusiasm. The forced departure of young males for soldiery deprived families of needed help from their sons and disturbed religious and pacifist groups who saw in conscription preparation for war, to which they were opposed on principle.

Another important factor that added to the dislocation was the spectacular increase in population after 1815 all over Europe. In the hundred-year period after the surrender of Napoleon, the German population alone rose from twenty-five million to almost seventy million.[1] Where was their living to come from? Emigration seemed the only way out.

The dissatisfaction of the German-speaking peoples during the decades prior to the Civil War reflected itself in the constantly accelerated emigration to the United States. The first significant increase was felt in 1832 when the number of German immigrants exceeded ten thousand.[2] The increment was undoubtedly caused by the failure of the Revolution of 1830. Between 1845 and 1860, the period of the highest increase, one million, two hundred and fifty thousand poured into America, leading the German historian, Heinrich von Treitschke, to the assertion that almost one-third of the population of North America was of German origin, for the reason that five million out of more than fifteen million immigrants were of Germanic stock.

The contribution of the Germans was of incalculable importance. As workers, they brought new and valuable skills to America. As farmers, they were careful husbandmen whose way of cultivating the soil was in distinct contrast to the wasteful methods of native agriculturists who were apt to feel that if one's acres became exhausted, one could go farther west. Among German workers there were skillful carpenters, printers, upholsterers, bakers, wagonmakers, locksmiths, glassworkers, and other craftsmen. German immigrants introduced the butcher shop and the corner bakery. Trained Germans opened pharmacies. German workers built musical instruments and kept them in repair. By perpetuating their cherished traditions, they brought subtle changes into American life. They introduced the first Christmas tree west of the Appalachians. Where evergreens were not to be had, a sassafras was made to do.[3] They formed *Biergärten, Turner,* and *Sänger Vereine;* they arranged *Volksfeste* and Sunday picnics which attracted Americans and acquainted them with the German *Gemütlichkeit.* Trained musicians started symphony orchestras and introduced the native population to symphonic concerts, and owners of brass instruments organized bands to provide entertainment in saloons and for festive occasions and funerals.[4]

Though the claim that the Germans contributed an unusually large contingent of intellectuals is a well-founded one, the bulk of German newcomers consisted of humble, hardworking folk who had no higher expectations than to own farms and make their living from the soil, if they had been farmers, or to become mechanics, small tradesmen, or common laborers, if they had worked in such capacities at home. It was in many cases an undreamed-of promise of American life that even from the humblest families a "Little Giant" could arise who was destined to make an impression on the nation. Such a man was John Peter Altgeld.

The American Setting

Throughout the nineteenth century the undeveloped land and the growing commerce beckoned invitingly to immigrants to join in the effort of developing the country. In 1848 the United States had gained a large portion of territory through the Mexican War, confirming some people in their belief that it was their "Manifest Destiny" to make the continent American. The riches of America seemed without end. Though until 1862 prospective settlers had to purchase land from the federal government at between $1.25 and $2.00 an acre, and at higher prices from the railroads and land speculators, settlement went on so rapidly that between 1846 and the outbreak of the Civil War six western states were able to meet population requirements for joining the Union.[5] The frontier was pushed beyond the Missouri River.

Prior to the outbreak of the Civil War, America's commercial development had reached a state designated by economic historians as "mercantile capitalism," but a new era was rapidly approaching. In the East farms and shops still commingled, but agriculture was becoming subordinated to industry, with New York, Chicago, Philadelphia, Boston, and Pittsburgh in the front ranks. A number of smaller cities had forged ahead as centers for shipyards, railroad building, and machinery and commercial manufacturing. Urban growth was proceeding with such rapidity (due to immigration and the movement of rural Americans to the cities, where jobs were more plentiful), that after the end of the Civil War the main urban centers would increasingly reveal the blight of spreading slums. There were no professional police organizations, fire departments, or public health services until past the middle of the nineteenth century. Fires, causing frightful destruction in many of the large cities (which were largely built of wood), were not isolated occurrences; nor were epidemics of typhoid, smallpox, and even cholera. The telegraph had been invented, but was only in limited use; the telephone and electric lights did not come into existence until the end of the century.

The majority of the work force consisted of wage earners who received incredibly small wages. Only a very small fraction of the people enjoyed large incomes. The richest man before the Civil War is said to have been John Jacob Astor, a German immigrant, whose fortune, made in New York City real estate and by profiteering in government bonds during the War of 1812, is supposed to have amounted to more than twenty million at his death in 1848.[6]

In the wake of swelling immigration, hostility to foreigners was gaining among native Americans, who were not averse to banding together in secret societies to stem the alien menace. Because of the tendency among members to refuse information with the retort "I know nothing," the movement was dubbed "Know-Nothingism." During its heyday in the 1850's, "Know-Nothingism" met with surprising success in electing local officials in Massachusetts, Pennsylvania, and New York—an indication of the deep resentment felt toward foreigners. Although the movement did not survive after 1860, its seeds remained dormant, to spring up again in other efforts to limit the privileges of the foreign-born, until in the early twentieth century it culminated in the termination of the historic policy of free and unhindered immigration.

The Civil War, the most significant event of the nineteenth century in America, affected immigrants as well as natives. Among the hundreds of thousands who fought in the Civil War, there were newcomers of all nationalities—Scandinavians, Italians, Dutch, Swiss—including some who had not even learned to speak English. A well-known combatant was Joseph Pulitzer, who was of Hungarian birth. More than a hundred and seventy-five thousand men of German parentage enlisted,[7] forming their own battalions under their own leaders. One was Brigadier General Carl Schurz; another was Major General Franz Sigel. The Irish, too, volunteered in enormous numbers (despite the Draft Riots in New York City in 1863) and formed their own regiments.

The foreign-born gained a tremendous advantage from the Homestead Act of 1862, enacted after the war had begun. This policy of granting anyone one hundred and sixty acres of unoccupied land, provided he pledged himself to become a citizen and to live upon the land for five years, acted as a magnet to the land-hungry peoples of Europe. To millions of Northern Europeans who had led a miserable existence on "pocket handkerchief" farms this lavish gift represented the *promise of America*.

A song that grew up—"Uncle Sam is rich enough to give us all a farm"—reveals the interpretation placed on "Uncle Sam's" munificence to agricultural settlers. City-dwellers, however, received no favored treatment. Their privilege was to work on the most onerous jobs at the lowest wages and to live in slums such as did not exist even in the factory towns of England. The consequence was that such evils as unemployment, labor unrest, savage strikes, and depressions were felt with particular severity in urban centers. These conditions increased in violence as the nineteenth century neared its end.

The Civil War had brought to an end America's golden youth.

I

John Peter Altgeld experienced all the convulsions of the latter half of the nineteenth century. He served in the Civil War, which left him with a permanent impairment. He made a fortune that he lost, and he died a poor man. He served as a judge, then as governor of Illinois, yet met an ignominious end. If not for the fact that he was born in Germany and was brought to America when he was three months old, he could have had the nomination for the presidency in 1896 on the Democratic ticket. He commanded such strong labor and Populist support that people believed had he been a native he could have won against McKinley in 1896. Instead, everything he had gained slipped through his fingers. His conviction that because the anarchists of the Haymarket Affair, condemned for throwing the bomb that killed and maimed policemen and bystanders, had not been *proved* guilty, they deserved a pardon, ruined his political career. Later, his stubborn insistence that President Cleveland had no right to send troops to Chicago against the Pullman strikers when the authorities had not requested such aid, finished the hope of receiving a second term as governor. Such slander and contempt were heaped on him that from then on he found himself powerless, except in one respect: he could see to it that the party denied President Cleveland the renomination to another term, which Cleveland wanted. This he accomplished, but it did not save him in the eyes of the people. Shakespeare's words uttered by Richard II in his despair, might have been repeated by Altgeld:

> I live with bread like you, feel want,
> Taste grief, need friends. Subjected thus,
> How can you say to me I am a king?

II

In 1847, Altgeld's parents, simple farm folk from southern Germany, decided to make the attempt to improve their situation by taking themselves and their firstborn infant son of three months to a rented farm near Mansfield, Ohio, which relatives had found for them. The unstable political situation in the German states worried them less than the economic bind which affected so many of those living off the soil.

During the next twelve years eight more children were born. They were years of severe struggles and privation. In addition to attending to his chores on his farm, the father worked at his trade as a wagon maker. John Peter was twelve when the father purchased a larger farm, on which he took a heavy mortgage. As the eldest in the family it devolved upon the boy to do more than a boy's share in helping to reduce the mortgage. While he attended school—for two summers and one winter—he revealed no special aptitude for studying. To a family obsessed with one ambition—eventually to own the farm without the shackles of a mortgage—the boy had acquired sufficient education.

His father was a severe disciplinarian who did not believe in sparing the rod. The thirteen-year-old boy was expected not only to plow and do the heavy farm work, but when there was not enough work at home, he was hired out to neighbors. The wages he received went to his father.

In appearance the boy was unprepossessing. Somewhat under medium height, he appeared shorter because of his short legs and a shuffling gait. Later, he would be referred to as "the little Dutchman." He had a slight harelip, about which he seemed to have been sensitive, because as a grown man he would hide it under a moustache. His eyes of deep blue were said to be "remarkable." When Brand Whitlock, lawyer, journalist, and, many years later, reform mayor of Toledo, Ohio, met Altgeld, then in his middle age, he noticed that his eyes stood out in his face and that they shone with a high intelligence. Whitlock was struck by his "sad and serious face," which seemed to him to be "a mask of suffering and despair."

The rough, homemade clothes he wore as a youth did not enhance the impression he created. He learned to accept ridicule, which might have been due to the prevalence of anti-foreign sentiment, then in its heyday. But his speech and appearance did not help. He spoke with a German accent, traces of which remained even in later years when he had become a fluent speaker. Howard Fast mentions that he "spoke the weird half-German, half-English of the backlands."[8] Even when he had become governor of Illinois, his foreign birth was frequently referred to with contempt. His enemies did not hesitate to speak of him as a "foreigner," "un-American," "a mysterious fragment of jetsam from the Lord knows where." To Theodore Roosevelt he was "the Illinois Communist."[9]

III

In 1863, at the age of sixteen, Altgeld enlisted as a substitute for someone who had enough money to buy his safety. The bounty of one hundred dollars he received from his country was turned over to his father, who gave him ten dollars.[10] After a short training period he was sent to the swamplands of the James River, where he contracted a severe case of fever, a variant of the ague, of which he almost died. He could have received a discharge, but he preferred to serve until the end of the war. What had he to return to? The effects of the fever were to return periodically throughout his life.

When he returned home after his discharge a strange ambition had come to the surface—the desire to go to high school. Though his father objected, he enrolled in the high school of Mansfield. He was still far from an inspired student, but he was interested in reading. At nineteen he was appointed a teacher. His salary of thirty-five dollars a month went to his father. At twenty-one, when he could consider his obligation to his father fulfilled, he decided to break the tie that bound him to his family and to seek his fortune further west.

The tendency to seek wider opportunities in the "West" predates Huckleberry Finn's half-hearted musings on whether or not to "light out for the territories," as well as Horace Greeley's advice, "Go west, young man." Since prerevolutionary days young Americans had developed the habit of leaving the settled states to seek greener fields, literally and figuratively, in the newer states, if not in the territories. It was not unheard-of for several sons of one family to leave the family hearth and to carve careers for themselves in widely separated states. An example is the Washburn family in Maine. Four sons migrated, each to a different state. All were elected to Congress where they came together again, each to champion the interests of his own state.[11]

Though German immigrants of Altgeld's peasant background were not politically minded, for to them politics seemed a too impractical and volatile profession, the plan by which the young man hoped to raise himself was to study law and to enter a political career. In this he again followed a custom that was typical of young Americans. Yet in later years, when the newspapers turned against him, their favorite attack was to point out that "he did not reason like an American, nor act like one."

His destination was St. Louis rather than Chicago, because at that time it was a widely held belief that it might outdistance the other city. Altgeld set out on foot, working for handouts, and when he was down to his last penny he took a job as a section hand on the railroad for what was then a magnificent wage—three dollars and a half per day. By then he had reached Missouri, where he was stricken by a recurrence of fever so severe that he had good reason to fear he would not survive. He possessed so much grit that as soon as he was on his feet again he set out for the North and a more salubrious climate. Though terribly weak, he walked one hundred miles through open prairie on bare feet.[12] He was near collapse when a farmer took him in out of pity.

After he recovered Altgeld began to pay back his debt to his benefactor by working on his farm, as he had promised. When the local teacher gave up his post, he persuaded the school trustees to give him the job. He taught, worked the farm, and at night read law. He was admitted to the bar and shortly after was appointed city attorney for the small town of Savannah, Missouri. A year later, in 1873, panic and depression struck the country, bringing collapse to the financial structure. Bankruptcies multiplied, unemployment rose drastically. In the West, farm priced dropped so sharply as to produce a glut of agricultural products. The farmer who could not meet his mortgage payment was likely to find himself homeless. The impact on the farmers was to give rise to that syndrome called "the Granger Revolt," which manifested itself on the one hand in hostility to bankers and financiers, particularly those with eastern connections, and on the other, in seeking political power through affiliation with the People's party, as Granger political units came to be called. Altgeld was able to observe the effect of the depression on the farmers, and from that time on his sympathies were on the side of all strugglers and toilers. Nominated for the office of prosecuting attorney by the People's party, he won against heavy competition. Thus began his political career.

But within a year, while depression was still holding the country in its grip, Altgeld chucked his job and with his entire fortune of less than one hundred dollars, departed for Chicago.

He had come to the conclusion that Chicago was a better place in which to make one's start than St. Louis. Four years after the disastrous fire of 1871, the city was growing spectacularly, but it was one of the unloveliest places in all America. A tremendous number of immigrants toiled in Chicago's factories, railroad yards, and meat packing plants. By 1890 sixty-eight percent of the population were foreign-born and another ten percent were children of immigrants.[13] The conditions described in the following excerpt may be taken as having been characteristic not only of Chicago but of other industrial centers of that time:

Chicago had become a city of intolerable extremes. At the top were men like Marshall Field, who could spend seventy-five thousand dollars on a birthday party for his son. At the bottom were innumerable families where ten year old children had to work along with their mothers and fathers to scrape together the necessities for the most miserable existence. Field had piled up his fortune while thousands of women clerks in his store earned less than a living wage. Swift had made his, but if a worker in his packinghouse broke a leg, the man was turned into the street and forgotten and another hired in his place. George Pullman built a model factory town and made many inventions and a great fortune—but in doing so he goaded his workers into striking and the strike set off one of the most violent labor conflicts in American history. When the demand for meat declined, Armour might turn out thousands of men, with no notice at all; if their families starved, that was no concern of the company. Such were the inexorable laws of trade. Men who could not rise to the top were smashed underfoot.[14]

IV

In the state of Illinois Altgeld was to play out the role for which his destiny had cast him. He returned to the practice of law in a tiny cubicle where he slept behind a screen. He drifted into real estate, then gathered a fortune and decided to make his first "bid for immortality"[15] by erecting Chicago's first skyscraper. A sixteen-story building that he called "Unity Block," it ruined him in the end.

The apogee of his career was his election to the governorship of the state. By then he had become so devoted to Chicago that he justified a veto on legislation he thought would squander Chicago's resources by remarking, "I love Chicago." In 1905, when he had been dead three years, his friend, Edward Osgood Brown, a judge, stated before the Chicago Historical Society: "He loved Chicago and he loved Illinois even more." More than fifty years after Altgeld's tenure as governor, a distinguished successor, Adlai Stevenson, also a Democrat, would express his feelings for Illinois as "a thrice-blessed land," a statement the more easily understandable in that Stevenson's family had been associated with the history of the state for generations.

In Chicago Altgeld met some of the men who were to have considerable influence on his thoughts and actions. Among them were Brand Whitlock, whose ideas received implementation when he became reform mayor of Toledo; Clarence Darrow, defender of labor and liberal causes; and George Schilling, radical labor leader and socialist organizer. Like Altgeld, Schilling was of German birth and came from much the same background. The effect of their ideas was to make him aware of the need for social reform, in particular, prison reform. As governor, he would concentrate on strengthening the charitable and penal systems, he was responsible for obtaining from the state legislature a law adopting the parole system; he abolished the striped garb of prisoners. He was also interested in building up the University of Illinois, whose budget he increased. Formed some twenty-five years before under the Morrill Land Grant Act of 1862, the university had still to win its reputation. Its growth meant so much to him that when at the end of his term as governor financial disaster struck him and the banker who had carried his loans defaulted with some of the university's securities, he was heartbroken and wrote: "I would as soon have been paralyzed as to have had anything happen to this institution."[16]

There can be no doubt that Altgeld was an ambitious man who was dominated by the need for personal success. Having married an educated, handsome woman, he wanted desperately to make an impress on his society. His wife was a graduate of Oberlin College, which was the first college in America to grant degrees to women as well as to admit Negroes. When he first made his bid for her, her family, which was of American lineage, indicated that he was not welcome; but when he returned as a wealthy and successful man he encountered no objections. She was to uphold him through thick and thin, sharing his triumphs as well as his humiliations.

With so much to make up for in his past, the acquiring of a fortune was not enough to satisfy Altgeld. The skyscraper was an attempt to gain prestige, but it proved too ambitious a project for his financial resources and before it was finished he had to mortgage or sell his other properties. He sank four hundred thousand dollars of his own money into it and placed the financing in the hands of a banker, John R. Walsh, who proved unscrupulous. When in his capacity as governor he vetoed what he called the "Eternal Monopoly Bills," in which the traction king, Charles T. Yerkes, and Walsh were interested, Walsh used every means to harass him financially. But the governor would not yield. It is ironic that Yerkes is said to have admired Altgeld so much that in 1899 he contributed to his campaign for mayor of Chicago without the candidate's knowledge.[17] But Yerkes' own vote went to the opposition candidate who was a Republican.

V

It has been said that Altgeld's prime ambition was to be elected to Congress, specifically to the Senate. He made the race in 1884 on the Democratic ticket, but that year Illinois stuck to its Republican tradition and he was defeated. The day on which he won the congressional nomination coincided with the appearance of his first book, *Our Penal Machinery and Its Victims*. Prisoners, he set forth with an immense sympathy reinforced by charts and calculations, were those who had no proper homes, who had lost one or both parents at an early age. They were the victim of circumstances. The intentions of the prison system, he stated, was to punish those unfortunates of society instead of rehabilitating them. Let us listen to him:

Therein lies the objection to our present system. It applies the *crushing process* to those who are already down, while the crafty criminal—especially if he be rich—is gently dealt with.[18]

His attitude predated the exposures of Alexander Berkman, the anarchist, which presented a horrifying picture of the inhuman treatment accorded to prisoners.[19]

In addition Altgeld urged specific reforms, such as immediate trials, the opportunity to earn enough in prison to support dependents over and above the actual expense of keeping an individual in prison, and the education of prisoners to prepare them for earning a livelihood. His sincerity so impressed Eugene V. Debs—that indefatigable champion of all victims of social injustice—that he wrote of him: "He was genuine, he was true, he could look God and man straight in the eye."[20]

His concern for the underprivileged of society revealed itself in subsequent articles which kept appearing in newspapers and magazines. Later they were gathered together under the title *Live Questions*. He condemned sweatshops and child labor; he advocated limiting the work of women to eight hours; he favored factory inspection and arbitration of strikes—all considered radical proposals at that time. The lynching of a Negro outraged him. It was considered such a strange preoccupation for a lawyer specializing in real-estate promotion that the only explanation would be his pinched childhood, which had made him receptive to the problems of the underdog in society. As governor he exercised his pardoning power so frequently, that he came to be called "Pardoning John."

The tragic Haymarket incident that took the lives of seven policemen and wounded fifty more people, policemen and bystanders, had taken place in May, 1886. In 1886 Altgeld was elected superior judge of Cook County. He won the office with the support of labor. Schilling had endorsed him as one of labor's sympathizers. Though he was in favor of the eight-hour day (one of the issues that underlay "the Haymarket Affair") and the unionization of workers (he employed only union labor on his construction projects), he had carefully refrained from antagonizing the capitalist elements. During the Haymarket trial he was silent, and he did not sign any of the petitions for clemency, which some of the most respected people of Chicago favored. He was acting the part of a conservative liberal. Schilling explained his silence in regard to the condemned anarchists as stemming from the realization that he could do nothing. Nevertheless, Altgeld found that the labels "radical," "anarchist," and "follower of Karl Marx," were beginning to be pinned on him, particularly by Joseph Medill of the *Chicago Tribune*, who was to prove increasingly hostile to him and his policies.[21]

In 1891 he resigned his judgeship, giving pressure of private business as the reason. Due to faulty construction the Unity building was costing him a great deal more than he had anticipated. It was now near completion and was to be opened in 1893. However, cynics spread the opinion that he had stepped down from the bench because his sights were on the Senate.

Instead, Altgeld found himself elected governor in 1892. He was the first Democratic governor of Illinois since the Civil War, as Adlai Stevenson was to point out in his inaugural speech when he became governor in 1948. Altgeld was hailed as the new "Little Giant" of Illinois. (The first had been Senator Stephen Douglas, Lincoln's opponent in the election of 1860, and he, too, had been of short stature.) During the campaign Altgeld had sought out miners and farmers and had indicated that he was sympathetic to their grievances, but had refrained from antagonizing the conservative elements. Though he acted the part of a liberal conservative with businessmen, the cry that he was a "millionaire fraud" and an "anarchist sympathizer," was increasingly heard.

His election in 1892 was a personal triumph. Although he had made no promises, it was expected by his supporters—among them George Schilling, Clarence Darrow, and Henry Demarest Lloyd—as well as by thousands of laboring people who had voted for him, that he would reexamine the evidence in the Haymarket case. Immortality was hovering in the wings; but so were obloquy and degradation. They had not as long to wait as immortality.

VI

Altgeld's inauguration was followed by a severe bout of illness, a recurrence of the ailment that was a legacy from the Civil War. Three months later Clarence Darrow appeared as an emissary from the governor's labor supporters to remind him that they were getting impatient because action in regard to the Haymarket prisoners was being delayed. Altgeld had appointed George Schilling secretary of the State Board of Labor Statistics, and Florence Kelley and Julia Lathrop, both reformers, as respectively chief factory inspector for the state and member of the State Board of Charities. As for Darrow, he had been placed with the city of Chicago in a legal capacity. Later, he was to be recommended for a legal job with the Northwestern Railroad, which Darrow would give up in order to defend Debs for his leadership in the Pullman Strike. Darrow was on his "second career" in labor law, which was to be followed by a "third career" in criminal law.[22]

To Darrow's reminder that the release of the prisoners was expected to be the governor's first act, Altgeld replied that he would act when he was ready and would then do what he considered "right." By then the governor had requested the files of the anarchists' case and the transcript of the court records and was studying them. Another advocate of pardon received this answer: "By God, if I decide they are innocent, I will pardon them, if I never hold office another day."[23] He was aware that if he ordered the release of the prisoners, he would be a "dead man politically."

Several months after Altgeld's inauguration, while he was occupied in studying ' the case, the judge under whom the anarchists had been tried and convicted—Joseph E. Gary—published in *Century Magazine* an article that was a whitewash of his role in the trial. He insisted that the eight defendants (four had been hanged and one had committed suicide in his cell) had been "rightly punished, not for their opinions, as liberals claimed, but for their deeds." It was a bold attempt to gloss over a case that even lay people considered suspicious. To someone who was a lawyer and had been a judge, Gary's reasoning would seem even more suspect. The article must have angered the governor, but he kept his feelings a secret. On the day after the unveiling of a monument placed before the graves of the anarchists at Waldheim Cemetery—on June 26, 1893—the pardon message freeing the three still imprisoned burst upon the public. The individual who had been the foreman of the grand jury and had been suffering from misgivings ever since, was entrusted with the delivery of the pardon to the prison officials. He wept when handed the document.

The pardon caused an uproar. A torrent of vilification swept over the governor. It came not only from the Chicago papers but from newspapers and magazines all over the nation. Among them were the *New York Times,* the *Washington Post,* the *Boston Herald,* The *Nation, Harper's Weekly,* and many others. Some called for impeachment. The words of one of the pardoned, Michael Schwab, that it was "the deed of a brave heart, and will live as such in history,"[24] did not deflect the fury of those who disagreed. An avalanche of epithets descended upon Altgeld. He was called "anarchist," "viper," "slimy demagogue," "un-American," "a disgrace to our Republic." The *Chicago Tribune* remarked: "He has apparently not a drop of true American blood in his veins. He does not reason like an American, nor feel like one, and consequently does not behave like one."[25] He was denounced by politicians, civic leaders, and ministers. Even in 1896, during the Democratic convention, he was referred to as "a genuine European Red."

Though Altgeld had expected an adverse reaction, the vitriol that was poured out surprised even those who were accustomed to antiradical sentiments. He was burned in effigy. The custom of inviting the governor to review an annual parade was ignored. An invitation to attend the commencement exercises at Northwestern University was withheld. When he and his wife visited a hotel in the East, the guests left the hotel, refusing to stay under the same roof with "that anarchist."[26] The malice shown by the newspapers was unbelievable. He was depicted in cartoons in the vanguard of a procession of anarchists, carrying a can of blood, or waving the flag of anarchy. Nor was the public allowed to forget it. In 1901, after the assassination of President McKinley, he was pictured alongside the murderer, Czolgosz, holding in his hand a torn Constitution.

VII

In view of the fact that even during the trial there had been an insistent call for clemency for the accused, and that an Amnesty Association had been specifically formed for the purpose of agitating for the release of the surviving three prisoners, the reaction of the press would be considered irrational, except for one fact: the nature of the pardon. Instead of a "mercy" pardon, of which even reactionaries might have approved, the eighteen-thousand-word pardon message was an unconcealed attack on the judge under whom the case had been tried. Entitled "Reasons for Pardoning Fielden, Neebe and Schwab," the document stressed "the unfairness of the judge," that he had permitted a "packed jury to render the verdict," that the evidence was "pure fabrication," that the defendants had not been proved guilty, and that the prosecutor "took his cue from the judge's remarks." In other words, the blame was place squarely on the judge. Even Jane Addams and Clarence Darrow, both friends of the governor, thought it had been unwise to attack the judge in such a conspicuous way. Brand Whitlock, who was devoted to Altgeld, thought it was regrettable that "so great a soul should have permitted itself to mar the document by expressions of hatred of the judge who tried the case." In a statement that was also a comment on Altgeld's later action in connection with the Pullman Strike, Edgar Lee Masters declared: "It might have been possible for him to have pardoned the anarchists and protested against the act of Cleveland in sending troops to Illinois during the American Railway Union Strike without ruining himself. Cleveland and the men in the penitentiary came into Altgeld's life without fault on his part and he dealt with them according to the nature that was given him."[27] Altgeld denied the charge that he had been influenced by his dislike for Gary, pointing out that he had denounced not Gary, but "Garyism."

The key word in Masters' statement is Altgeld's "nature." It was his nature to be impulsive, stubborn, and reckless. He had demonstrated his recklessness and stubbornness in his "Unity" building, when, to everyone's surprise he had committed his whole fortune to it, contrary to the counsel of friends. That he was hotheaded, and unyielding, "with a huge capacity for bitterness," he was to prove again during the presidential election of 1896, when he made the most of his opportunity to revenge himself on President Cleveland for having shown him less than the full respect to which as governor of Illinois he considered himself entitled.

"He never chose the easy way," was Masters' explanation, "he meant to undo it [the 'judicial crime' that had led to the execution of four men and the imprisonment of three] as to the living men in prison by a historic rebuke of the society and the judge who had committed it." When Altgeld was aroused, expediency was swept aside. "He hated the bad so much that it obscured the love of the good," Masters explained. Thus, it seems to have been his "nature" that brought on his political destruction and, eventually, his untimely end.

What had blown up the storm over the pardon of the Haymarket victims was not so much that Altgeld had freed them, but that he had violated the unspoken rule not to assail a judge. This was a serious misdemeanor in a country where respect for the judiciary is a cornerstone of government, and it provided the rationale for the accusation that his behavior was un-American. He might have been forgiven in time if henceforth he had acted with caution. But caution was distinctly not an Altgeldian trait.

VIII

The other portentous event which afforded his "nature" the chance to assert itself again occurred during the Pullman Strike of 1894. A man of Altgeld's views would naturally have sympathized with the strikers, who had not only always been poorly paid, but who were now asked to accept a wage cut without a reduction in the rent or in the price of goods charged in the company store of Pullman's "model town." Furthermore, George Pullman had refused and was continuing to refuse arbitration, which Altgeld always recommended in labor disputes. Even conservative Republicans advised arbitration. One of them was Marcus A. Hanna, who would later become McKinley's backer for the presidency. He sent his brother to George Pullman to urge mediation. When told that Pullman remained obdurate, he stormed: "The damned idiot ought to arbitrate, arbitrate, arbitrate! . . . A man who won't meet his men halfway is a Goddamned fool!"

IX

In this impasse between George Pullman and his employees, the American Railway Union had committed itself to aid the striking workers by refusing to move trains carrying Pullman cars. According to Debs and others, the strike would have been won if Richard Olney, Cleveland's attorney general in his second administration, had not thought up the idea of attaching sleeping cars to mail trains. He had been a railroad lawyer and was "railroad and corporation minded." It was an explosive situation, yet neither the mayor of Chicago nor the sheriff of Cook County requested state aid from the governor. The reason might have been that Altgeld's attitude was suspect. Henry Demarest Lloyd, a labor sympathizer, testified in a newspaper article in the *New York Morning Journal* that Altgeld assured him:

If it becomes necessary I could and would put 100,000 men into the city of Chicago inside of five days. The whole state would answer the call as one man.... [and that] Governor Altgeld acted in this crisis with the most scrupulous faithfulness to his official obligation.[28]

However, without application from the legislature of the state or its executive, President Cleveland decided to intervene by sending federal troops. The excuse was that the mail had to go through. This action without the request of the proper authorities was interpreted as an invasion of "States' rights" and was considered an enormous affront to its governor. This is implicit in the following comment in the pages of the *Nation,* whose editor was the foreign-born Edwin Lawrence Godkin, a political conservative: "...he can scarcely fail to wince under the treatment he received from the president."[29] In two lengthy telegrams to the president, Altgeld requested that the troops be withdrawn, because the action was "unnecessary" and "unjustifiable" and because he was fully able to handle the situation. It took courage to defy the president, but courage Altgeld possessed in plenty. He knew the president would receive all the support and that he would be the recipient of severe criticism. The press did not disappoint him. A torrent of abuse again descended on him.

The exchange of telegrams did not result in the withdrawal of troops. The strike was lost; Debs went to jail for six months for ignoring a government injunction and emerged a "political Socialist" who for the rest of his life was to blast away at the capitalist structure. Altgeld was worsted, but only temporarily. The first step he took was to bring into the limelight the ridiculously low taxes Pullman had been paying. He also publicized the miserable treatment accorded to the defeated strikers, many of whom were not taken back and were homeless and starving. The upshot was that the Illinois Supreme Court declared George Pullman's "model town" illegal, forcing him to give up the company town where he had been able to extort from his employees high rents and inflated prices at the company store. Altgeld could now afford to be completely outspoken in his championship of labor and in his condemnation of "the privileged few."

X

It was to be expected that a man of Altgeld's "nature" would seek the opportunity to retaliate for the insult to his dignity by President Cleveland. The election of 1896 provided the opening he sought. By the time the convention drew near, it was clear Cleveland had alienated a large number of Democratic regulars who resented that he was a "gold-standard" man who had repealed the "Sherman Silver Purchase Act"—the favorite "child" of the western states—thus placing the country on a gold standard exclusively. In the view of farmers and the Populists who favored "cheaper money," the president had committed the nation to "dearer money." Others criticized him for having failed to revise the despised McKinley tariff. It appeared that a real revolt among Democrats was shaping up.

Altgeld had favored bimetallism since the early days, when the grievances of Grangers had impressed him as being well-founded. After his feud with Cleveland he became an even stronger supporter of the coinage of silver as a means of increasing the amount of money in circulation. To circumvent those members of the Democratic party who were in favor of maintaining the gold standard— "the Gold Democrats"—he prevailed upon the Illinois State Democratic Committee to call a special convention to act on the silver question. Illinois declared itself for bimetallism and thus struck the first blow at Cleveland. Other midwestern states followed the lead of Illinois by calling special conventions which repudiated the gold standard. The rebellion against Cleveland and his "hard money" policy was forced into the open.

When Altgeld departed for the national nominating convention as chairman of the Illinois delegation, he controlled forty-eight electoral votes, the highest of any state after New York and California. Since the Constitution requires that the president be a native American, all he could expect was to be able to influence the nomination. But it was readily admitted that if he had been a native he would have received the nomination. In becoming the leader of the "free silver" forces, he was able to circumvent the president, who was known to be eager to remain in office. This was Altgeld's revenge for Cleveland's behavior during the Pullman Strike. In vanquishing the president, he proved how inexorable an enemy he could be.

The great significance of the convention of 1896 is that its platform included many revolutionary planks, some of which became the reform measures of the early twentieth century. Whether the adoption of the platform which embodied many of the Populist demands was an Altgeldian achievement is a matter for conjecture, but it is significant that the second paragraph stated:

During all these years the Democratic Party . . . has found its best expression in the maintenance of the rights of the States and in its assertion of the necessity of confining the General Government to the exercise of the powers granted by the Constitution of the United States.[30]

It was a direct reference to the overstepping of the constitutional prerogative by the president in the Pullman Strike of 1894.

The nomination of William Jennings Bryan was to Altgeld, as it was to many others, an unexpected upset. What he had intended was to block the renomination of Cleveland, not to make Bryan the standard bearer of the party. He favored Senator Richard Bland of Missouri, whose career had been dedicated to leading the silver forces. What had brought Bryan to the forefront was the opportunity to make a speech that had not been scheduled. It was the emotional "Cross of Gold" oration and it so moved the delegates that they forgot about practical matters and the debt they owed to "Silver Dick" Bland and nominated a neophyte who, in Altgeld's opinion, possessed little more than the gift of oratory. Altgeld tried to hold out against the swing to Bryan, but on the fourth ballot he was forced to deliver the votes of Illinois to the "boy orator from the Platte." Bryan's defeat in 1896 and his subsequent failures in 1900 and

1908 confirmed Altgeld's soundness of judgment. But in spite of his doubts about Bryan, Altgeld traveled to New York City to give a memorable speech on his behalf in Cooper Union, and exerted himself to the limit to help him win.

XI

The Democrats lost, and McKinley and the gold standard won. Fortunately, the effects of the depression ushered in by the Panic of 1893 lifted and additional gold came in from Africa and other sources. Altgeld had not sought renomination, but he permitted it when he found himself renominated by acclamation. Not only had his health suffered, but his personal finances were in precarious shape. He too lost, but in his race for governor he received ten thousand more votes in the state of Illinois than Bryan did. His defeat caused newspapers all over the country to gloat and to shower him with expressions of contempt. The last insult was the refusal of the inauguration committee to let him make his farewell speech. He had released it to the press, and could not cancel it when he found he would not be allowed to speak.

In 1896, when Altgeld stepped out of office, six more years of life were left to him. During these years several more blows were inflicted on him. He lost his building. He would have saved himself financially if during his last days in office he had accepted a bribe for a half a million dollars in exchange for not blocking some monopoly bills. With his building lost, his whole fortune was swept away. In 1899 he allowed himself to be persuaded to run for mayor of Chicago, but was badly beaten.

There was nothing left for him to do but to return to the practice of law. At first he established his own law office, but in 1901 he joined Darrow & Thompson as a senior partner. In 1902 Darrow and he helped to set up a new bar association, having refused to join the Chicago Bar Association on the grounds that it was sympathetic to monopoly.

In 1901 he published a short volume entitled: *Oratory: Its Requirements and Its Rewards.* He started another volume of philosophical essays which was to be called: *The Cost of Something for Nothing,* but it was not to be published until after his death.

Altgeld died suddenly in March, 1902, after making a speech when he was overtired. At his death he received some praise from newspapers and individuals who had heaped obloquy upon his head during his public career. Darrow, his partner during the last year of his life, made a memorial address during which he observed cynically that one reason for Altgeld's greatness was that he had never had "the misfortune of being educated." (Nor had Darrow.) Immortality was hesitantly emerging from the wings. "Time has its way," as Vachel Lindsay was to say in his commemorative poem, "Eagle Forgotten." In the words of Edgar Lee Masters, "[Altgeld] had been beaten on everything for which he had fought. He had sacrificed himself, his wife's security, because he could not silence the voice that kept interposing itself with the insistent question: 'What is right?' "[31] At his death, he, at one time considered a millionaire, did not leave much more money than to cover the cost of his funeral.

ABRAHAM JACOBI
1830-1919

Impassioned Physician

*A political fugitive from the Revolution of 1848, he helped by his
high moral and ethical standards and his professional competence
to advance the medical profession in America and to bring it to the
high level of achievement for which it is celebrated throughout the
world. The realization that the diseases of childhood require specialized
study and attention led him to pioneer in a study of pediatrics and
to train a generation of physicians who would devote themselves
to the diseases of children.*

The Revolution of 1848

A second round of uprisings occurred in 1848. Paris again
fired "the first revolutionary cannon" (in the words of Abraham
Jacobi), which caused the abdication of Louis-Philippe, *"le roi
bourgeois,"* whose support had come from the middle class. He
was followed by the nephew of Napoleon I, Louis Napoleon,
who had enlivened his exile in England with grandiose dreams
of inheriting his uncle's powers and title. At first elected president of the French Republic, three years later, in 1851, he
made himself emperor of France by a *coup d'état.* He chose
as his name Napoleon III.

By 1848 the liberal elements of Germany, Austria, Hungary,
and Italy had grown sufficiently strong to rise in a series of
revolutions that shook the status quo to its foundations. One
month after the uprising in Paris, the Austrians rebelled against
the archconservative Count Metternich. The frightened em-

[67]

peror of Austria promised a constitution, a parliament, and a liberal franchise. But the promise was soon rescinded. The Austrian revolt was led by university students and young professional men, one of whom was Dr. Ernst Krackowizer. In America he would become a close friend of Jacobi, who had participated in revolutionary activities in Germany and had drawn a prison sentence in reprisal.

The Austrian insurrection was followed by an uprising in Italy. The American writer, Margaret Fuller, known as one of the early "bluestockings," happened to be in Italy on a journalistic mission when the rebellion broke out. It was to be expected that she who had been reared in the non-conformist tradition of New England should thrill to the call of freedom. She became romantically attached to one of the fighters against the Austrians, Count Angelo Ossoli, and married him. The Austrians defeated the rebellious Italians and Margaret Fuller took ship for America; but she, her husband, and baby were drowned in a shipwreck off Fire Island, near New York City. The manuscript of her Italian experiences, which she was bringing back with her, was lost. Freedom for the Italians was still several decades away.

The Hungarians did not fare much better than the Italians, although they met with greater success at the start. A Hungarian republic was set up under Louis Kossuth, but the Austrian emperor soon succeeded in overthrowing it with the help of the Russian Czar, whose overriding motive was to shore up the monarchical principle. Not until 1867, almost twenty years later, were the Hungarians given their own constitution, parliament, and administration, and then under an Austrian sovereign who would be emperor in Austria and king in Hungary. Thus was born the dual monarchy, Austria-Hungary.

Within a week after the outbreak of the revolt in Vienna, the revolution spread to Prussia and the German states. It became a movement for greater political liberties as well as unification of the states. The rebels met with unusually swift success, for in less than six months the first parliament was convened for the purpose of drawing up a constitution. But they fell into hopeless quarrels, which Austria exploited for the purpose of blocking German unification. Basic to Austria's objections was that unification would have swept out the Germanic Confederation that bound Austria and Germany together. Austria's role in the confederation was pivotal, and its dissolution would have reduced her importance. The republican members attempting to draw up a constitution for Germany deserted when the majority agreed to a limited monarchy, and the rest melted away. Very little of lasting significance was accomplished, but the cracks had widened.

The reactionary governments of Prussia and Austria attempted to repair the chinks in their armor by restoring the deposed princelings to power and by launching a ruthless manhunt for those who had taken part in the revolution or who had abetted it in any way. Some were executed; others imprisoned; those who could, fled—some to England, more to the United States. One of the latter was Carl Schurz, another, Franz Sigel, both of whom were to fight in the Union army as generals. One who chose to remain in England was Karl Marx.

Among the refugees America received was a group of highly trained individuals—physicians, lawyers, newspaper writers, editors, teachers, and businessmen. Of those who brought money with them, many bought homes in the "West"—in Missouri, Wisconsin, Illinois—and retired to rural obscurity, at least for a period of time. The Germans organized their own newspapers and schools and would have liked to establish a German state in America, if it had been possible. Many became teachers on all levels. Mrs. Schurz, for instance, is credited with having opened the first Montessori school for young children in Wisconsin. But many of these newcomers were unable to find positions for which their education fitted them and were forced to support themselves as waiters, bootblacks, street sweepers,[1] etc. Thousands would accept their situation in decades to come as more and more aliens poured into the United States.

Among the physicians there were some who had worked with the most famous men of their time. Their superior training became available to American hospitals and medical training centers. None made a contribution of greater significance or received greater honors than Abraham Jacobi.

Development of American Medicine

The earliest practitioners of medicine in the colonies were the ministers of New England, whose services in behalf of the sick were known as "Evangelical Conjunction." The most common diseases of a deadly nature which afflicted the colonial population were smallpox and diphtheria. Among children the death rate from dysentery and contagious diseases—measles and scarlet fever—was also very high. Death among young children was so frequent that many families had more children in the cemeteries than in their homes. The life expectancy at birth was only about twenty years.[2]

Smallpox occurred in the colonies as epidemics. Indians were particularly susceptible. As William Bradford of Plymouth Plantation remarked: ". . . a sorer disease cannot befall them; they fear it more than a plague."[3] When it broke out among them, ninety percent died for the reason that they lacked the immunity many of the colonists had developed through repeated exposure.

New England attempted inoculation against the disease very early. In the early 1700's Cotton Mather, the Puritan clergyman, of whose sixteen children nine died in infancy (four of smallpox),[4] publicly preached the advantage of inoculation. Zabdiel Boylston, a self-educated physician, inoculated his own son and others despite prohibition by the town government.[5] Cotton Mather, who was a member of the Royal Society in London, forwarded statistics on inoculation to the secretary of the society. The practice of inoculation in the colonies became so widespread that early in the Revolution George Washington ordered it to protect the whole army.[6] It is considered the first significant contribution of the New World to medical science.

During prerevolutionary times and the years of the early Republic, American physicians were practical men who maintained hospital facilities in their own homes and frequently were apothecaries as well. Prior to 1765, there were fifteen physicians who had studied in Edinburgh.[7] Throughout the eighteenth century and to a lesser degree during the early decades of the nineteenth century, Edinburgh and London remained the centers for the training of American physicians. The trend was to follow empirical rather than theoretical methods. Relying on the lessons of experience rather than on what they had read in books, they achieved astonishing successes. For instance, in 1809 a backwoods doctor, Ephraim

McDowell, who had studied in Edinburgh for a year, performed a successful operation for removal of the ovaries.[8] Because it was believed that the best way to pick up knowledge was by contact with the sick, would-be physicians apprenticed themselves to men in practice and learned what they could from observation at the bedside.

Five medical schools were in existence before 1800 and two before the Revolution. The first was the medical department of the College of Philadelphia, which was added to the college in 1765. (The college itself was founded in 1749.) The chief sponsors of the department were Dr. John Morgan and Dr. William Shippen, Jr., of Philadelphia, both of whom had studied in Edinburgh and London, as had Dr. Benjamin Rush, who joined the faculty soon after his return from abroad. Of great advantage was the Pennsylvania Hospital, which had been organized in 1751 by Dr. Thomas Bond with the aid of Benjamin Franklin. A hospital founded still earlier, in 1736, was Bellevue Hospital of New York City.

The second medical school in the country and the first in New York was that of King's College, organized in 1767 with a faculty of two. The school was a casualty of the Revolution, and even when revived in 1792 as Columbia College, attendance was sparse. In 1807 the medical department broke away to become the independent College of Physicians and Surgeons. Not until 1891, when Columbia College became Columbia University, did the medical school become part of the university's complex.

The medical school at Harvard University was founded in 1788, three years after Harvard College had become Harvard University. The plans were drawn up by Dr. John Warren, the younger brother of Dr. Joseph Warren, who had lost his life at Bunker Hill. The Warrens started a medical dynasty that was closely tied to the growth of the Harvard Medical School. The Medical Institute of Harvard University was conducted in Cambridge until 1810, when it was moved to Boston. Enormous benefits accrued to the medical school when the Massachusetts General Hospital came into existence in 1821.

The other two medical schools created before 1800 were that of Dartmouth College at Hanover, New Hampshire, in 1798

(Dartmouth itself was founded in 1770), and that of Transylvania University in 1799, the year after the organization of the university by the General Assembly of Kentucky.

Upward of twenty-seven medical schools came into existence between 1800 and the outbreak of the Civil War and more than one hundred by the end of the century.[9] Some were outgrowths of existing institutions, some were chartered by the states, and many were proprietary, that is, privately founded corporations of groups of physicians and surgeons without hospital connections. It was the "Flexner Report" by Abraham Flexner in 1910 which exposed abuses in medical education and brought about much-needed reform in teaching and in the curricula and standards of American medical schools.[10]

An important addition to medical education was the New York University Medical College in 1841. Another New York school, chartered in 1850, was the New York Medical College, which had an ambitious plan to enforce higher standards than those practiced in many of the other schools in the country. Though it had no hospital connection, it had a small ward for bedside teaching. It was here that Jacobi began the teaching of pediatrics at the bedsides of sick children.

Entrance requirements and standards of teaching were generally low, as this statement reveals:

. . . any student could enter a medical school with or without a college education if he gave evidence of a knowledge of Latin and elementary physics. He [the medical student] was required to attend two terms of lectures; at the most the school term lasted four months, usually only three—November through January. After he had had three years of . . . apprenticeship—and if he were twenty-one, he submitted a thesis and took a perfunctory oral examination.[11]

It was the procedure William James had followed in 1869, except that he did not apprentice himself to a physician. He spent two years in sporadic study in Germany, wrote a thesis, and after an oral examination by nine professors, one of whom was Dr. Oliver Wendell Holmes, received the M.D. degree. He never practiced medicine, but became an instructor in physiology. Later he turned to psychology and philosophy.[12]

Yale Medical School, founded in 1812, was somewhat more

demanding in requiring two years' attendance for college graduates, for all others three. In the hinterland, requirements were
very lax. A medical practitioner who began the study of medicine after serving in the Civil War states:

There was no preliminary or entrance examination. Any white
male who could read and write and who had mastered the rudiments of English was eligible. Neither Latin nor Greek was
essential. ... The requirements for graduation were a satisfactory examination at the end of two college terms of seven
months each. The division of subjects was anatomy, physics,
surgery, medicine, obstetrics, chemistry and materia medica.
No instructions at the bedside, no ward practice.[13]

Because the opportunity for clinical study did not exist in
America during the early part of the nineteenth century, Americans were compelled to go to European capitals, where medical
schools had grown out of hospitals. After the War of 1812,
medical students began going to Paris. There they either repeated the course at the Ecole de Médecine, or followed the
professors through the · wards of hospitals—the Charité, the
Pitié, the Salpêtrière. One of these students was Oliver Wendell
Holmes, who returned from Paris in 1836 to receive his M.D.
degree from Harvard, later becoming New England's most distinguished physician. Another was Mary Corinne Putnam, who
in 1871 became the first woman in America and Europe to
graduate from the Ecole de Médecine. Later in the century the
"Vienna School" drew large numbers of Americans to its All-
gemeines Krankenhaus.

Treatment and diagnosis were primitive by today's standards.
Bleeding and application of leeches were resorted to. Fevers
were diagnosed as "miasmata."[14] No distinction was made between typhoid and typhus. In 1899 Jacobi remembered that in
the early 1860's, while he had served at the New York Medical
College, a surgeon "performed operations on the cadaver and
on the living patient at the same revolving table in the amphi-
theatre and in the same purple velvet gown, and I do not remember, perhaps even with the same knife."[15]

An immense spur to progress in the field of medicine was
provided by the passage of laws that provided bodies for dis-

section. New York State passed "Anatomy Acts" in 1788-1789 that made a limited supply of cadavers available, and in 1790 the first Congress of the United States passed similar legislation.[16] Only bodies of unclaimed persons who would otherwise have to be buried at public expense were offered to medical schools. Nevertheless, it was difficult to secure bodies, in contrast to Paris, where a cadaver could be had for fifty sous[17] and "body snatching continued past the eighteen hundreds."[18]

Important progress in medicine was made as the nineteenth century progressed. A significant advance was the invention of the stethoscope and the method of auscultation by the French physician, René Laennec, during the first decades of the century. Another was the invention of the ophthalmoscope by Hermann von Helmholtz. One of the most important breakthroughs occurred in America when Dr. William Morton of Boston discovered anesthesia in 1844. The first operation under the influence of ether was performed at Massachusetts General Hospital in 1846 by Dr. John Collins Warren, a descendant of Dr. Joseph Warren.

Uniform educational standards did not come into existence until the end of the nineteenth century. By 1895 a modern licensing system by boards of examiners was in effect. In 1892 Harvard extended the study of medicine to four years. In 1893 the College of Physicians and Surgeons made the four-year course obligatory. But the greatest advance in raising medical standards was made by the Johns Hopkins Medical School when it was founded in 1893. It had a hospital of its own and laboratories. For the first time, a college degree was required for entrance to a medical school.[19]

The last decades of the nineteenth century produced some epoch-making discoveries in the fight against disease. One of the greatest blessings was the discovery of diphtheria antitoxin and the isolation of the tubercle bacillus. Medical progress in America kept pace with that of Europe, and in the twentieth century it would begin to outshine the scientific advances in European medical centers. In 1900 Jacobi declared: "I have observed [the American profession] to evolve without governmental aid, out of its own might, to become equal to any on the globe."[20]

I

Abraham Jacobi belongs to the category of immigrants who brought to the United States the benefits of fully developed professional talents. A refugee from the aftermath of the Revolution of 1848, he was in a position to put the skills acquired at the expense of his homeland to immediate use. His career forms one of the numerous examples of the "brain drain" from which America has benefitted since the beginning of our history.

Born in 1830 in a mean little town in Westphalia (which Prussia had acquired in 1815), Jacobi had a cramped childhood. His father, a small shopkeeper, vented his ill nature on his family. He was not in favor of turning his son into an educated man; but Jacobi's mother, doughty in her resolve that he should rise to a higher position in life than his parents, made it possible for him to finish the course of study at the town gymnasium.

As a medical student at the University of Göttingen he joined a revolutionary group. In those days students preparing for the medical profession went from one medical center to another to study with professors of their choice. Thus, the young man proceeded from Göttingen to Bonn, without finding roadblocks in his way. But when he presented himself for his examination in Berlin, he was arrested on a charge of *lèse-majesté*. He was then not quite twenty-one years of age. As a medical student he had met Carl Schurz at a clandestine rendezvous arranged by a third party. Later he found himself on the same train that took Schurz to the fortress at Spandau (used as a jail for political prisoners to this day), where Schurz planned to make a daring attempt at liberating one of his teachers who was being held for trial. Schurz's "cops-and-robbers" plan succeeded, giving him the immense satisfaction of saving a gallant man and outwitting the Prussian police at the same time. This daredevil stunt completed, Schurz betook himself to England, where he acquired a wife, and with her he emigrated to the United States in 1851. Jacobi, who had become identified with Schurz in the eyes of the authorities, was apprehended.

What Jacobi gained from this escapade was Schurz's lifelong friendship, which became one of the joys of his life, particularly in their late middle age when Schurz settled permanently in New York. Of Schurz it could be said that, like Goethe, he had a *"Frohnatur"*—a joyous disposition, whereas Jacobi was reserved and serious to the point of melancholy. They also presented a contrast in appearance. Schurz was tall, thin, and long-legged, whereas Jacobi was short and slight. Though Schurz had escaped the blighting experience of prison life, in his later years he experienced disappointments and setbacks in plenty. He did not escape the thorns of life, but he covered up his misfortunes with geniality and easy laughter.

Jacobi received a two-year jail term which kept him in prison from his twenty-first to his twenty-third year. We have it from Oswald Garrison Villard, son of Henry Villard (who liked to think of himself as a "Forty-Eighter" by virtue of having come to America in 1853, at the age of eighteen), that Jacobi's cell was dungeonlike in its darkness and that he wore chains for months. Jacobi's unusually thick hair had enabled him to smuggle a pencil into his cell, but as he lacked paper, his pencil did him no good. At the end of his jail term his mother was permitted to visit him. While he struggled with the awareness of how poorly he had repaid her for her sacrifices, she consoled him by telling him that if he had done what seemed right to him he had followed the proper path.

Upon his release a friendly jailer warned him that the authorities intended to pick him up again and to imprison him for an indefinite term. He had barely time to see his mother before he fled to England as his first stop. It was America that drew him, just as the Rhine maidens of the mythical German past were supposed to have lured travelers to follow their siren song. In the dreams of immigrants, America, too, had something of the mythical about it, and many arrived there with utterly unrealistic expectations that could not fail to bring heartache and disillusionment to them. Not to Jacobi, for he found what he looked for in America. Oswald Garrison Villard expressed what Jacobi must have felt when he wrote in the *Nation* on the occasion of his death:

These Forty-Eighters had dreamed about America as they dreamt about heaven in the days when they plotted the overthrow of their governments. It meant to them paradise—liberty, equality, freedom and humanity, the most exquisite words in any language—as they wore their chains and wondered when the executioner would sever their heads from their bodies.[21]

Jacobi's prison experience embittered him, but it also helped to turn him into a more compassionate human being. As a physician he would treat patients with the utmost kindness and consideration. He did not believe that a patient should be told that he was incurably ill. In one of his later statements he said, "I found it easy to imagine myself in the place of a patient, and to spare his feelings if I could not preserve his life. When you cannot save, you can still comfort."[22] But the memory of jail and of the injustice he had suffered was never extinguished from his consciousness. To the end of his life he hated Prussianism and its characteristics.

II

Jacobi was twenty-three when he landed in Boston in 1853. New England appealed no more to him than Old England. He decided to push on to New York, where a large German population would make his acclimatization easier and where he could hope to make a niche for himself as a German physician. It was a surprise to him that he encountered no prejudice, even among physicians of old American lineage. Within a short time he was translating European articles for the *New York Journal of Medicine* and within a year he was contributing original articles on pediatrics. Those patients who were able to paid him twenty-five cents for an office visit, fifty-cents for a home visit, and five dollars for a confinement. It is not likely that he pressed patients for payment in the manner of some physicians who would not make a home call unless paid in advance,[23] for in the words of a colleague, he was the "patron-general of all poor devils."[24] Another source states that Jacobi maintained free office hours for the poor."[25]

Why Jacobi became interested in pediatrics can only be guessed. It may have been an effect of his attunement to new currents in the field of medicine, or it may have been a response to the fact that infant mortality was tremendously high. One infant in five died before its first birthday, and almost as many during their second year. He lost his own first child and his first wife; he was to lose his second wife and six more children—three stillborn and one born prematurely of his second marriage, and a stillborn child and a boy of seven by his third wife. Out of eight children only one daughter grew to maturity.

In 1857—four years after his arrival—Jacobi's interest in pediatrics had crystallized sufficiently for him to offer a series of lectures on pedology at the College of Physicians and Surgeons. Soon thereafter he was offered a professorship in "Infantile Pathology and Therapeutics" at the newly reorganized New York Medical College, where he started a clinic for children and taught at their bedsides.[26] Dr. Harvey Cushing commented on his appointment: "In 1858, seven years [sic] after his escape from Germany as a political refugee [Jacobi] has suceeded in making such a name for himself as a children's specialist that the first professorship in pediatrics in the country was established in order that he might fill the position."[27] Dr. Ernst Krackowizer, by then a close friend of Jacobi's, interpreted his acceptance of the job as an attempt to induce other hospitals to open departments for the treatment of children's diseases. If it was a stratagem, it proved effective, for a year later Bellevue Medical College created the post of "Clinical Professor of Infantile Pathology."[28]

It has been said that the recovery rate among Jacobi's patients was higher than was usual, and the reason given was the painstaking care his patients received. He was known to spend hours and nights at the bedside of patients so that he could treat them in response to momentary changes in their condition. He remained at his post until 1864, when the institution was forced to close because of competition from schools with lower standards.

III

What was it that made Jacobi a pioneer in modern medicine? In the first place, he was a genuine pathbreaker; secondly, he was immensely courageous in his advocacy and defense of unpopular viewpoints. One of his theories that went counter to medical practices of his day was that children's diseases are not lighter versions of adult ailments, but maladies specific to children. Consequently, he believed that reducing the dosages given to adults was not *ipso facto* the proper way to treat them. Another of his theories that caused suspicion if not hostility among medical practitioners was that nurseries must be detached from obstetrical and gynecological wards in order to reduce the high mortality among infants from contamination. Children, he insisted, must be studied and treated separately. A third theory that aroused the ire of his colleagues was that teething was not a cause of death, as it often appeared on death certificates, but a normal physiological function. These were radical views for a man who was otherwise conservative and appeared so: Jacobi's clothes were uniformly of an unfashionable cut and the firmness of his views was a contradiction to the smallness of his stature.

An issue that illustrates the extent to which Jacobi was ready to battle for his convictions and that brought him a great deal of enmity, was a dispute with the Nursery and Child's Hospital, which he deliberately forced into the open. After serving the institution without pay for ten years, during which he had antagonized the directress and her aides by demanding changes in diet and hospital conditions, he came out with the startling statement that an infant's life was in greater danger in a foundling home or hospital than in a dirty tenement. He was basing his claim on records he had kept which indicated that the survival rate in foundling homes for infants four to five months old was fifty percent lower. This, he stressed, was not due to negligence, but to the fact that infants did not thrive well in public institutions, despite the best care and attention.

His suggestion was that infants be farmed out to country families under the supervision of the state. In his perception that foster homes would be more beneficial for an infant than the best regulated hospitals, he was decades ahead of his time. In 1870 this notion reacted with the force of a bomb explosion. How could the wealthy be approached for contributions to foundling homes if it was better for infants to remain in private homes, regardless how squalid? But instead of resigning quietly as he was asked to do, Jacobi insisted upon a hearing before the medical board. It was a foregone conclusion that he would lose the battle, inasmuch as the president of the board was a brother of the directress and her son-in-law was a member of the board. He did lose, but he made a report before the New York County Medical Society, and was appointed chairman of the committee that was to study his proposal for the care of the foundlings.

In 1870 he joined the College of Physicians and Surgeons as Clinical Professor of the Diseases of Infancy and Childhood. He was then forty and within two years he was considered a recognized authority in his field. Among the physicians he trained many became noted pediatricians who were invited to join the teaching staffs of medical schools. When Johns Hopkins was established in 1893, two of his former students were appointed members of the faculty.

Jacobi's reputation rested not only on his professional renown, but also on his attitude toward patients. According to Dr. Hans Zinsser, he was one of "the most beloved and distinguished figures in the New York medical profession at this time," and was known as "the Jewish Jupiter." To Dr. John Allen Wyeth, who worked with him at Mount Sinai Hospital, Jacobi was "the Nestor of Medicine." To the son of a friend he was "Atlas," because his prominent head atop his slight body suggested a man who was carrying the world's responsibilities upon his shoulders. Physicians looked upon him as "the Dean" or "the Grand Man of Medicine." His assistants venerated him. One of them established with his own funds an "Abraham Jacobi Ward for Children" at Roosevelt Hospital.[28] In 1910 a ward for children was endowed at the German Hospital (now Lenox Hill) on the occasion of his eightieth birthday. He had helped to found the German Hospital in 1869.[29]

Most of his theories became universally accepted. For instance, he was a champion of breast feeding. Where this was impossible, he advocated the use of boiled milk, stating specifically: "Heat the milk until you see the bubbles." He considered it essential at a time when neither pasteurized milk nor proper refrigeration was available, especially among the poor. Among infants living in tenements the ailment known as "summer complaint" took on epidemic proportions during the hot summer months. Jacobi was frequently consulted by boards and associations responsible for the care of children. On the request of the Public Health Association he wrote a booklet, *Infant Diet*, which was considered the most authoritative statement on how to preserve the health of infants. Another, *The Improvement of the Condition of Poor and Sick Children*, was written at the request of a sanitarium in Baltimore. In it he repeated with an urgency that cannot be missed: "They [children] require absolutely plain, simple, wholesome, digestible, nutrient food only, only, only."[30]

IV

At the age of forty-two Jacobi married for the third time. Already widowed twice, he was also to survive his third wife. She was Dr. Mary Corinne Putnam, whose parents were descendants of New England settlers. Her father, George Palmer Putnam, was the founder of the publishing firm G. P. Putnam's Sons, and a cousin of Sophia Peabody Hawthorne. She was twelve years younger than her husband, and a woman of advanced views. After receiving her first degree from the New York College of Pharmacy (now a part of Columbia University), she went on to the Female Medical College in Philadelphia and from there to Paris for further study. She was the first woman to graduate from Ecole de Médecine in Paris. Before she committed herself to a medical career she had written several stories for The *Atlantic Monthly*. She supported herself in Paris by writing for American magazines. In 1871 she returned home, where a teaching job at the Women's Medical College of the New York Infirmary (founded by Elizabeth Blackwell, the first American woman doctor) as well as marriage were awaiting her. She had always wanted to marry a physician. The circumstances of her first meeting with her future husband illustrate how advanced Dr. Jacobi's views were for his time.

When Mary Putnam returned from Europe the medical profession was completely in the grip of a narrow view in regard to women physicians—"doctresses" or "she-doctors" as they were called. Medical schools did not accept women, and the custom of refusing to be associated with a "doctress" on a medical case was not unusual. It was considered a breakthrough when Johns Hopkins admitted three women after Mary E. Garrett offered to raise a hundred thousand dollars, provided women were admitted on the same basis as men.[31] It was therefore a triumph for Mary Putnam when in 1871 she was accepted to membership in the New York City Medical Society. She was a self-possessed young woman when she presented herself to be inducted into that august body. It was assumed that

Jacobi, newly elected president of the society, had approved of her application. He proved his broad-mindedness in the welcoming remarks he made to the twelve new members by expressing his belief that women would become valued members of the medical profession.

Within six months they were married in a civil ceremony, for Jacobi was an avowed atheist. After the very simple rites he took her to his summer home at Bolton Landing on Lake George, of which she became as fond as he was. It turned out to be a very good marriage that benefited both. She was an undemanding wife and was extremely proud of him. He was "Ajax" to her—the man whom all the bolts of Jove could not frighten. She undertook to turn his *Infant Diet* into an enlarged edition which bore under the title and name of the author the inscription: "revised, enlarged and adapted to popular use by Mary Putnam Jacobi, M.D."[32] It became a much-used text and reference book.

Mary Putnam Jacobi's contribution to medicine was outstanding. Three years after her marriage she entered the competition for the coveted Boylston Prize from Harvard and won it. It was a contest in which the identity of the contributors was not revealed to the judges. She remained on the faculty of the New York Medical College, which became a teaching institution in 1867, until 1899, when she resigned. But she kept her connection with St. Mark's Hospital and with Mount Sinai, where she had helped her husband to establish a pediatric clinic, to the end of her life. Besides, she bore three children, one stillborn, a son who died at the age of seven, and a daughter who survived her parents. When Mary Putnam Jacobi died in 1906 from a brain tumor, she was universally respected by physicians of both sexes.

V

The fearlessness Abraham Jacobi displayed in endorsing new theories in medicine became one of the identifying features of the man. He was one of the first American physicians to recommend the use of diphtheria antitoxin, which began to be produced in 1893. Diphtheria was deadly not only to children under two years of age, but it also claimed a huge number of victims among older children as well. When his only son succumbed to diphtheria at the age of seven, it was a loss from which the father never recovered. How bold it was to recommend the use of antitoxin in those days is pointed out by a medical historian who says: "It required a man of great moral and physical courage to introduce antitoxin therapy on a significant scale. The hazards Jacobi risked (and physical violence in the tenements of New York was not the least of these) have never been placed in print, nor was he the man to recount them himself."[33]

Not only did Jacobi endorse diphtheria antitoxin when many other physicians preferred to be cautious, but he also supported Dr. Edward Trudeau, who had been his student, in his pioneer work in the field of tuberculosis and participated actively in the National Association for the Study and Prevention of Tuberculosis with his friend, Dr. William Osler, later Sir William Osler, Regius Professor at Oxford. As he approached the end of his life he did not hesitate to advocate birth control and to call for a clean bill of health for those intending marriage. These recommendations did not fail to bring him severe criticism.

The high regard in which Jacobi was held by colleagues and friends was vividly demonstrated on the occasion of his seventieth birthday, when over four hundred people gathered to honor him. His most intimate friends were Dr. Ernst Krackowizer and Carl Schurz. He attended Dr. Krackowizer in his illness which brought him to an untimely death, and in 1906 he took care of Carl Schurz in his terminal illness. After the death of Krackowizer he offered a moving testimony at the Academy of Medicine on the life, character, and accomplishments of his colleague and friend.[34] His address revealed not only his sentiments in regard to his friend, but also a remarkable ability to express himself in English. While he retained his accent, he had learned to make the English language expressive of his deepest feelings and his broad humanity: "A delightful vein of quaint, elusive irony"[35] did not go unnoticed.

VI

The ability to use the English language like a native was not unusual among the foreign-born. Another who "felt" in English, despite a conspicuous German accent, was Carl Schurz. He was not only an impressive orator in English as well as in German, but was also an extremely able writer who handled his adopted language with marvelous effect. Jacobi was so devoted to Schurz that when his daughter was born he wished to name her after Schurz's wife, Margarethe, who had recently died after the birth of her fifth child. The child was named Marjorie, because her mother preferred it, but she remained "Grete" to her father. In 1892 Jacobi prevailed upon Schurz to build a summer home close to his own, on land Jacobi owned.

After that they were inseparable, particularly during the summer months when both occupied their homes on Lake George. Summer was vacation time for the aging physician. For the rest of the year Jacobi exemplified Carlyle's dictum: "Blessed is he who has found his work; let him ask no other blessedness." This "blessedness" was not Schurz's, for the vicissitudes of his life were such that he found himself seesawing between public service and journalism. It is a fair guess that his first love was service to the nation and that he fell back on journalism when the opportunity to participate in political activity appeared closed.

The year Schurz joined his old friend at Lake George in 1892 was the year Schurz had succeeded the reformer George William Curtis as president of the National Civil Service Reform League. Jacobi, who had always taken an active interest in politics and social questions, became a charter member of the league. That summer they could always be seen walking together, exchanging views in their beloved German, or Schurz would be singing the German songs both loved, while Jacobi listened. Schurz was also an accomplished pianist who was apt to find release for his emotions through the music he played. For instance, when he found himself balked in his attempt to swing the nomination of the Reform party to Charles Francis Adams in order to oppose President Grant for a second term, he is said to have flung himself at the piano and played Chopin's Funeral March.[36] The attachment that bound Schurz and Jacobi together was well known to their acquaintances: on Jacobi's eightieth birthday, when Schurz had been dead four years, a birthday gift from Oswald Garrison Villard and a group of mutual friends was a portrait of Schurz.

The relationship between Schurz and Jacobi was strengthened when Jacobi's only daughter became engaged to Schurz's young associate, George McAneny. They had met at Schurz's home while Marjorie was a student at Barnard, and McAneny acted as secretary of the National Civil Service Reform League. Later, McAneny became borough president of Manhattan.

During his later years Schurz suffered several serious blows. The death of his only son and the youngest of his children at the age of twenty-five proved to be the final calamity. When Schurz succumbed to pneumonia at the age of seventy-seven, Jacobi was in attendance, but he could not save him. Jacobi survived him by thirteen years.

VI

In politics Jacobi was violently anti-Prussian and antiimperialist and devotedly pro-American. The extent of his hatred for the German regime can be gauged by his response when the University of Berlin offered him a professorship in pediatrics. He declined with a stinging reminder of the injustices that had driven him and others like him across the ocean. In 1900 he put his attitude to America in these words:

I am rooted in the country that was my ideal when I was young, my refuge when, alone and persecuted, I stole away, and always, clouds or no clouds, my sunny hope forevermore.[37]

Flattery and servility to people in power were detestable qualities to him, and the latter, especially, seemed to him characteristic of the Germans. When World War I broke out, he openly condemned Prussianism and militarism as the cause of the war. Another of the foreign-born who fearlessly asserted that the political leaders of Germany had plunged the world into "this horrible bath of blood" was Walter Damrosch.[38]

On his seventieth birthday, Jacobi heard himself praised by some of the most respected personages of his time. The occasion was a dinner at Delmonico's. Present were his wife, the president of the Academy of Medicine, Dr. William Hanna Thompson, Dr. William Osler (soon to leave for England, where Henry James would consult him), president Seth Low of Columbia, and, of course, his old friend, Carl Schurz. While the doctors extolled his contribution to medicine, Schurz, one of the speakers, stressed his sense of social responsibility and his adherence to moral principles. Jacobi received a *"Festschrift,"* composed of fifty-three papers by the greatest medical figures of all countries, who had contributed them specifically to honor his birthday.

When Jacobi's eightieth birthday rolled around, his wife and Carl Schurz had been dead four years, both having died within three weeks of each other. It was then he was given Schurz's portrait. At the reception arranged by the New York State Medical Society at the Academy of Medicine, one thousand people were present to observe the unveiling of a life-size bronze medallion by his granddaughter. Mount Sinai Hospital honored the occasion by putting on display a bust of him by the sculptor Jo Davidson and dedicating a library room to their distinguished member. It was then that a ward was endowed for more than fifty children at the German Hospital.

VII

By then Jacobi had received every conceivable honor but one, and that was to come to him a year later, in 1911. In 1882 he had held the office of president of the State Medical Society. Twice he had been chairman of a department of the American Medical Association that was concerned with the diseases of children. He had been honorary president of the International Medical Congress in Paris. He held honorary degrees from Columbia, Yale, Harvard, Washington, Jefferson, and other universities and honorary membership in many medical societies in foreign lands. The last honor came to him when he was elected president of the American Medical Association. He was the first foreign-born Jew to hold this prestigious office.

Toward the end of his eighties he was still working at his profession. He also began an autobiography, which he called *Jugendserinnerungen.** He was still fighting for causes of which he approved. Such a cause was Nathan Straus's milk depots, which had been opened in 1893 with his cooperation, for he wanted to see the pasteurized milk they provided made avail-

---

* *Recollections of Childhood* (Author's Translation)

able to the city's children. The opposition by milk companies and milk dealers almost forced Nathan Straus to close his depots, but Jacobi succeeded in his ambition through the efforts of his son-in-law, George McAneny, then borough president of Manhattan, in prevailing upon the city to take them over.

The peace of his old age was upset when Jacobi was eighty-eight. The cause was a fire in his summer home in the middle of the night, which forced him to jump out of an upstairs window. He escaped serious injury, but the house burned to the ground and he lost his letters, books, and mementos. The four chapters of his autobiography were also lost. Realizing that he was too old to start it again, he let it go, like one who is forced to let something slip from his grasp.

Still he went on, though he was getting more and more tired. Four days before his death he saw his last patient, a baby, for whom he wrote his last prescription. It was as if he could not have enough of being a doctor. He had said in 1905 when he was seventy-five years old: "If you asked an old man who had been through hard, lifelong work and heartrending scenes, through success, maybe, and endless failures and disappointments, if you asked him what he craved to be if he began life again, he would, I think, reply, 'just a modern doctor.' "[39] Jacobi remained a doctor to the end of his life, and as "modern" a doctor as it was possible for him to be.

The heritage he left were eight volumes of *Collectanea Jacobi*,[40] published in 1909 when he was nearing his eightieth birthday. They contained his medical writings, essays, public letters, and speeches. There is also a hospital in New York City which is named after him. However, the most valuable legacy he left to the American people are the hundreds of disciples whom he had trained to carry on in the specialty he had developed.

EDWIN LAWRENCE GODKIN
1831-1902

Impassioned Journalist

The founder and editor of the Nation, *he reached a commanding position in journalism as the spokesman for several generations of intellectual readers who were impressed by his viewpoint and fearless independence. Later, as editor of the* New York Evening Post, *he implanted it with a policy of high-minded journalism and pursued a relentless course in opposing policies which ran counter to his moral and ethical sense. In exposing the iniquitous influence of Tammany Hall on New York City's municipal affairs, the* Evening Post *under his editorial direction was responsible for breaking Tammany's stranglehold and for helping to elect a reform administration.*

England After the Napoleonic Wars

For Great Britain the elimination of the Napoleonic menace signified the beginning of a new phase of political and industrial supremacy. In 1837 a new queen, Victoria, ascended the throne of Great Britain. Because of her long rule—until 1901— and the eminence of Great Britain during her reign, the age took its name from her and became known as the "Victorian Age." Her regime, identified with stability, prosperity, and British leadership in international affairs, was also conspicuous for a series of social reforms long overdue. It was a period of peace, except for two "little" wars, the Crimean War of 1854 and the Boer War at the end of the century. Though the latter lasted from 1899 to 1902, it had little discernible effect on the English way of life.

[89]

For the English upper classes the sun stood at zenith, but knocks at the door of privilege were becoming insistent. The effect of the Industrial Revolution, in full swing by then, was to make the urban classes more strongly aware of the inequities of the English social and political system. They were demanding greater representation in Parliament through the admission of new towns in the industrial North, as well as reforms in local government. The Reform Bill of 1832 liberalized the franchise, but did not extend it to the laboring classes. The enfranchisement of the working classes became one of the main objectives of a working-class movement, called Chartism. The membership in the Chartist organization grew so rapidly and demands for reform were so clamorous that the ruling classes were frightened. In the end, however, the movement that had seemed so threatening to the privileged collapsed as quickly as it had arisen, although most of the Chartist demands were over the years incorporated in the British Constitution. Disappointment over the failure of Chartism brought many of England's skilled workmen to America. Their "know-how" formed an important contribution to the progress of American industry.

Political and economic reforms in England were legislated piecemeal throughout the nineteenth century and into the twentieth. An important concession to the working classes was the repeal in 1846 of the Corn Laws, which were a form of protective tariff for the benefit of landowners. This meant that the agricultural interests were sacrificed to the development of industry and commerce. Bread became cheaper in England. Also, the American farmer found a wider market for his wheat.

A thorn in the complacency of nineteenth-century England was the continuing agitation by the Irish for Home Rule, which culminated in 1912 in the enactment of a Home Rule Bill. The demand for Home Rule was not limited to Irish patriots in southern Ireland, but was also supported by Anglo-Irish elements in the North whose forbears had been English. One of those was the father of Edwin Lawrence Godkin.

On the international political chessboard England dominated. Russia, Prussia, and Austria were concerned with internal matters. The upstart, Louis Napoleon, who had lived in England before his recall to France after the abdication of Louis-Philippe in 1848, could only play second fiddle in the orchestration of

Europeon politics, even though in 1851 he became Emperor Napoleon III of France. Thus, in 1854 he was proud to be permitted to join England as an ally of Turkey against Russia in the Crimean War.

The Crimean War was an effort to contain Russian ambitions in the Black Sea. The czar had demanded of Turkey that he be recognized as the protector of all Christians in the Ottoman Empire. It was a Russian ploy to gain a foothold in the Balkans. England supported Turkey in the rejection of the Russian ultimatum and was therefore forced to send military aid to Turkey. The fall of the Russian fortress of Sebastopol, achieved mainly by French troops, ended in a Turkish victory. England was able to impose permanent neutralization of the Black Sea and to ban Russia from acquiring a naval base in that region.

Godkin was the war correspondent who reported the Crimean War for the *Daily News* in London. It marked the start of a journalistic career of distinction. At the end of the war he emigrated to the United States.

The United States at Mid-Century

The decade of the 1850's was characterized by unusual activity in the economic, political, and social spheres. The building of the railroads, a prerequisite for industrial expansion, which later proved an enormous boon to the northern cause, was proceeding at a constantly accelerating rate. The drilling of the first oil well, near Titusville in northwestern Pennsylvania, occurred in 1859 on the very eve of the Civil War. Telegraphy had been discovered in the 1830's, but not until the mid-forties was the first telegraph line built—from Washington to Baltimore, for which Congress had contributed thirty thousand dollars, not a munificent sum of money even for that day. The sewing machine had made its appearance, and the constant improvement in agricultural machinery held out hopes for greater productivity and more leisure for farmers. In 1848 a cable had been laid across the Atlantic Ocean, enabling President Buchanan and Queen Victoria, at whose court Buchanan had served as ambassador from the United States, to hold a conversation. The cable soon snapped and would not be repaired until after the war was over.

On the political side there was defiance and oratory. In spite of all efforts to keep the issues dividing North from South below the boiling point, sectional controversy was in constant danger of spilling over. In the face of such provocations as the Kansas-Nebraska Act of 1854, the Dred Scott decision in 1856, the continuous flaunting by the North of the Fugitive Slave Law, and, finally, the John Brown insurrection, all efforts at compromise proved futile. In 1854 that astute immigrant, Carl Schurz, after listening to some of the debates in Congress, came to the conclusion that the "decisive contest" was rapidly approaching.[1] He was not the first foreigner to foresee a bloody conflict. In the late 1830's Ole Rynning, a Norwegian immigrant leader prophesied that "there will in all likelihood come either a separation between the North and the Southern states or else bloody civil disputes."[2]

The intellectual currents were also running strongly at midcentury. The chief stimulation came from the writers of New England and New York. The most influential voices from New England were Emerson's, Thoreau's, Hawthorne's, and Melville's. In New York Bryant and Poe attempted to make themselves heard. Newspapers and magazines also vied for reader attention. Though newspapers had been popular since colonial days, the beginning of mass circulation dates from the 1830's, when "penny newspapers" came into existence. That Americans were newspaper readers did not escape the notice of Frances Trollope, for she declared superciliously: "Where newspapers are the principal vehicles of the wit and wisdom of the people, the higher grades of composition can hardly be looked for."[3]

By the 1840's the East could boast of several influential newspapers that competed furiously, and not always ethically, for the attention of the reading public. These were: the *New York Tribune,* established by Horace Greeley; the *New York Sun,* then under Benjamin H. Day, later purchased by Charles A. Dana; and the *New York Herald,* under the direction of James Gordon Bennett. The *New York Times* was not established until 1857 and did not reach a commanding position until after 1896, when it was taken over by Adolph S. Ochs. In New England, the *Springfield Republican* was a very respected paper; in Chicago the *Daily Tribune* under Horace White exerted great influence. There were also magazines appealing to popular tastes, including some that catered exclusively to women. Those destined to wield great prestige among the educated were the *Atlantic Monthly*, founded in 1857, and the *Nation*, founded by Godkin in 1865. During the latter half of the nineteenth century the newspaper and magazine fields were to provide several men of foreign birth with the opportunity to distinguish themselves. Godkin, the editor of the *Nation*, was Anglo-Irish; Joseph Pulitzer, who turned the *New York World* into an enormously popular newspaper, was Hungarian; Edward Bok, who took over the *Ladies' Home Journal*, was Dutch; and Samuel McClure, whose *McClure's Magazine* became the most powerful muckraking organ, was an Irishman from the North.

I

Frances Trollope was resting on her laurels as a writer of travel books and living in splendor in one of Florence's palaces when Edwin Lawrence Godkin decided in 1856 to investigate the opportunities that awaited a young man of breeding and education in America. Mrs. Trollope was then seventy-eight and the anguish caused to sensitive Americans by her book, *The Domestic Manners of the Americans*, had faded. Had she been alive in 1865 when Godkin began to publish the *Nation*, she would probably have agreed that he was just the kind of person to supply to Americans "the higher graces of composition" she had found wanting in the 1820's. It would undoubtedly have seemed fitting to her that it should be one of the educated Anglo-Irish who would raise the cultural levels of the Americans.

The year in which Godkin was born—1831—coincided with the appearance of Mrs. Trollope's unflattering book on the Americans. His birthplace was northern Ireland. His father, a Presbyterian minister, was a "Home Rule" man who lost his pulpit because of his membership in the "Young Ireland" movement. As a consequence, he turned to journalism. Godkin's mother's ancestors had been Cromwellian settlers. Though young Godkin was in favor of "Home Rule" and said of England that it had "an atmosphere I detest and a social system I have hated since I was fourteen,"[4] some of his contemporaries maintained that he was more at home in the English than in the American system. After graduating from Queen's College in Belfast, he went to London to study law at Lincoln's Inn. But he also sought employment as an editorial writer with the highly respected publisher, John Cassell, with whom his father had literary connections. For him he wrote his first book, A *History of Hungary*, at a time when the revolutionary fever, which had also infected that country, formed exciting news. In it he revealed himself to be sympathetic to the aspirations of those struggling against political oppression and against reactionaries seeking to maintain the status quo. A letter he addressed to the editor of the *London Daily News*, in which he defended the claims of the Greeks to Turkish territory, created such a strong impression on the editor that when the Crimean War broke out he remembered Godkin and asked him to go to the Balkans as their newspaper's correspondent. He was then twenty-two.

Two years later he returned with a deep hatred for war and for those who promoted war, which was to remain with him throughout his life. (As editor of the *New York Evening Post* he asserted that some day the soldier would find himself properly ranked next after the hangman.)[5] The fact that since his college days he had considered America his own "Promised Land," explains his decision to try his fortune across the seas. The United States seemed to him a country where "at last the triumph of humanity over its own weaknesses and superstitions was being achieved and the dream of Christendom was at last realized."[6]

Arriving on the eve of Buchanan's election in 1856, Godkin traveled for the next year on horseback through the South, forwarding to the *Daily News* travel letters that contained his impressions of all classes of the South—planters, "poor whites," and Negroes. Mississippi on a wet day struck him as the dreariest and most monotonous of places. Of the "poor whites" he remarked as follows:

The population is scanty; and the houses, such as they are, for the most part are inhabited by that most wretched, most cadaverous, most thinly clad, most lean, most haggard, most woebegone, forlorn, hopeless, God-forsaken-looking portion of the human race, the poor niggerless whites of the slave States. I have seen many varieties of the genus "homo," and many varieties of the misery to which he is at all times liable, but I think I have never seen men in whom hope, energy and courage, to all outward appearances, seemed so utterly extinguished as in these. . . . They are despised alike by negroes and planters.[7]

Though he made an effort to understand the attitude of planters to their Negro slaves, he was repelled by slavery. Coming on a group on the way to Texas, he described a cavalcade of slaves struggling through a quagmire:

East or West, in Alabama or Texas, hard work, coarse food, merciless flogging are all that await them, and all they can look to. I have never passed them,—staggering along in the rear of the wagons, at the close of a long day's march, the weakest further in the rear, the strongest utterly spent—without wondering how Christendom, which eight centuries ago rose in arms for a sentiment, can so long look calmly on at so foul and monstrous a wrong as this American slavery.[8]

At the end of the trip Godkin decided to remain in America and return to the study of law at the office of David Dudley Field, a prominent New York attorney. Within two years of his arrival he was admitted to the bar, and a year later he married Frances Elizabeth Foote, whose family was socially and politically prominent in New Haven. She was destined to die young. The loss of a child affected her so severely that in 1875 she succumbed to illness.

II

Godkin attempted to practice law, but the magnet which drew him was journalism. He had become acquainted with many leading journalists and intellectuals living in New York. Among them were William Cullen Bryant, editor of the *New York Evening Post* and a poet of distinction, Horace Greeley, editor of the *Tribune*, Charles H. Dana, who had acquired the *New York Sun* in 1868, and George Ripley, who had been one of the organizers of Brook Farm and was now book reviewer for the *Tribune*. One of Godkin's earliest and most intimate friends was Frederick Law Olmstead, the designer of Central Park and Riverside Park in New York City, Prospect Park in Brooklyn, the grounds of the national capitol, the park systems of Boston, the 1893 World's Fair in Chicago, and the grounds of Stanford University, the University of California, and other campuses. Olmstead became one of Godkin's backers in establishing the *Nation*. Godkin also made friends among the New England literati, among whom were Charles Eliot Norton, the James and Adams families, and James Russell Lowell. He was so taken with Lowell that he offered the following judgment of him and of American men in general: "There is something very charming about Lowell—something of the European flavor, which, you will forgive me for saying, makes an American when he has it, the best of style of man in the world."⁹ In his condescension there is a faint whiff of Mrs. Trollope.

When the Civil War broke out Godkin was on a tour of Europe with his wife and infant son. In a series of letters to the *Daily News* in London he undertook to explain the views of the North to the English people. The letters are said to have made such a strong impression on the British people that many of them were won over to the support of the Union. During the last three years of the war he acted as regular correspondent for the *Daily News*. His dispatches were so strongly flavored in support of the North that he was accused in England of having been "employed" by the American authorities. His praise for American naval and military heroes was extravagant. Grant's conduct of the war was to him "admirable" (he did not admire him as president); Sherman was "a real genius," and David Farragut, who defeated the Confederate fleet in the Battle of New Orleans, was his "example of what fighting sailors really are." In addition, his letters revealed a sympathetic understanding of the northern point of view and the principle of the inviolability of the Union. In 1863, for instance, Godkin explained the sentiments of the North in this way:

People in England don't understand, and never have rightly understood, the nature and origin of that tremendous devotion to the Union of which we have heard so much during the past two years, and of which the Northern people have given such terrible proofs. It is partly, no doubt, due to the fact that it is associated in their minds with that national power and greatness, the passion for which so many writers consider very reprehensible in an American, though in an Englishman they deem it worthy of admiration. And it is partly due to the remembrance and deep appreciation of the blessings which they have enjoyed under its shadow, the peace, plenty, prosperity, security and liberty, which it has bestowed on three generations.[10]

The idea of editing his own magazine was suggested to Godkin by his friends, Norton, Olmstead, and others. He was associated with the *New York Times*, then owned and edited by H. S. Raymond, and had the promise of a financial interest, when the opportunity to found his own magazine suddenly materialized. Forty stockholders raised one hundred thousand dollars; one half came from Boston, one quarter from New York, and another quarter from Philadelphia. Godkin left the *Times* and threw himself into the preparations. The name of the magazine may have come from an Irish newspaper he had read during his youth. Patterned after the respected English magazine, the *Spectator*, the *Nation* was to be a weekly journal dealing with politics, literature, science, and art. Some of its backers had been abolitionists, specifically one James McKim of Philadelphia. McKim's aim was to support Negro development in the South; another to create an editorial position for a young man of abolitionist background whom his daughter was about to marry. Godkin was to be the editor and he was to have complete freedom in determining editorial policy.

The first issue appeared in July, 1865. By the time the third issue was off the press the circulation was five thousand and the reading public possibly five times that number for it was presumed that the magazine was passed around within the family circle. It was a very auspicious start. But within a year disagreement developed among the stockholders: some did not consider an Englishman an ideal interpreter of strictly American viewpoints. Olmstead, Godkin, and McKim reorganized the magazine under the ownership of E. L. Godkin & Co. Thereafter, no further difficulties were encountered.

III

From the very beginning the new magazine exercised its strongest influence on the educated reader. The circulation soon rose to ten thousand, which was taken to mean that it was read by fifty thousand people. Godkin was considered an expert in foreign affairs and, in the judgment of many, a master of prose style.[11] The magazine became a standby for college professors, editors, and college graduates all over the nation. A regular reader was Thomas Woodrow Wilson. In the South and Midwest subscribers waited so eagerly for each issue that they made special arrangements to hasten delivery. College teachers recommended it to their students. Among its contributors were such illustrious personages as James Russell Lowell, the poets Longfellow and Whittier, Phillips Brooks, and Charles Eliot Norton. One of the English contributors was James Bryce, Oxford professor, who was to publish *The American Commonwealth* in 1888 and still later in 1907, was to be named ambassador to the United States.

Many subscribers were no less distinguished. Among them were: Emerson, poet, author, and lecturer (at first he was not enthusiastic about the project); Francis Parkman, the eminent historian; William James, professor of physiology and psychology at Harvard University; President Charles W. Eliot of Harvard, and William Curtis, editor of *Harper's Weekly* and later president of the National Civil Service Reform League. While traveling abroad James Russell Lowell wrote: "All the time I was without it, my mind was chaos and I didn't feel that I had a safe opinion to swear by." Another time he wrote: " 'The Nation' is my weekly refreshment and you preach the best lay sermons I know of." James Bryce declared it was "the best weekly not only in America, but in the world." (It was obtainable in Geneva, but not in Paris.) To Charles Dudley Warner, literary critic, journalist, and Mark Twain's collaborator on *The Gilded Age,* the arrival of the *Nation* marked "the Weekly Day of Judgment."

Five years after the inception of the magazine, Godkin had acquired such a reputation that Harvard University offered him a professorship in history. He was tempted to accept, for like William Dean Howells,* then associated with the *Atlantic*

---

* William Dean Howells had been briefly associated with the *Nation*. When he received an offer to become assistant editor of the *Atlantic Monthly*, he left for Boston, having on a previous visit fallen in love with the literati of Boston and its intellectual atmosphere. Howells became one of the most prolific novelists of his time and the most respected adviser of the newer literary figures of the late nineteenth and early twentieth centuries.

Monthly, he loved Cambridge and its atmosphere. However, his friends objected to his leaving the magazine and their counsel prevailed. Said Olmstead: "The *Nation* is worth many professorships," and Lowell told him that Harvard could obtain another professor of history, but that "we can't find another editor for the 'Nation.'" Yale University asked him to deliver a course of lectures in political economy or social science, which he had also to decline, for he did not want the magazine to "die," as he was told it would if he left it.

A frequently encountered statement is that anyone employed by Godkin learned to write lucidly and effectively. He trained many journalists and after 1881, when the *Nation* and the *Evening Post* were purchased by Henry Villard and Godkin became editor of both, such prominent newspaper men as Lincoln Steffens and Norman Hapgood worked under him. The relations between him and his staff are said not to have been uniformly harmonious. He has been judged as having been unduly censorious, particularly with Lincoln Steffens. Steffens joined the *Evening Post* in 1892 without any previous newspaper experience and left after five years to take over the down-at-the-heel *Commercial Advertiser*, which picked up amazingly under his direction.

As editor, Godkin was above criticism. His editorials are judged to have been models of "lucid style." James Ford Rhodes, a noted historian and Pulitzer Prize winner, considered him "a born writer of paragraphs and editorials." To Henry F. Pringle, professor of journalism at Columbia University, Godkin was "a mediocre journalist but a great editor." Commercialism, sensationalism, and sentimentality in journalism were his special detestation and he is said to have been contemptuous of those who indulged in them. The story was told that when Godkin discovered that a sentimental article by Lincoln Steffens had been printed in the *Post* during his absence, he flew into a rage and would have asked for Steffens' dismissal, if the literary editor had not upheld Steffens.

Even Godkin's enemies conceded that he possessed unusually keen powers of observation and that he was fiercely courageous and independent. To his fellow journalist who became his biographer, Rollo Ogden, he was a "prophet-publicist." Theodore Roosevelt during his prepresidential years had a less favorable opinion of him. In one of his dignified moods the future president contented himself by declaring that Godkin was "not a good patriot," but during a more belligerent moment he became "a malignant and dishonest liar."[12] (To be called "liar" by Theodore Roosevelt was no unusual experience.) The patriotic Rough Rider regarded the Spanish-American War as a holy crusade, whereas Godkin, like many of America's intellectuals, condemned the war so vehemently as to say, "American ideals were the intellectual food of my youth and to see America converted into a senseless Old World conqueror, embitters my age."[13] Godkin's antiwar editorials are supposed to have aroused McKinley's cabinet members to the point of suggesting that the editors of the *Post* and the *Nation* (and of the *Boston Herald* and the *Springfield Republican* as well) be prosecuted for treason.

Godkin criticized the English no less bitterly for starting the Boer War than he condemned America for entering into the war against Spain. He attributed as much guilt to Kipling for inciting "Jingoism," as Mark Twain had heaped on Sir Walter Scott for encouraging southern romanticism, which had in his opinion caused the South to precipitate the "War between the States."

IV

There was much that was contradictory about Godkin. He had been called a "Mugwump" by some, "a liberalist in the old tradition" by others and by many a "conservative." That none of these descriptions fitted him exclusively can be inferred from this statement: "To the advocates of democracy he pointed out its flaws; to the critics he appeared as its champion."[14] His attitude toward Negroes seems also to have been ambiguous. In regard to political rights for them, he favored that they be educated before being entrusted with the responsibilities of citizenship, an attitude that pained Senator Charles Sumner, who insisted on the necessity of the Negro franchise.[15] Sumner even asked one of Boston's abolitionist backers of the *Nation* to suspend the magazine, arguing that "it does more hurt than good."[16] "I would insist on equality for him [the Negro] at any cost," Godkin wrote in a letter, "but do not let us ruin the country in order to set him up in business." To his friend Charles Eliot Norton he wrote in 1865:

I do not oppose the admission of such negroes as shall prove their fitness. . . . What I ask and meant to ask, was not that the blacks shall be excluded as *blacks*, but that they shall not be admitted to the franchise simply because they are blacks and have been badly treated. I want to have the same rule applied to them that I would, if I could, applied to white men.[17]

Oswald Garrison Villard, the son of the founder of the *Post* and *Nation*, worked under Godkin and must have known him well. Some of his statements confirm the impression that Godkin was ambivalent in his behavior. Villard testifies Godkin fequently appeared reserved and haughty. Villard, no plebeian himself, admitted that "it is impossible to deny that there was some snobbishness in him, probably some residue of his life in Ireland and England, for he always looked down upon people who were in small trades."[18] He also mentions with more amusement than reproof that it was not unusual for Godkin to fail to recognize and greet men who worked on the paper with him and had served it for years. He also mentions that Godkin although he favored higher education for women, was not in favor of suffrage for them. This alone would have prejudiced anyone whose mother (like Villard's) was wont to march, attired in white, at the head of a column of women agitating for political rights. Villard's mother had been Fanny Garrison, the daughter of William Lloyd Garrison, and to her husband and son she could do no wrong.

Another opinion of Villard's was that Godkin "showed no real understanding for the need of a labor movement." When Governor Altgeld of Illinois pardoned the three anarchists in 1893, the *Nation* attacked him as viciously as his other detractors.[19] Godkin observed that the pardon message "reads almost as if the Governor himself were an anarchist." An indication of his antilabor stand may be deduced from the fact that he approved of President Cleveland's decision to send federal troops to break up the Pullman Strike. Also, his support of the gold standard and his opposition to Bryan and the Silverites may be taken as a sign of conservatism.

Others said of him that he was excessively opinionated, stiff-necked, and positive; that he was too critical; that he acted as if he could not be mistaken; and that he never retracted any personal charges, even if proved incorrect.

Godkin seems to have been snobbish even in regard to the readers of the *Post*, for his attitude was that it was better to influence "a few enlightened minds rather than a million numb-skulls." To Ralph Pulitzer, first-born son of Joseph Pulitzer, who worked on the *World*, a Godkin editorial was "a fine sermon to empty pews;"[20] but he read the *Post* faithfully and considered it the best paper for intellectuals.[21]

In Godkin's point of view there is a faint echo of Jeffersonian agrarianism, in that he was apt to consider the man who made his living from agriculture more virtuous than the individual who prospered through commerce. He condemned life in the big cities because of the disparity between excessive wealth and dire poverty, and also because he was aware that the cities were rife with corruption. Yet, while he was hostile to excessive wealth, he realized that materialism was the direct consequence of the opportunities to be found in a young and growing country.

Godkin's epithet for the period in which he lived was "Chromo Civilization." It is a variation of Mark Twain's and Charles Dudley Warner's designation of "the Gilded Age." It was a time when near illiteracy was no handicap to becoming a millionaire. When a railroad magnate like Collis Huntington, president of the Central Pacific Railroad openly bragged "My ledger is the only book I have gone through for five years,"[22] and when "Commodore" Vanderbilt, among others, could not write a sentence without violating the simplest grammatical and spelling rules, it is no surprise that a man of Godkin's type should have looked upon many American business leaders as "uncouth."

V

When Henry Villard acquired the *Nation* in 1881, he also took over the *Evening Post*, which had been under the editorship of William Cullen Bryant until his death three years before. Henry Villard had come to the United States from Germany in 1851 and after some of the usual struggles to which immigrants were subjected, he made his start as a journalist in the offices of the German newspaper, the *Staatszeitung*. During the Civil

War he was a war correspondent and later he covered the Franco-Prussian War for some of the American papers.

Though he became a railroad magnate and a Wall Street financier, Villard's attachment to journalism remained strong. Altruistic motives, as he explains in his autobiography,[23] prompted him to purchase the *Post* and the *Nation*. His editors, who were to be Carl Schurz, Godkin, and Horace White (of the *Chicago Daily Tribune*), received the promise that they would have complete freedom to determine editorial policies. He kept his promise. Relinquishing all financial control by placing the majority stock under the jurisdiction of three impartial trustees, he turned ownership over to his wife. The purpose was to forestall any allegation that the *Post* was under the control of Wall Street. The *Nation* became a weekly edition of the *Post*, but the quip was that the *Post* became a "daily edition of the 'Nation.'"[24]

It was as chief editor of the *Post* that Godkin reached the summit of his powers. He made the paper widely respected among readers who wanted news and not gossip. His dicta prevailed even when circulation and advertising managers foresaw dire consequences if certain editorial policies were followed. Many of them did prove financially hurtful to the paper. In 1888 the *Post* supported Cleveland in his bid for reelection, but a scandal over the disclosure of an illicit love affair shocked Godkin. Though he supported Cleveland again in 1892, Godkin condemned him bitterly as a "Jingo" when the Venezuelan crisis brought England and the United States close to war. He did so not because of pro-English sentiments, for his condemnation for England in starting the Boer War was equally strong. When Pulitzer and Hearst came out strongly for war with Spain, he castigated them for their "disgraceful behavior."

VI

In the security of his prestigious job, Godkin began in 1884 to concentrate his editorial attacks on the corruption of New York City's municipal government. It was in his opposition to Tammany Hall that he earned a permanent place among the reform journalists of his day. Other media—the *New York Times* and *Harper's Weekly*, for instance—had been fighting Tammany since Tweed's days in the 1870's. Thomas Nast's cartoons in

Harper's Weekly, representing Tammany as a tiger and/or as a bloated human beast, had brought the magazine prestige as well as added circulation. Godkin entered the fray during the "reign" of Richard Croker, who followed "Boss Tweed." An Irish immigrant, Croker had been brought to America at the age of three and had passed through various stages of dependence on Tammany Hall. Croker's professed motto was "honest graft," but he failed to inhibit the practice of "dirty graft" by other members of the Tammany machine. In spite of Godkin's fulminations against Tammany during the 1880's, Tammany delegates were elected with unfailing regularity. In 1890 Godkin hit upon a new scheme—to discredit Tammany by publishing the biographies of Tammany chieftains with all the unsavory facts that would reflect on their backers, many of whom were leaders in the business world. To no avail did the staff point to the unpleasant consequences that might follow. Godkin ignored them icily. The biggest editorial guns were aimed at Croker and Hugh Grant, mayor of New York between 1888 and 1892, the strongest of Tammany sachems since the days of Tweed.

Hugh Grant was an amiable but weak young man of wealth whom Croker manipulated with ease. Like Croker, Grant had begun as alderman of New York City, but he was beaten on his first try to become mayor. In 1888, however, Croker decided to overthrow Mayor Abram Hewitt and to install Grant in his place.[25] Grant was reelected in 1890, but was dropped in 1892. In 1894, after "the Lexow Investigation" studying corruption in the city government had shaken Tammany Hall to its foundations, he was dusted off by Croker and deliberately sacrificed to run against William Strong, a reform candidate. Strong won. Croker took himself to England to wait it out. He reappeared in 1900 to assume leadership of Tammany Hall again. In 1901 Seth Low was elected mayor on a reform ticket, and Croker departed for England permanently.

When these and other unsavory machinations were revealed in the *Post,* the Tammany clique was so infuriated that suit was brought against Godkin for criminal libel and he was arrested. But the grand jury exonerated him, and instead of the conviction for which the Tammany bosses had angled, he received a loving cup inscribed: "From Friends in Grateful Recognition of Fearless and Unfaltering Service to the City of New York." It has been said that the attacks on Tammany Hall by Dr. Charles Henry Parkhurst, clergyman and reformer, from his pulpit in the Madison Square Presbyterian Church were directly inspired by the articles in the *Post* and that "the Lexow Investigation" was the result of his fulminations.

VII

The years between 1895 and 1900 were Godkin's "pessimistic years." He had lost many of his illusions about democracy. When he resigned from the *Evening Post* in 1900 he wrote: "I came here fifty years ago with high and fond ideals about America. . . . They are now all shattered and I have apparently to look elsewhere to keep even moderate hopes about the human race alive."[26]

For twenty-five years after coming to the United States Godkin did not return to England. After his first visit, which he said "intoxicated" him, he went back frequently. In 1897 he received an honorary degree from Oxford University. Three years later he suffered a cerebral hemorrhage which forced him to resign from his editorial duties. He improved, however, and was again visiting England when death overtook him in 1902. He was buried in England, but the inscription over his grave, composed by his friend, James Bryce, stated that he had been a citizen of the United States for forty years. As a tribute to Godkin's life and work, a sum of twelve thousand dollars was subscribed by friends and admirers to endow a lectureship at Harvard University in his name. The first lecturer was Bryce, who a few years later was appointed ambassador to the United States. The Godkin lectureship has provided a forum for some of the most respected public figures. One of them was Adlai Stevenson, who in 1954 delivered a series of lectures on world affairs that were published under the title, *Call to Greatness*.

Godkin was the author of several books on such subjects as wealth, poverty, and labor in America. The titles of his books mirror his concern: *Reflections and Comments; Problems of Modern Democracy; Unforeseen Tendencies of Democracy*. But his most lasting achievement was the *Nation*, which Oswald Garrison Villard retained after he sold the *Evening Post* in 1918, becoming its editor. The *Nation* was finally sold when

Villard retired in 1933, but it has remained what Godkin intended it to be: a spokesman for liberal thought and social justice. In this and in the influence of his moral persuasions upon a host of journalists, publishers, and public figures to follow his lead, lies Godkin's gift to intellectual America. It is best expressed by William James, who said: "To my generation,* his was certainly the towering influence in all thought concerning public affairs, and indirectly his influence has certainly been more pervasive than that of any other writer of the generation, for he influenced other writers who never quoted him, and determined the whole current of discussion."[27] This is great praise from a very respected source.

---

* William James died in 1910 at the age of sixty-eight.

JOHANN MOST
1846-1906

Radicalism Comes to America

He was persona non grata in Austria, Germany, and England when he decided to transfer his activities to America. His particular contribution was to introduce and spread the doctrines of anarchism in America at a time when labor dissatisfaction was at its highest.

A bombastic orator and an alumnus of European prisons, his is the distinction of belonging among the infamous rather than the famous of America's immigrants.

The Emergence of the German Nation

Otto von Bismarck (1815-1898) was the architect of the German Reich. While most Germans considered him a hero, to the followers of Karl Marx he represented the ruination of their hopes. A reactionary in politics and a stout defender of Protestantism, he was serving in the Prussian parliament when the revolution of 1848 broke out. Summoned in 1861 by King William of Prussia to become prime minister, he began to dream of consolidating the German states into one nation under the banner of Prussia. The process by which he accomplished it was through three lightning wars.

The first occurred in 1864 when, in participation with Austria, Prussia quickly defeated Denmark. King Christian IX of Denmark had taken the unwise step of claiming for his country the duchy of Holstein, a member of the Germanic Confederation.

But after Denmark's defeat, Austria continued to maintain troops there under an Austrian governor. Bismarck seized upon the occupation as a *casus belli,* for he had been seeking an excuse for ejecting Austria from the Germanic Confederation. Austria was humiliatingly defeated by her former ally and deprived of her membership. Bismarck then created a North German Confederation of the states north of the River Main, with the king of Prussia at its head. But national unity was not yet, because four south German states that had sided with Austria were outside the union and free to form their own association.

These four states had to be brought into the Confederation if Bismarck was to achieve his purpose. He realized that a challenge to their patriotism as Germans would probably produce the result he desired. Conveniently, a crisis arose in 1870 between Prussia and France. It could easily have been composed, but Bismarck deliberately maneuvered the situation in such a way that Napoleon III of France would declare war. It happened just as he had hoped. The outcome was a lightning victory for the Germans that astounded the world, and a disastrous defeat for France. Napoleon, who became a prisoner of the Prussian armies at Sedan, was overthrown; a French Republic was set up and a civil war followed in which radical elements placed themselves behind barricades and fought a monarchist faction. For two months, until hunger forced the revolutionaries to capitulate, Paris was in a state of siege. Germany's terms were an indemnity of one billion dollars[1] and the cession of Alsace and parts of Lorraine. The fate of the revolutionaries was to be shot summarily or to be condemned to imprisonment at hard labor, many of them to France's penal colony in the jungle of French Guiana.

Germany climbed to nationhood over the prostrate body of France. As Bismarck had foreseen, the southern states of Germany were aflame with nationalism and gladly joined the new Reich. The king of Prussia was named emperor; Bismarck became chancellor. A new constitution granted two democratic features: universal manhood suffrage and a lower house, the Reichstag, to be elected by popular vote. The rest of the system was conservative, because the chancellor and the other ministers were responsible only to the emperor, to be appointed and dismissed by him.

The German Social Democrats were by then well entrenched. The focus was Karl Marx, who had been expelled as a result of the unsuccessful Revolution of 1848 and was living as an exile in London. His first work, *The Communist Manifesto,* published in London in the German language, gave to Marxian socialists their slogan: "Workers of the World, Unite!" Revolutionary intrigues were constantly being hatched, and upon their being discovered, or even suspected, participants, even sympathizers, were forced to flee. In this way thousands of German proletarians found their way to America.

After unification the Social Democratic party increased its number of seats so rapidly that Bismarck became alarmed. One of the earmarks of socialism, which made it so hateful to him, was its internationalism. To the chancellor nationalism was the fulcrum on which the German state rested, and was therefore sacrosanct. The tendency of the Social Democrats to oppose purely national goals smacked of treason to him. For instance, Wilhelm Liebknecht and August Bebel, both militant socialists, refused to support a war loan in 1870, first abstaining from voting, and later taking an even more positive stand by voting against further military expenditures. They also expressed their opposition to the annexation of Alsace-Lorraine.[2]

Bismarck's method of inhibiting the growth of socialism was a two-pronged one: he rescinded privileges that had been gained, but he initiated legislation which brought benefits to the German people that were of the greatest significance. In 1878 antisocialist laws were passed that suppressed the socialist movement. At the same time, Bismarck stole the thunder of the socialists by posing as the protector of the working people. Germany received a system of workingmen's insurance, safeguarding them against sickness, accident, and old age, that became the model for all other European nations.

As a result, unrest and opposition in Germany quieted down. The pride and satisfaction of the Germans in having become the most progressive country in Europe showed itself in a sharp drop in emigration. Whereas until 1850 fifty percent of America's immigrants came from Germany, and after 1860 thirty-five percent, after 1890 the number declined to ten percent. In Alexander Berkman's* words, "the idealistic elements" (by which he meant leftists and intellectuals), were replaced by a more conservative class of newcomers, for whom America was utopian enough without an added injection of revolutionary idealism.

The Germans introduced socialism to America. Later Russian immigrants strengthened the movement. But though socialism had a considerable impact during the post-Civil War period, when industrialization took a tremendous swing forward, it was not able to penetrate deeply enough into American life to survive as a potent political force for more than a few decades. In America, its chief accomplishment was to cause the two traditional parties eventually to adopt some of the principles that were the backbone of socialism.

America in the Throes of Industrialization

Long before the mid-nineteenth century it had become obvious that Jefferson's hope for a predominantly agrarian society, composed of sturdy yeomen owning and cultivating their portions of land, would not prevail. This dream of a bucolic paradise is most poignantly expressed in a word picture by a pre-revolutionary settler of French birth, Crèvecoeur, who described the pleasures of a father working the fields with his small boy —just old enough to make gurgling noises—whom he had strapped into a seat made for him in the back of a plow.[3]

By 1850 the physical United States presented a picture of millions of acres in the West still untouched by human habitation. But the East and parts of the Midwest were crisscrossed by railroad lines and canals and rivers were filled with traffic. The stir and excitement in the seaboard cities and in dozens of new towns suggested that the American dream was more likely to be realized through commerce and industry than through a rustic way of life.

Even the earliest settlers showed a predilection for commerce. Jefferson recognized it as something that had been

---

* One of the leading anarchists (of Russian birth) in America.

brought over on the first ships. After the War of 1812 immigration began to increase significantly. Though many of the newcomers were drawn to America by the hope of creating a home in the open spaces and proceeded with all possible haste to the "West," many more preferred to seek work in the burgeoning cities. The majority of pre-Civil War immigrants came mainly from Ireland and Germany. In Germany, lack of economic opportunity and political unrest had forced them out; in Ireland, hunger had made life unendurable. While large numbers of Germans were drawn to the states of Missouri, Illinois, Wisconsin, and other midwestern areas, where some of them purchased farms and became *"Lateinische Bauern"* ("Latin-speaking farmers"),* those who were artisans, craftsmen, and industrial workers searched for employment in the cities. The Irish, too, preferred the cities, where jobs for unskilled workers were available, although great numbers of them were shipped off to work on the railroads, the canals, and the roads under construction.

Immigrant workers, accustomed to accepting a class-conscious way of life, were more likely than natives to be satisfied with their status of workmen. Though uncounted numbers of newcomers who possessed specific technical "know-how" secured positions of importance and not infrequently met with the kind of success that brought them wealth, most immigrants considered good wages, a certain amount of security, and opportunities for their children the acme of a satisfactory life. Such gains were by no means to be taken for granted.

The native worker was less apt to regard himself as a permanent member of the work force. There was always the hope that a worker today would be an employer next year, or sooner. As the acerb W. E. B. DuBois remarked: ". . . everywhere the poor planned to be rich and the rich planned to be richer."[4] Considering the frequency with which such transformations occurred, such expectations were not unwarranted. It was the mudsill theory in operation—from the cabin with an earthen floor to the house on the hill, if not to the White House, from worker to employer as soon as possible.

---

* They were men of such superior education that they were said to be able to converse in Latin.

In the drive to succeed, the worker-turned-employer did not hesitate to become an exploiter or to climb over the backs of his workers, particularly when they were immigrants. Otherwise, how could he hope to get on? It was characteristic of nineteenth-century employers to pay the lowest wages, sometimes because they were convinced that more money than was essential for survival was apt to soften the moral fiber, and to oppose unions and strikes until hunger forced workers to return to their jobs. Even Andrew Carnegie, whose profits enabled him to give away close to three hundred and twenty-five million dollars during his lifetime,[5] did not consider it wise to spread surplus earnings in the form of increased wages, for, he asserted, "If distributed in small quantities among the people [it] would have been wasted in the indulgence of appetite, some of it in excess."[6] Instead, he declared, ". . . the best means of benefiting the community is to place within its reach the ladders upon which the aspiring can rise." Among such "ladders" were libraries and institutions of learning.

In spite of the optimism of native workers that wealth was around the corner, some began to realize even before the end of the eighteenth century that it was to their benefit to form and join workers' organizations. The need became more evident as the work force increased and depressions made unemployment a recurrent problem. In 1842 Judge Lemuel Shaw of Massachusetts had declared trade unions to be legal as well as the pursuit of their objectives "in such a manner as best to subserve their own interests."[7] It was the first decision in favor of workers. While labor made some gains during times of prosperity, it invariably lost them in the next recession, because widespread unemployment made existing wage scales unenforceable. The period between 1800 and the Civil War was punctuated by four depressions, of which that following "the Panic of 1837" was the most severe.

The Civil War removed all impediments to rapid industrialization. To Lewis Mumford, the war "shook down the blossoms and blasted the promise of spring. . . . The Brown Decades had begun."[8] Freed from the constrictions imposed by the South, the North and West pressed for a far-flung transportation system that permitted tremendous industrial acceleration. The war also provided an incalculable boon to those who wished for no grander opportunity than to create homes where no white man had lived before. The Homestead Act, passed in the midst of the war, opened the national domain to prospective settlers and supplied natives and newcomers alike with one hundred and sixty acres of land free of charge.

During the war years the doors were opened wide to an orgy of corruption and thievery unmatched before. After the war the pioneers of industry completed a vast industrial empire in such a short time that America became the wonder and the envy of the world. To immigrants, post-bellum America remained "the Golden Land," but the period would become known otherwise as "the Gilded Age," hardly a term of un-alloyed admiration.

This rapid success was accomplished also through ruthless exploitation of natural resources and labor. In the Contract Law of 1864[9] the industrialists gained the advantage of being permitted to import European labor. The existence of an un-limited labor supply enabled unscrupulous economic planners to maintain high productivity uninterruptedly at the lowest possible wages. So many millions kept pouring in, expecting a share of the good life they identified with America, that be-tween 1860 and 1890 the immigrant population more than doubled—from over four million it rose to over nine million.[10] In 1890 sixty-eight percent of Chicago's population was foreign-born. What awaited them was a terrible letdown. Because most of them were not skilled at any particular work, they were considered fit only for the menial jobs—"foreign jobs"—as they were called, paying the lowest wages, requiring long hours, and frequently exposing them to occupational hazards. The cities, unprepared for such an influx, could offer only the most miserable housing. For most aliens it was a desperate struggle to keep their heads above water. There was no protection for them, for the government was pledged to remaining aloof. The unions? Many of them, organized on craft lines, considered im-migrants undesirable. Besides, the unions had a hard struggle just to maintain themselves in a system that was dominated by employers who did not hesitate to employ strikebreakers and Pinkerton spies, and to use every possible means with which to break efforts at labor organization. Immigrants were so deeply enslaved, so inescapably caught in the vise of relentless exploitation, that they became susceptible to propaganda by radicals who openly espoused militant resistance.

During the closing decades of the nineteenth century occurred some of the fiercest labor battles in the history of the American people. The struggle between workers and the employing class was aggravated by two severe economic breakdowns that occurred during the last twenty-five years of the century—in 1873 and again in 1893. Beginning with 1875, a bloody strike in the anthracite mines was followed by a violent disturbance on the railroads. Both were precipitated by wage cuts resulting from the depression following "the Panic of 1873." These strikes were a prelude to three convulsions which took place during the next two decades: the Haymarket Affair of 1886 in Chicago, the Homestead Strike of 1892 in the Carnegie mills near Pittsburgh, and the Pullman Strike of 1894, also fought out in and near Chicago. Of the three, the Haymarket incident had the most far-reaching effect.

What gave the Haymarket Affair its sinister significance was that the consequence of the tragic event seemed to justify the anarchist interpretation of the state as unjust and tyrannical. When a bomb was thrown in the midst of an assembly that was peaceful until interrupted by the police, eight known anarchists were arrested for the killing of a policeman and injury to hundreds among bystanders and police, some of whom died subsequently. Despite the fact that the guilt of the accused was never proved, four men were executed.

In the absence of proof, horrified liberals agreed with anarchists that in taking the lives of four people for their beliefs the state had committed "judicial murder." Chicago, which already possessed an unenviable reputation for its exploitation of labor and the skull-cracking tactics of its police, became for many people the most iniquitous city in the United States. But the anarchist tide, which reached its crest during the cataclysmic events connected with the Haymarket incident, was turning. Though, according to the high priestess of American anarchism, Emma Goldman ("Red Emma"), the outcome of the event attracted new disciples from all over the world, the futility of the movement became obvious to many of the dissatisfied elements. For the practical and down-to-earth there was a lesson in that calamity they could not fail to heed.

I

When Johann Most, considered "the father of anarchism" in America, arrived here in 1882 at the age of thirty-six, he had had a long career as a radical agitator. From his early childhood on he had been the victim of so many calamities that a man of his romantic disposition might well have thought a malevolent fairy had stood at his cradle and decreed his various misfortunes. His birth in 1846 in Augsburg, Bavaria, *"polizeiwidriger Weise"* ("against police regulations"), as he himself cynically put it, preceded the marriage of his parents by two years.[11] His father, a lawyer's scribe, was looked upon by the authorities as too poor to take on family responsibilities. His mother, a gentle, well-educated governess, taught the boy to read and write before he was five.

He was such a bright boy that he won a prize at school every year. But at the age of eight disaster struck. He was attacked by a bone disease which settled in his jaw, and which eventually was diagnosed as bone cancer. Removal of part of his jaw left his face, which had been even-featured and normally attractive, a caricature of itself. Later in life he attempted to minimize the effect of the operation with a thick beard, but he still appeared so hideously disfigured that even those who had no reason to be ill disposed toward him could not hide their revulsion.

The tragedy was not only that his disfigurement caused people to shrink from him, which gave him an ineradicable inferiority complex, but that it also killed his hope for a career he wanted above any other and for which he seems to have had a conspicuous talent. What he wanted to be was an actor of the romantic type, and this ambition never left him.

While he was young Most nurtured the hope that if he could only find a director who would conquer his aversion and put him on the stage, he could make people forget about his face. But he could never overcome the handicap of his mutilation, nor could he forget the lure of the theater, which persisted even in middle age, when he acted in benefit performances that stirred people to their very depths. Emma Goldman, who at first was his devoted disciple and admirer, then broke with him, and in their later years attempted, unsuccessfully, to regain his trust, remarked of him:

Who knows what Most's career would have been but for the neglect and stupidity of the provincial German doctors? One must have heard him on the platform, or seen his counterpart of old Baumert in Gerhart Hauptmann's *The Weavers* . . . to realize what an unusual actor was lost in him through his deplorable facial defect.[12]

The second tragedy in his life was the loss of his mother. Her death by cholera while he was still a child deprived him of the only person who might have helped him to endure his deface-ment. He was a high-strung boy, full of turbulent spirits, who needed to be taught how to cope with the realization that there was something repellent about him, and who required loving guidance and care. His misfortune was compounded when his father remarried, for his stepmother was a termagant who mis-treated him. She deprived him of play, expecting that he per-form all kinds of menial chores. She starved him as well, so that he was compelled to steal or beg for food. His hatred for his stepmother poisoned his life. Associating tyranny with her, he grew to despise and to oppose all tyrants.

Most was also plagued by difficulties at school. In Bavaria, which was predominantly Catholic, religious instruction was required by law. His parents, freethinkers, had brought him up to scoff at religious training, but he had to learn the catechism if he wanted to avoid corporal punishment. Another scourge was a teacher so brutal that he made school unendurable for him. His revenge was to organize a strike against him, for which he was expelled, ending the hope the father had entertained that the unfortunate boy might reach security and status in a re-spected profession. Most's expulsion made it clear to him how obnoxious he was considered to be. Henceforth, it was to be hammered into his mind until he accepted it as a fact of his existence.

II

Apprenticed to a bookbinder by his own choice, because he loved books, Most found he had exchanged one misery for another. His master was cruel and his mistreatment continued. By law he had to attend religious instruction until he was eighteen. His refusal led to his being dragged to jail for twenty-four hours. He was so difficult that his master was glad to release him from his apprenticeship at seventeen, a year earlier than required by law. A slight and undernourished youth, he set out as an itinerant journeyman. During his three *"Wanderjahre"* he covered all of Germany, parts of France, Switzerland, and reached northern Italy in search of work and adventure.

At the same time he read voraciously in history and in the classics. When he found employment, he was likely to be expected to work fourteen hours a day for the equivalent of a Gulden a week. He was frequently turned away with silent aversion or with the explanation that his presence might cause the master's wife (who might be pregnant)[13] to be frightened out of her wits, or that he might drive customers away. Because of the lack of normal relationships, his bitterness became more pronounced. He could only dream of the stage which was inaccessible to him.

By the time he found a steady job in the French-speaking part of Switzerland, Most had developed a strong sense of social concern in compensation for his years of misery. As Longfellow observed: "The thoughts of youth are long, long thoughts." His starved spirit drew him to the labor movement. He joined the International Working Men's Organization, a division of Karl Marx's First International. As soon as he started to organize his fellow workers, he was fired.

III

The next arena for his activities was Vienna. Smarting from its defeat by Germany in 1866, Austria was floundering help-lessly before demands for increased political liberties that were being advanced by newly formed proletarian and liberal groups. Some of the demands were granted, but agitators remained dissatisfied. Most was twenty-two and the political climate suited him to perfection. He plunged into speechmaking against the government and was punished with a jail sentence of one month—his first as an adult. For radicals jail was rarely a calamity, for it provided them with the opportunity to improve their education at state expense. All over Europe and in America as well, radicals acquired knowledge in jail. For instance, Emma Goldman used her first prison sentence at Blackwell's Island to learn nursing by assisting the prison doctor, and to increase her knowledge of literature and philosophy. After her release from prison nursing was her profession until she established a magazine, *Mother Earth*. One of her friends, who had been jailed in Europe, acquired such a sound background in French during a prison term that he was able to teach Emma in turn. Alexander Berkman was another who benefited in one way from his long prison sentence of almost thirteen years.[14] At the trial for his "*Attentat*" on Henry Clay Frick he knew so little English that he had to depend on a German interpreter. In jail he learned to use the English language to such good effect that he became an extremely able writer and editor. Most found conditions in the Austrian jail so far from unpleasant that he considered his existence "*angenehm*" ("pleasant"). Thus, he put his period of detention to good use.

Jail so enhanced Most's reputation that upon his release he found himself in great demand as a speaker and labor organizer. He embraced the opportunity to thunder against the government with such enthusiasm that in less than two years he was again arrested, this time for leading a revolutionary demonstration before parliament. He received a sentence of five years, but was freed after one year in a general amnesty for political prisoners. Prison was still not unpleasant. This time he composed a revolutionary poem, "Die Arbeitsmänner" ("The Workers"), which became the favorite of German workers for two generations. He also condensed Marx's *Das Kapital*. Engels criticized the abridgement sharply in a letter, but Most claimed that it introduced the German proletariat to Marx. By the time he left prison he had acquired such renown in his circle that the socialists were glad to use him as an organizer. In those days he was not yet an anarchist but a militant socialist, who expected to achieve reform by propaganda. He plunged into his work with such zeal and met with such success that the Austrian government decided to expel him, using as justification the fact of his being a "foreigner."

Most himself tells the story that he confronted the official who informed him of his expulsion with an all-too-visible sneer at the implicit assumption that the Austrian state was omnipotent and would last forever. His doubts were well founded, for a little more than a dozen years after his death Austria was dismembered as a consequence of its defeat in World War I. Most was twenty-seven when he took his way back to his native Germany. The experiences of the last years had raised his self-confidence and had turned him into a persuasive orator and editor. Assuming the editorship of a south German labor paper, he began immediately to attract attention. His rise was meteoric, but not without impediments. During the first year he was summoned to court forty-three times.[15]

His election to the Reichstag during his first year in Germany represented a great triumph. But he was not awed by this representative assembly; his powers of derision won and he dubbed the parliament "the theatre of the marionettes." He was not to remain unmolested for long, for in the same year he was arrested for a seditious speech in Berlin. At some time during this period Most acquired a wife, but his marriage did not last. His explanation for its failure was that jail and marriage were incompatible. Receiving a sentence for eighteen months, he decided this time to concentrate on writing and to have his work smuggled out of prison. A pamphlet entitled *The Solution of the Social Problem* indicated he still held the socialist view that "propaganda of the word" was sufficient to win a majority to labor's side.[16]

While Most was in prison Bismarck's "Exceptional Laws," aimed at the suppression of the Social Democratic party, went into effect. The new legislation was the consequence of two attempts on the life of the octogenarian emperor, William I (grandfather of William II, who abdicated at the end of World War I), which Bismarck accused the party of having instigated. His real reason for outlawing it, however, was that the party had become too powerful. He dissolved the Reichstag and ordered new elections. As for Most, he was expelled from his native land.

IV

Most was then thirty-two, a fiery orator and an able writer and editor. London, which was home to many radicals from

Russia and Germany, seemed like a good place to him. Isaiah Berlin describes England as:

> the country most hospitable to political refugees, civilized, tolerant of eccentricities or indifferent to them, proud of her civil liberties and her empathy with the victims of foreign oppression.[17]

Among the Russian revolutionaries who lived in London for many years were Alexander Herzen and Mikhail Bakunin. For more than forty years London was also the home of Prince Kropotkin, who in 1917 decided to return to Russia, only to find himself ignored by Lenin.[18] Long-time residents of London were Karl Marx and Friedrich Engels. Most arrived with the reputation of being "the irresponsible wild man of the German press," a description bestowed upon him by the more responsible journalists of Germany. He himself admitted he was *"der best gehasste und der verleumdetste Mann fast zweier Generationen"*[19] ("the most hated and most maligned man of almost two generations").

As an orator Most possessed personal magnetism and an unusually melodious voice. The ability to sway an audience was one of his greatest assets. He was aware that the spell of oratory could make people sympathetic to him and wipe out the shock of his first impression, and he played upon their emotions with the skill of the actor he was. His means of impressing an audience were his voice and his daring use of invective, which had the effect of dousing his listeners with ice water. Conversely, those who refused to let themselves fall under his sway, or who were alienated by his message, reacted with an even greater revulsion that expressed itself in derision and outright cruelty. Consequently, Most was apt to be driven to an even more daring display of vitriolic language.

He might have found exile in London acceptable if he had been able to support himself. He had hoped to do so with his pen, but the Social Democrats of Germany had decided to conciliate the chancellor by assuming the role of citizens who were one hundred percent law abiding. That meant that those party newspapers and magazines that had survived would not accept Most's articles for fear of courting suppression. How was he to maintain himself? The idea of starting a magazine was a natural one, for as the Trotskyist Max Schachtman observed:

". . . a radical group without a paper is a contradiction in terms." Most hoped to be able to circulate the magazine he started, *Freiheit*, on the continent. He did not consult his German comrades, and as soon as the first issue appeared it was disavowed by the leader of the Social Democrats in Germany, Wilhelm Liebknecht (the father of the more famous Karl Liebknecht).

It was an even more severe blow when the German socialists undertook to publish their own official paper in Zurich. They also started a whispering campaign against Most, implying that his drinking habits made him unreliable. In addition, he made a poor impression on Marx and Engels, who dubbed him "a dealer of revolutionary phrases."[20] Most, whose violent nature made it impossible for him to behave with circumspection, retaliated with intemperate remarks against the leadership. He also proved indiscreet in revealing secrets which endangered the safety of the German leaders. After living in London for a year and a half and indulging in the kind of backbiting at which he was a master, he was expelled from the party. It meant a loss of prestige and a loss of readers he could afford even less.

It was during this period that Most began to veer away from socialism. Heretofore, he had given no sign of being attracted to anarchism. It was either because of bitterness or because of a genuine change of heart that he began to search for other gods to follow. He found one in Louis-Auguste Blanqui (1805-1881), a much persecuted French revolutionary, and another in Mikhail Bakunin (1814-1876), the foremost exponent of violence for its own sake. Blanqui and Bakunin had much in common, for both were dedicated apostles of revolution with all its violent consequences. At one time Marx and Bakunin had cooperated with each other, but many of Bakunin's zealous followers had come to favor a break with Marx. Most allied himself with the disciples of Bakunin. It might have been a genuine conversion, but his embrace of Bakunin might also have been due to resentment felt toward the German socialists who had repudiated him. Such a reaction would not have been inconsistent with Most's vindictive nature.

His new convictions were soon put to the test. In 1881, while he was a resident of London, the nihilists of Russia finally succeeded after several attempts in assassinating Czar Alexander II by aiming at him the anarchists' favorite weapon of assault, a homemade bomb. Ironically, Alexander had begun his reign as one of the more humane rulers of Russia who had emancipated the serfs and had thus earned himself the title, "the liberating czar."

When Most picked up the news of the assassination, he went berserk with joy. He wrote a gloating editorial which, beginning with the words, "Triumph, Triumph," overflowed with praise for the perpetrators of the murder. The editorial was surrounded by a conspicuous border of red. The vulgarity of his language offended the English authorities. He was arrested and given a term of sixteen months in an English prison. It was his fourth sentence as an adult.

V

During his imprisonment Most came to realize that further political activity in England was impossible. The overwhelming question, "Whither now?" was not to be evaded. While in jail he received an offer (which in view of his detention he had to decline), to edit a labor paper, *Arbeiter Zeitung* in Chicago. He was tired of Europe. Why not America? There, he was inclined to believe, guarantees of freedom of speech and freedom of the press promised immunity to disseminaters of unpopular doctrines.

Upon his release from prison the opportunity to leave Europe magically presented itself. It was an invitation from a radical German group, "the New York Social Revolutionary Club," to come to America on a lecture tour. But it seems he must have decided to remain in America, because before setting out, Most forwarded to a member of the club enough material for an issue of *Freiheit* to be assembled before his arrival.[21]

He was thirty-six when he reached the United States in 1882—a lightly graying man of slight appearance. Though Chicago and New York had nuclei of German radicals, his was the distinction of becoming the first immigrant to teach and popularize the anarchist credo.

One of his first disciples was the disillusioned teen-ager, Alexander Berkman, who was then suffering the bitter disappointments to which immigrants were prone. His background in Russia predisposed him towards anarchism. Though Most later condemned Berkman for attempting to kill Henry Clay Frick, he remained, for Berkman, *"mein Freund und Lehrer"* ("my friend and teacher"), as Berkman stated in an introduction to a biography of Most by a German comrade, Rudolf Rocker.

Through Berkman Most met the young Emma Goldman, who was also disillusioned and unhappy. She was shocked by Most's face, but she was carried away by his voice and oratory. Most was no less astute about Emma than she was about him. He recognized that it was her tempestuous childhood that had predisposed her toward becoming a rebel. Calling her *"Aschenprödelchen,"* after the bedraggled heroine of one of Grimm's fairy tales (Most was an incorrigible romanticist), he speculated whether she would not have turned out differently if her childhood had not been filled with violence and privation. She in turn came to question whether he would have become a revolutionary if fate had not conspired against his ambition to become an actor.

He indoctrinated her with such success that eventually she wrested the torch from his unwilling hands, surpassing him in intellectual vigor and in glamor, though physical attraction was not her most conspicuous characteristic. During the crucial decade between 1882 and 1892, when the American working class was most susceptible to radical propaganda, Most was the "pope" of the anarchist movement and the issues of *Freiheit* were his encyclicals. Thereafter he was a fading star.

VI

By the time Most arrived in America his habits and personality were as malleable as flint. He was vain, arrogant, suspicious, impatient, revengeful, intolerable of dissent, and incapable of self-discipline. Inured to slander, his combativeness was monumental. Admiration was so essential to him that he never forgave an injury to his ego, as Emma Goldman was soon to find out. That he possessed an overflowing measure of magnetism is obvious from her description:

The rapid current of his speech, the music of his voice and his sparkling wit and biting sarcasm, combined into something elemental that swept me along . . . It was overwhelming.[22]

When she met him she had been following the Haymarket trial, but she was not yet an avowed anarchist. Under his tutelage she was "swept" into anarchism. He recognized her potentialities and trained her to become a superb speaker whose hold on audiences of all kinds was no less powerful than his.

Obsessed by hatred for authority, Most seized control of the anarchist movement in America. His original intention may have been to direct his thunder against European institutions, but the oppression of workers he observed in America was sufficient to give his capacity for invective full play. The two foci of labor unrest were Chicago and New York. Chicago was better organized and had more anarchists than New York. *Freiheit* was established in New York, but Most expected to bring his message to Chicago and other industrial centers through "lecture trips" (or "*die Agitationstur*," in his words). His method was to heat up his audiences with inflammatory utterances against the system that permitted "the beast of capitalism" to exploit workers. He also depended upon propaganda to increase his subscription list.

He played his first important role at the Congress of Pittsburgh in 1883, arranged by anarchists and members of the Socialist Labor party, a militant forerunner of the Socialist party. What had brought them together was the desire to promote labor unity. The unity Most achieved was to put the whole assemblage into the radical camp.

Fired by his utterances, the meeting accepted his manifesto (*unsere Grundsätze*), which preached that "the class struggle must have a revolutionary character to succeed."[23] This meant by implication that the use of force was inevitable. Under his excoriation of the "American slave system," papers that heretofore had been merely prolabor, as, for instance, the *Arbeiter Zeitung* of Chicago, edited by August Spies, turned anarchist. Spies was to be one of the four who would be executed for his alleged connection with the Haymarket Affair. Another paper that was converted to anarchism was *Alarm*,[24] edited by Albert Parsons, whose life also ended on the scaffold for his imputed participation in throwing the bomb. Parsons was the only native among the four executed.

The closing decades of the nineteenth century were not a time of polite journalism. Fisticuffs between rival editors of major newspapers were not infrequent and vitriolic verbal assaults were the order of the day.[25] Hence, Most's tendency toward intemperate language fitted the spirit of the times. Besides, he was lulled into a sense of false security by the assumption that the principle of freedom of the press insured him immunity. For that reason, he allowed himself to become so intoxicated by the vision of enhancing the anarchist cause singlehandedly that he let caution go entirely to the winds.

One of his boldest moves was to print recipes for manufacturing explosives at home. In order to learn more about the production of bombs, he took a job in a factory producing explosives and smuggled out materials that were to make the production of homemade bombs easier. At the same time he suggested other means of sabotage. In a handbook that he called *Revolutionäre Kriegswissenschaft* (*Revolutionary War Science*), he offered not only instruction on how to make bombs and how to start fires, but also how to put deadly chemicals into the food served to the rich.[26] When Louis Lingg, another of the Haymarket defendants, was brought to trial, the evidence against him was that he had reprinted recipes for homemade bombs in his paper and that ingredients for the production of bombs had been found in his shop. During the Haymarket trial sympathizers pointed to the lack of proof in connecting the accused with the deed, but Most declared in *Freiheit* that the bomb was thrown by someone associated with the movement, thus adding fuel to the suspicion that the accused were indeed the perpetrators of the outrage. He also declared the crime itself to be "fully justifiable."[27]

VII

During the four years preceding the Haymarket incident, Most experienced no interference. A week before the riot occurred he made an incendiary speech at a public meeting in New York, urging the listeners to collect bombs, rifles, revolvers, and the like, in preparation for a conflict he judged to be inevitable.[28] The Haymarket explosion was seen by many as a direct response to Most's preachings. No wonder the authorities associated him with the event, for one of his comments appearing in the *New York Herald* of May 6, 1886, went as follows:

Hip, hip, hooray for Chicago! . . . It is the beginning of the social revolution in America. The worker has become aggressive. The sufferers have determined to suffer no longer. The spiritual dynamite which I have sown for years in the breasts of the American workmen is bearing beautiful and bloody fruit. They have met the hordes of the oppressors; they have coped with them and disabled twenty-three. May the accursed dogs all die lingering deaths, full of pain and torment.[29]

Most was arrested and received a conviction of a one-year term at Blackwell's Island. The conditions in the American prison did not strike him even as tolerable. The English prison had been much less comfortable than those in Austria and Germany, but not as bad as he found this one to be. He confided to Emma Goldman when their friendship was still unclouded that nothing he had endured during his former periods of incarceration could compare with the humiliation, petty cruelty, and inhumanity to which he was subjected at Blackwell's Island. In Europe, political prisoners were looked upon as more "high class" than common criminals, and were therefore treated with some consideration, whereas in America Most found he was considered no better than the rest. What outraged him particularly was that his beard, which served him as a means of covering his misshapen face, was shaved, thus exposing him to the kind of mockery his appearance called forth. The soft-hearted Emma did not withhold her sympathy, which he so obviously craved. These were the "honeymoon days" of their friendship, when Most was still her "hero" and "the most remarkable man on earth" and when he was still harboring hopes that their relationship would turn out to be more than platonic. This hope was thwarted when Emma fell in love with the youthful Alexander Berkman.

During the trial and the conviction of the Haymarket victims, Most was behind bars. When he was released he would not keep still and was soon arrested again. The execution of four of the accused (one, Louis Lingg, committed suicide in his cell) served Most as an occasion for a particularly vitriolic speech. According to Emma Goldman, his speech was misrepresented by the *New York World* and copied by other papers. By then America had become thoroughly outraged over the dangerous doctrines brought in and disseminated by immigrants, as this poem reveals:

Anarchists

We took them in unclothed, unfed, unhoused,
  The poorest poor of Europe's weltering mass;
They were the dregs of populations roused
  By goad of tyrants to a desperate pass.

And Europe spewed them forth upon our shores.
  They came from every foreign kennel, fled
In at our windows and wide open doors,
  Unfit for freedom and to license wed.

Not theirs to fell the forest, not to tame
  Nature; they come to agitate and blab.
Who are the leaders of this race of shame?
  Herr Most, the blatherskite, and Julius Schwab![30]

At his trial, the prosecuting attorney introduced Most's pamphlet *Kriegswissenschaft* into the evidence against him and Most was again convicted for a year. He was released only a short time before Berkman's attempt to assassinate Henry Clay Frick for the brutal treatment of his workers in the Homestead Strike.

His second prison term in the United States must have shaken his confidence in the wisdom of preaching "direct action" against oppressors of labor. At forty-six Most may have felt weary and disappointed in the results of his preachments. This man who, Berkman claimed, had declared in his hearing, "If I had a hundred resolute men at my disposal I could achieve a revolution in New York tomorrow,"[31] disavowed Berkman's attempt on the life of Frick, declaring that propaganda by deed was not practicable, because it endangered the revolutionary movement. His doctrinal attitude had undergone still another change. He was becoming partial to the theories of the syndicalists, of whom the Frenchman, Georges Sorel (1847-1922), was the principal exponent. Though syndicalism preached the general strike, in itself a violent form of protest, it was less drastic than anarchism. Like the anarchists, the syndicalists advocated collective ownership of the means of production, but would place them in the hands of an association of producers. When the Wobblies adopted the syndicalist program in 1905, Most was said to have been sympathetic to them, which indicates that his sympathies must have swung over to the view that the salvation of the working classes lay in the radical trade-union movement.

While Berkman frothed impotently in the Western Penitentiary of Pennsylvania over his repudiation by his "first teacher in anarchy," Emma, whose temper was so ungovernable that she admits she threw a chair at one of her lovers, was free to take action. Confronting Most at a public meeting with a horsewhip hidden under her cloak, she demanded that he retract his condemnation of Berkman. When he remained silent, she drew out and whip and applied it to him in front of the audience. Finished, she broke the whip to pieces, threw them into his face and stalked off.

To her it was no simple slip-up on the part of Most to have criticized Berkman. In her eyes Most had committed a double crime. He had belittled what she regarded as a "noble act" on the part of her lover, one that would cost him, a youth of twenty-one, almost fourteen years of freedom and, in addition, he had disavowed the core of the anarchist credo. She never retracted her anarchist principles, but in her later years she changed her mind about producing bombs at home, for she spoke with horror of the possibility of accident and the danger to innocent people.

Most, who was proud and arrogant, never forgave her for her humiliation of him. Though he was antireligious, he believed fully in at least two Biblical axioms: "An eye for an eye" and "Thou shalt have no other Gods before me." Furthermore, he had a conspicuous talent for retaining grudges. Perhaps he could not forget the time when Emma had been his adoring disciple and that, when he asked her to accompany him on a lecture trip, she did.[32] Emma, who was as forgiving as she was impulsive, must have regretted her action, for she tried to conciliate him on several occasions; but he always turned stonily from her. Her last attempt to show her respect for the man who had set her on the path she was to follow until she collapsed and died (at a meeting), was to pay him tribute at a memorial gathering after his death.

By the 1890's the influence of his paper was waning. Most was becoming "a general without an army" and a prophet whose disciples were steadily diminishing. Alexander Berkman later stated that *Freiheit* was slipping because the Germans emigrating to the United States at the end of the century had lost their idealism, but he would not admit that the anarchist movement itself had lost its potency.

During the 1890's Most acquired a wife, Helene—on whom he became dependent—and two American-born children. His children, it has been said, were the butt of jeers and taunts, which they learned to accept with indifference and stoical composure. By 1897 it became obvious to him that he could not make a living and he was forced to accept a job as editor of a labor paper launched by German trade unions in Buffalo. *Freiheit* became a weekly supplement of the paper.[33] But Most could not get along with his employers and within two years he was back in New York.

VIII

It was lucky for him that he returned when he did, because two years later President McKinley was murdered in Buffalo by Leon Czolgosz, a demented anarchist. Had Most remained the editor of the Buffalo paper, the assassination of the president would have been laid squarely at his door. He was arrested anyway, and later convicted, but a direct link between his propaganda and the actual crime could not be established. His arrest was due to an article which appeared in *Freiheit* two days before the attack on McKinley. The article, called "Murder Against Murder" had been written in 1850 by Karl Heinzen, a revolutionary long since dead, and had been intended as a filler, but Most had omitted to cite the name of the author and to give the date when it was first composed. Appearing as it did, it was assumed that it came from the pen of Johann Most and that it was intended as an inflammatory piece of propaganda. As soon as the news of the attempt on the life of the president was released, Most knew he was in trouble. He tried to recall the edition, but a few copies had been sold, one to a member of New York's police force.

McKinley had had other enemies among newspapers, and these had attacked him with the lack of restraint characteristic of the period. One of them was William Randolph Hearst's

Journal, which had printed a ditty about "stretching McKinley in his bier," and had published many anti-McKinley editorials and cartoons. Though Hearst was burned in effigy in many cities throughout the nation,[34] he was left unmolested by the police. But not Most. He was immediately arraigned on the charge that the murder was a direct consequence of his propaganda. Though Morris Hillquit, Most's lawyer, fought so hard to have him acquitted that he was commended by the trial judge for his efforts, he could not save his client.[35] Most was condemned to serve a year in prison.

While serving his sentence, he edited *Freiheit* from prison. The articles that appeared in these issues were judged to have been the best he wrote in five years. The tone was quieter and more restrained than it had been in years. When he returned from prison, he found the magazine in a moribund condition. His wife participated in the desperate struggle to keep it alive. In 1906 he was forced to embark on a tour to raise money, a procedure to which many radical editors regularly resorted when the need for additional capital became desperate. They took it for granted that their supporters would not let them down and their trust was generally vindicated. It boiled down to the question: "If you will not help, who will?"

It was a method that Emma Goldman found successful in keeping alive her magazine, *Mother Earth,* as well as Alexander Berkman, who after his release from prison betook himself to San Francisco to issue the magazine *Blast.*

In Cincinnati, Most caught a severe cold, which he neglected until an attack of erysipelas forced him to stop. He is supposed to have wandered feverishly through the home of a comrade where he stayed, calling for the ministrations of his wife. He was sixty at his death and had served one-sixth of his life behind bars in Austria, Germany, England, and the United States. Hillquit remarked of him: "As he had studied the social conditions of different countries in his earlier years as a wandering artisan, so he explored their jails in later life as a traveling agitator."[37] He had been hounded in every country where he had lived and worked.

Freiheit died with him, for Helene Most declared at the memorial meeting held after his death that she would not continue publication of the weekly that represented the sum of

Most's accomplishments during his turbulent life. No objections seemed to have been raised, perhaps because it was realized that no one could take his place. Some of the comrades must have felt relieved, for they would have been duty bound to support the paper.

IX

There can be no doubt that after the authorities in America became aware of the type of propaganda Most disseminated, he was mercilessly persecuted. Even Morris Hillquit, who had no love for anarchists, admitted that Most was convicted not for complicity in the murder of McKinley, "but for his general anarchist propaganda."[38] His own trial was a repetition of the tactics used during the Haymarket trial. Hillquit had taken on Most's defense not because he sympathized with him, but because he wanted him to be tried fairly. Americans despised anarchists, not only because most of them were foreigners who violated American hospitality, but also because they seemed to be hiding behind the guarantees provided by the Constitution, while at the same time undermining the very institutions that insured protection. It is an indisputable fact that Americans have consistently rejected social and political ideas imported from Europe. Native Americans were not inclined to embrace radical ideas, though a few did. The treatment accorded to those who did was no more gentle than that meted out to foreigners.

Most was lucky to have lived when he did and to have died a natural death, because the hatred for radicals increased during the years preceding World War I and came to a climax after the conclusion of the war, when there was a repetition of persistent labor violence. This time the instigators were the Industrial Workers of the World, called Wobblies, among whom were many native Americans.

Many of them fared much worse than Most did. By the 1920's the hatred of employers and police authorities toward these troublemakers had become so virulent that the guarantees supplied by the Constitution were disregarded. Natives as well as foreign-born found themselves indicted without regard for due process. Some were lynched. Had Most lived in the twenties he might have shared the fate of Wobbly leaders Frank Little and Wesley Everest, who were put to death by lynch mobs, or he might have been executed in the shameful manner of Joe Hill, the Wobbly poet, who gave the movement its inspiring songs.[39]

Anarchism was an imported movement that could not fail to alienate the bulk of the American people, because they were convinced that they had the best and freest government in the world. As Friedrich Engels realized, the teachings of anarchism proved powerless against the "bourgeois prejudices" of Americans. Though the influence of anarchism was comparatively short-lived, the remembrance has remained in the American subconscious. It gave Americans a permanent case of jitters that has made them virulently suspicious of anything even faintly redolent of radicalism. The anarchism of the late 1960's—a completely indigenous movement—was no easier to swallow than the anarchist doctrines propounded by the despised "scum" of Europe.

From Yugoslavia:

NIKOLA TESLA
1856-1943

Electrical Genius

He was a scientist to whom Walt Whitman might have addressed the words: "to you the first honors always: / Your facts are useful and real." Arriving here with an invention that hastened the rapid transmission of power, he brought about a revolution in electrical science. That invention was alternating current. Beside alternating current Thomas Edison's direct current was as slow as the tortoise's progress beside that of the hare.

His genius foresaw other developments that were too fantastic to be believed. Had he succeeded he would have brought some of nature's functions under control. Because of the many vicissitudes of fortune which he underwent, his story forms one of the strangest illustrations of success and failure in the American environment.

The Southern Slavs Turn to America

Among the Slavs are included the Russians, Poles, Czechs, Slovaks, and a group of South Slavs whose homelands were the Balkans and other small groups bordering the Russian Empire in the East. Until the beginning of the Greek War of Independence in 1821, the entire Balkan peninsula was controlled by the Turks. The loss of Greece in 1832 began the precipitous decline of the Turkish Empire. The cause was not only the opposition to Turkey of the various ethnic groups living in the Balkans, but also Turkey's internal weakness that cul-

[133]

minated in the "Young Turk" revolution of 1908. Both Russia and Austria angled to replace the Turks as overlords in the Balkans. During the second half of the nineteenth century the whole region boiled over periodically into armed conflict.

The opposition arose largely because the greater part of the Balkans was inhabited by Christians of the Orthodox religion who bitterly resented being ruled by a sovereign of the antagonistic Moslem faith. But though they were not averse to playing Russia and Austria off against one another, both of whom were eager to pose as the deliverers of Christians from Moslem rule, they were too fiercely nationalistic to put themselves under the protection of either Russia, the defender of Greek Orthodox Catholics, or Austria, staunch champion of Roman Catholicism. What these Balkan countries desired was complete political independence. After Greece had won her freedom from Turkey, Serbia, tiny Montenegro, and Rumania followed, and, later in the century, Bulgaria. As the self-appointed protector of the states practicing the Greek Orthodox religion, Russia had hopes of becoming the dominant power in the Balkans. But the European powers—Germany, France, and England—had no intention of permitting it. In making Austria their cat's-paw, they hoped to balance Austria against Russia.

In this competition Russia and Austria maneuvered constantly to secure advantages over each other. Confrontations were frequent. One of these occurred in 1908. At the end of the nineteenth century Austria had been assigned to occupy and administer the Balkan province of Bosnia, which was almost entirely Serb, but not to incorporate it into the Austrian state. Nevertheless, after a secret arrangement with the Russian foreign minister, Austria annexed the region in 1908. It proved to be one of history's most fatal errors. Austria acquired an additional dissident group; Russia was alerted to the possibility of further depredations by Austria; and Serbia, which had hoped to add Bosnia to her own territory, seethed with resentment. Thus was laid the groundwork for the outbreak in 1914 of World War I and for the eventual dissolution of the Austro-Hungarian monarchy. In 1919 an independent Yugoslavia (country of the South Slavs) would rise from the ravages of the war.

One of the reasons for the hostility of the Slavic minorities to Austria was their jealousy over the power held by the German and Hungarian groups who constituted the two largest blocs in the Austrian Empire. The population ratio of Austria-Hungary before World War I was: twelve million German-speaking Austrians, ten million Magyars; five million Serbs and Croatians; and one million two hundred thousand Slovenes (residing in Carniola, north of the Austrian province, Croatia).[1] In addition, there were the Slavs of Bohemia and Moravia and several small Slav groups on the eastern periphery of the dual monarchy. The Hungarians, having been granted equal rights with the Austrians under the constitution of 1867, were willing to keep up the myth of a united empire.

The situation in which the Slavs found themselves was entirely different. Because the number of Slavs was comparatively small and because illiteracy among them was high, the Slavs had the smallest representation in the Austrian parliament. The German elements and the Hungarians pooled their efforts in keeping down the political aspirations of the Czechs and Slovaks in the north and the Slovenes, Croatians, and Serbs in the south.

There was constant dissatisfaction among the South Slavs caused by disagreement within the various groups. Speaking different tongues and ruled by antagonistic traditions, they would not cooperate with one another. By comparison with Russia's treatment of minority groups, Austrian rule was benevolent. But the Slavs considered themselves oppressed, though religious toleration was guaranteed by law and educational opportunities were unrestricted, provided students did not participate in hostile demonstrations against the monarchy. One who did was Louis Adamic.[2] Upon being expelled from his gymnasium for having taken part in a protest meeting, he found his way to America.

It was during the period of highest political unrest—between the 1870's and 1914—that immigration from the Balkans increased markedly. Another reason was that after the Civil War American agents began to penetrate the hinterland of Europe to recruit workers for industrial companies and the railroads. These people, who were so poor that they rarely handled money, proved susceptible to the tales of American wealth and opportunity spread by the agents. The Slavs exchanged their pastoral life for work that often took them into the bowels of the earth and for homes in mining towns and slums. They began to arrive by the tens of thousands, mostly men, tall, stalwart, and handsome, capable of prodigious feats of hard work. What did they find here? Work in the copper mines, in the steel factories, in the coalpits, in the railroad yards. Most of them had never seen buildings more than a few stories high, but in America many were drawn to construction work on skyscrapers.[3] Because the last decades of the nineteenth century were years of intense railroad building, a large number of Slavs became railroad laborers.

Not all entrants intended to remain in the United States. Many hoped to be able to accumulate a little hoard of money with which to better their situation at home. Some returned home coughing, or tubercular, or with a limb missing as a result of an industrial or mining accident, to live out the rest of their lives sitting in a chair placed against a sunny wall of their cottage.

Among Yugoslavs who wrested recognition of their talents in America were some eminent singers, both men and women; a sculptor of uncommon genius, Ivan Meštrović; the journalist and writer, Louis Adamic; and several scientists, among whom the most famous are Michael Pupin and Nikola Tesla. A teen-age boy when he arrived in 1874, Pupin received an American education which he augmented with graduate study in Cambridge, England and in Germany. Tesla appeared ten years later, a graduate of several famous European schools who was hoping to find financial backing for an invention he had worked out in Europe.

American Industrial Science Comes of Age

The development of American science is interwoven with the names and accomplishments of individuals of both foreign and native birth. Immigrant craftsmen brought the first technical skills to the colonies and it was their specialized knowledge on which the first commercial enterprises were based. It cannot be said that individuals with technical skills came predominantly from any one particular nation or group of nations. The first who brought technical "know-how" to the colonies and the young Republic were, of course, mostly of British background.

Through the post-Napoleonic German influx America gained newcomers who were highly trained in mathematics, engineering, optics, pharmacopeia, and medicine. The Swedes contributed outstanding engineering talent, of whom John Ericsson was an early representative. During the Civil War he designed the first "ironclad," the *Monitor*, and thus helped to tip the balance in favor of the Union. Later, as the diversity of national groups increased, outstanding scientists were found among the Italians, the Russians, the Slavs, and others. In the twentieth century, when Fascist persecution threatened doom to religious and political minorities, some of the greatest scientific minds escaped to the United States and placed their knowledge and experience at the disposal of the nation.

The interest in science lagged but little behind the beginning of the American experiment. The Massachusetts Bay Colony was barely ten years old when John Winthrop Jr. (1606-1676), son of the redoubtable John Winthrop, first governor of the colony, began to concentrate on how to apply principles of science to the development of a primitive society. Born and educated in England, he imported to his home in Connecticut apparatus for experimenting. He encouraged the start of an iron industry and the manufacturing of glass, salt, and other products. The first colonial to be elected a Fellow of the Royal Society of London, he can be said to have been the first of the foreign-born to bring the benefits of science to his countrymen.

A hundred years after the birth of John Winthrop Jr. in England was born the first native American to achieve world fame as a scientist, Benjamin Franklin (1706-1790). He was the first person in either the Old or the New World to whom may be applied Tesla's definition of invention as the "harnessing of the forces of nature to human needs." Franklin's father, a tallow chandler of Boston, had considered sending his son to Harvard College, which would have educated him for the ministry or might have fitted him for a secular calling. The expense of a Harvard education decided him against it. When young Franklin found himself apprenticed to his half brother, who was a printer, he started to educate himself. In the 1740's, when he was in his middle thirties, he secured a Leyden jar that had been sent to the "Junta" (a club he had organized for the purpose of self-improvement) by their purchasing agent in London.[4] Franklin was fascinated by it. By then he had already invented the "Franklin stove" as well as a new kind of clock. Later he began to experiment with electricity. In his kite experiment, which led to the discovery of how to protect houses against lightning, he employed an empirical method that was to remain characteristic of most American inventors for more than a century thereafter.

This method of "tinkering" was followed by Thomas Alva Edison as late as the 1870's. Edison, who had had a minimum of formal schooling, started out as a railroad newsboy. After becoming a telegraph operator, then as promising a career as that of the computer engineer today, he invented the incandescent lamp (1879) and, among other contrivances, the phonograph, the microphone, and the stock ticker. Like other American inventors before him, he followed a procedure that was based on trial-and-error.

Among the earliest results of tinkering was Eli Whitney's cotton gin in 1793. This gadget not only revived the moribund institution of slavery, but made it more profitable than it had ever been. Whitney had studied at Yale, but it was while he was a tutor on a Georgia plantation that his interest was aroused by the difficulties of separating cotton fibers from the seed. What his invention achieved was that a single slave could produce fifty pounds of cleaned cotton daily.

Because inventive creativity was spurred by accelerating economic development, inventions became more numerous after the nineteenth century got under way. An early one (1830) was Samuel Colt's model of a revolving pistol that he whittled between Boston and Calcutta, while plying the seas as a sailor boy. Another was the process of vulcanizing rubber, invented by Charles Goodyear in 1836. A third was the sewing machine in 1846, the work of Elias Howe, a cotton-mill manufacturer in Lowell. In 1867 a Milwaukee printer, Christopher Latham Sholes, produced the typewriter.

The first native theoretical scientist to devote his life to science as a teacher, experimenter, and director of the Smithsonian Institution in Washington, was Joseph Henry (1797-1878). The son of a Scotsman who was a day laborer, he entered the Academy of Albany and remained there to teach until he was called to the College of New Jersey (now Princeton). When the Smithsonian was established in 1846 by a bequest from the Englishman, James Smithson, Henry accepted the post of director. In the words of Michael Pupin, his admiring disciple, Henry let himself "be torn from his beloved laboratory out of patriotic duty, so that his skilled hand . . . could organize . . . and defend it [the Smithsonian] against the scheming politicians."[5] From then on Henry's main task was to promote the advancement of scientific research in America.

But before he moved to the Smithsonian, he had made his mark as one of the outstanding scientists of all time. His achievement was the conversion of magnetism into electricity. The breakthrough preceded Faraday's by a year,[6] but Faraday was the first to announce it to the world. Faraday conceded that Henry and he had arrived at the same conclusions independently of each other.

The discovery paved the way for Samuel Morse's invention of the telegraph. It was made possible by Henry's electromagnet wound with a copper wire and a nonconductive silk thread.[7] Morse had studied chemistry at Yale. Though electricity had always fascinated him, he turned to painting. While teaching fine arts at New York University, he continued to "tinker" with electricity in the college's laboratory. A mutual friend brought Henry's suggestions back to Morse. Though Henry supplied the direction, Morse completed the project himself. Having refused to patent his invention, Henry never received anything from Morse's discovery. He commented:

The only reward I ever expected was the consciousness of advancing science, the pleasure of discovering new truths, and the scientific reputation to which these labors entitle me.[8]

In 1838 Morse demonstrated his invention before President Van Buren and government officials[9] and asked the government for an appropriation of thirty thousand dollars with which to construct a fifty-mile line. It was a large sum compared with the six thousand dollars which the Advisory Committee on Uranium recommended in 1940 for the purchase of graphite and uranium oxide for the research Enrico Fermi was doing on splitting the uranium atom.[10] At least the appropriation for

Fermi's project went through without delay. Morse had to wait for years until the money was made available to him and the first telegraph line could be built. In the meantime he nearly starved.

This serves as an illustration of the lukewarm interest the American government took in scientists and their inventions. Not until the twentieth century did government begin to take an active part in promoting scientific discoveries. During the Spanish-American War Nikola Tesla offered to the government his invention of a "robot" to be operated by remote control by means of his wireless system. The offer was not accepted, and he was laughed at.

A breakthrough of the most far-reaching importance was the invention of the telephone by Alexander Graham Bell in 1876. This again was a contribution of one of the foreign-born. Bell, a Scottish immigrant, was a teacher of deaf-mutes who had become interested in acoustics. The idea of transmitting human speech by electricity had occurred to others, but it was Bell who developed the first practical instrument for doing so. His invention was taken over by the American Telephone and Telegraph Company. Two years later, in 1878, the first New York telephone directory was issued with two hundred and fifty-two subscribers.[11] In a little more than ten years almost half a million telephones were in use in virtually every American city.

The last decades of the nineteenth century brought giant progress in pure and applied science. Though American colleges and universities had long before become the main training centers for aspiring scientists, the pool of scientific personnel continued to be augmented by trained newcomers from foreign countries. American technological schools had been offering instruction in engineering and pure and applied science since the early part of the nineteenth century, but the number of graduates in these fields was limited. For instance, at the end of the Civil War graduates of engineering schools, excluding West Point, numbered fewer than three hundred.[12]

What stirred interest in science was the rapid rise of industry and the awareness that the introduction of scientific methods into factories and assembly lines could not fail to be of great benefit. Scientists as assistants of industry were proving very useful. Walt Whitman must have been aware of this when he declared: "Hurrah for positive science, / Long live exact demonstration."

In no field were the opportunities for those trained in physics, mathematics, and engineering greater than in communications and public utilities. Toward the end of the nineteenth century three mammoth companies rose to great prominence. One was the General Electric Company; another, its strong competitor, the Westinghouse Electric and Manufacturing Company. The third, the American Telephone and Telegraph Company, quickly gained a virtual monopoly over all telephonic communication in the country. All three were controlled by men of vision who foresaw that scientific research would bring enormous advantages to their products. All three created research centers to which they brought the best talent among native and foreign-born scientists. Three immigrant scientists were destined to become world famous under the aegis of these companies. One was Charles Steinmetz, a German, who was on the research staff of General Electric and ended his career as a teacher at Union College. Another was Michael Pupin, a Yugoslav, who during his teaching career at Columbia University invented the "Pupin coil," which was said to have saved the American Telephone and Telegraph Company a hundred million dollars.[13] The third, also a Yugoslav, sold his invention to George Westinghouse and produced a revolution in the generation and transmission of electrical power. He was Nikola Tesla. His story follows.

I

Nikola Tesla did not leave his homeland to escape persecution as Adamic did, nor discrimination as a Slav, which was Pupin's motive. All avenues to success and recognition that were open to able young Europeans were open to Tesla. He had received a superb education. The specific reason for his emigration was the hope of finding a backer for his polyphase alternating current system, which he had perfected in Europe. Had he found a backer in Budapest, where he worked out his idea, or in Paris, his second place of employment, or in Strasbourg, where he demonstrated his apparatus, he might not have come to America when he did. Also, he would not have received a million dollars for his invention. This might have proved a blessing, for it might have kept him from thinking in millions forever after. But eventually he would have had to come to America. The magnet that drew him was Niagara Falls. As a boy in his teens he had looked at a picture of those swirling waters and ever since then the hope of converting the power of the falls into electricity had remained with him.

Deeply disappointed that no one in Budapest, Paris, or Strasbourg showed any interest in the staggering possibilities of a motor that could be used without a commutator, Tesla set out for New York in 1884. He was twenty-eight. He could hope for only one thing—that America would provide him with the chance to put his talents to their widest use.

It took only four years, during which he underwent several serious disappointments, to sell the patent rights to his invention. After that, he was free to devote himself entirely to pure research, which yielded some spectacular results. In addition to the polyphase system of alternating current, his inventions include arc lighting, the "Tesla coil," which is now used in radio and television,[14] the Tesla "oscillator," which he foresaw could detect oil and ore deposits,[15] a method in use today, the "carbonbutton lamp," which held "principles of the atom-smasher to be,"[16] the neon-tube types of light, "wireless power," which he did not complete, and other ideas his pullulating brain threw off like electric sparks. A later generation of scientists would resume the work he began and bring some of his ideas to completion.

II

Tesla was born in 1856 in a small hamlet of the Austro-Hungarian Empire, bordering on Serbia. His father was a priest of the Serbian Orthodox Church. He had turned to the church in preference to an army career. Like Goethe, Tesla was the inheritor of two distinct characteristics, each attributable to one of his parents. His father, a man of erudition, had a prodigious memory that he passed on to his son. From his mother, who was illiterate, Tesla received a high degree of creative ability that she had inherited from her father and grandfather, who had invented many practical implements for household and agricultural uses. Another factor in his growth was that he had an extraordinarily gifted older brother. His death provided him with a spur to prove himself worthy of his example.

At the *Untergymnasium* (lower school) he showed such surprising aptitude for mathematics that in order to prove he had not cheated at a test he was required to take a special one composed of problems made up on the spot. Before he was many years older he could visualize and solve any problem in his head. Later he would require no models, drawings, or experiments to arrive at a solution to a problem. He needed only to be able to visualize it.

A delicate boy, Tesla had several severe illnesses; one at the age of ten, when he became acquainted with Mark Twain books, which, he said, hastened his recovery; another in his late teens when he returned against his father's orders to his native village, then in the grip of a severe cholera epidemic. He was close to death when his father, desperately trying to provide a stimulus to make him want to live, promised that if he recovered he could study electrical engineering instead of seeking a career in the army. He spent a year in getting his health back, then proceeded at the age of nineteen to the famous engineering school, the Polytechnic Institute at Graz, Austria.

There Tesla stumbled upon the problem that came to obsess him and whose solution brought him the most lasting recognition. One day, when a piece of electrical equipment requiring a commutator to change the direction of the current was being demonstrated, the realization came to him that if the current could be made to come out of the dynamo with an alternating direction, the commutator would be superfluous. When he voiced his thoughts aloud he was ridiculed. In a heavily sarcastic tone the instructor replied that Herr Tesla was welcome to try it. Though he devoted day and night (it was his habit to sleep only four hours, if that long) to thinking about it, the solution eluded him. But it remained an *idée fixe*. Years later he explained in an autobiographical sketch why he was so tenacious in trying to solve the problem. He said: "We have certain finer fibers that enable us to perceive truths when logical deduction or any other willful effort of the brain is futile."[17] He believed not only in "finer fibers," but in occult manifestations as well.

The problem of how to do away with the need for a commutator pursued him while he continued his education at the University of Prague and after he went to work for the American Telephone and Telegraph Company in Budapest. There a tendency that would become characteristic of him rose to the surface. After inventing what would today be called an improved loudspeaker that would have brought him a considerable sum in royalties, he disdained to patent it.

In Budapest, Tesla suffered his third serious illness, which manifested itself in reactions indicating a disturbed nervous system. His sight and hearing had always been very keen, but now he became abnormally sensitive. He could hear the sound of a watch ticking three rooms away enormously magnified. Years later, in 1899, in his Colorado laboratory, he claimed he could hear thunder at a distance of seven and eight hundred kilometers.[18]

He also experienced other disturbing sensations. This is how he described them: "In the stillness of the night a vivid picture would thrust itself and persist and despite all my efforts to banish it, it would remain fixt in space—though I pushed my hand through it."[19] It led him to believe that it should be possible to project on a screen the image of any object one conceived and make it visible.

By an effort of will he made himself better. One day, while he was walking about and admiring a glorious sunset, the solution to the problem that had dominated his thoughts burst upon him with the force of a loud and unexpected clap of thunder. As he stood transfixed, the principle of the rotating magnetic field, which underlies the polyphase alternating current system, came to him at once in all its details. This was to be the way in which he was to conceive many of his ideas—whole, with every item in place. Afterwards he would work them out in his laboratory. He explained that his method was not to rush into active work, but to build a project up in his imagination, to change the construction in his mind, then "to put his ideas into concrete form to find invariably that they worked . . . not a single exception in twenty years."

When the telephone station in Budapest was sold (it had been a private concession), Tesla went to work for the Continental Edison Company in Paris, to which he had been recommended. He carried the plan for his new machine in his head.

In Paris he became the company's troubleshooter. One assignment, for which he was promised special compensation, took him to Strasbourg. There he found time to construct his machine —the dynamo that would generate the alternating current and the new induction motor. Everything worked out perfectly, according to the way he had visualized it. He showed the model to a group of wealthy citizens, but they reacted with total indifference. Nor did anyone in Paris show any interest in his invention. When he reminded the officials of the company that he had been promised a special bonus, he was given what he called "a castle in Spain."

Bitterly resentful about having been cheated, Tesla was instantly prepared to follow the suggestion of one of the officers of the company that he try his luck in the Edison laboratory in New York. He packed his scant possessions, including his notebook containing his poetry, and was ready to depart. On the way to the boat he was robbed of all his possessions, including his wallet, which contained his steamship ticket; but because he remembered the number he was allowed to board the boat. He arrived in New York with the equivalent of four cents, the smallest amount on record for any immigrant. It was not sufficient to pay for the ride by horsecar to the Edison laboratory.

III

So he walked. On the way he passed a machine shop. He was sufficiently interested to look in. What he saw was that a man was trying to repair a motor and that he was obviously exasperated over it. In he walked and asked if he could help. The man was willing. Tesla fixed the motor.

"Let me pay you," said the man, handing him a twenty-dollar bill. "It's worth that to me."[20]

Tesla must have thought that Americans were very generous, an idea to which Europeans were prone. Also, it must have seemed a very auspicious beginning. But his optimism did not last long. Edison took him on, but he made it clear that he was not interested in anyone else's invention. Edison was then in the process of establishing powerhouses, useless for any but low-voltage direct current, in various cities. He must have been condescending to this foreigner, almost a decade younger than himself, who had the temerity to want to improve on his invention, which was being hailed all over the civilized world. Tesla, on the other hand, must have felt some of the disdain of the highly trained European for this self-taught backwoods thinker, who had "very little theory and calculation" at his disposal.

The following conveys the condescension with which Tesla must have regarded the older man:

If Edison had a needle to find in a haystack, he would proceed at once with the diligence of the bee to examine straw after straw until he found the object of his search. I was a sorry witness of such doings, knowing that a little theory and calculation would have saved him 90% of his labor.[21]

An important reason for Edison's disparagement of Tesla's invention was that he was convinced alternating current would be too dangerous because of the high voltage required. He would fight the young European's invention until forced to secure a license to use alternating current from George Westinghouse, who bought Tesla's invention. Edison would never forget the error he had made in underestimating his young assistant, nor was Tesla inclined to ignore Edison's belittlement of himself. While he paid homage to Edison in public, in private his comments were barbed.

The young man demonstrated his value in the Edison laboratories by proving himself a capable troubleshooter, and by making improvements on electrical equipment, which Edison promptly patented. Unlike Tesla, Edison was not one to overlook the protection offered by the patent office. The young foreigner proved an extremely hard worker. Once he worked eighty-four hours continuously in order to get a piece of equipment installed and in perfect working order.[22] By then he believed he had mollified his employer, for he had understood Edison to say it would be worth fifty thousand dollars to him if his dynamos could be made to perform more efficiently and at lower operating costs.

The young foreigner took him seriously. After improving several pieces of apparatus to Edison's satisfaction, Tesla reminded him of the bonus he had been promised. Edison's reply was that he did not understand American humor.[23] In high dudgeon Tesla walked out of the Edison laboratories. He had been cheated—first by his Paris employers and now again in New York.

But he remained credulous enough to allow himself to be lured by a group of promoters who were willing to form a company under his name and to install him in his own laboratory. He hoped to interest them in backing his alternating current system. But they were no more interested than Edison had been. What they wanted was an arc light for street and factory lighting, which would be an improvement on existing illumination.[24] He was given a small salary, some high sounding promises, and a stock certificate without voting power. After producing a satisfactory lamp, he was forced out. His certificate, he came to realize, was worthless. It was the third time he had been defrauded of his rightful expectations.

It was then that the young foreigner reached the nadir of his career. Unable to get a job in his field, he was forced to dig ditches at two dollars a day. This experience seared him for life, for even after he had become famous he could not bear to speak of it. This was not an unusual reaction among educated Europeans, for living by the labor of one's hands seemed to them a belittlement of their education and training. The unskilled, who had no justification for feeling proud, were apt to think back on their humble beginnings with less embarrassment.

One of these was Andrew Carnegie who, after becoming a multimillionaire, admitted freely he had begun as a bobbin boy at one dollar and twenty cents a week[25]—approximately fifty years before Tesla. But the only qualification the thirteen-year-old boy brought with him when he came to America was his willingness to work diligently at anything.

At this lowest point in his fortunes when Tesla must have wondered if his invention would ever receive recognition, the break he had been waiting for was on the near horizon. The foreman of the gang of which he was a part had also seen better days. He took Tesla to see an official of the Western Union. The miracle happened; the man was impressed and he persuaded other men to join him in organizing the Tesla Electric Company and to establish the inventor in his own laboratory.

Immediately Tesla began to build dynamos and motors for single-phase, double-phase and polyphase currents, and worked out the mathematical theory underlying the application of the apparatus to the whole range of low and high-frequency currents. In May, 1890, he was granted the first string of patents. In the next two years the number of patents grew to forty.[26] Within two weeks after the appearance of the first two patents the attention of the whole electrical profession was centered on him. On the invitation of the American Institute of Electrical Engineers he delivered a lecture that he called "A New System of Alternating Current Motors and Transformers." It turned him into a celebrity.

IV

A fabulous reversal of fortune followed. George Westinghouse, a bold and imaginative industrial pioneer, grasped the possibilities of the alternating-current system and offered Tesla one million dollars for his patents. In addition, he agreed to a royalty of one dollar per horsepower suggested by the inventor, who proved thereby that he had good business sense. It was arranged that Tesla was to work as a consultant in the Westinghouse laboratories at a very good salary. To the inventor the turn in his fortune meant delivery from bondage, specifically, the opportunity to concentrate on whatever he chose. No one would cheat him again (but he would cheat himself) and no one would order him around. Though half a million would go to the men who had financed him, he believed that the other half a million would be sufficient to banish money worries forever. Besides, he was to receive royalties which anyone could see would amount to millions.

Everything went as planned, except that friction developed between Tesla and the Westinghouse laboratory staff. So what if the inference was that he was not able to work harmoniously with others?—that he was too adamantine to work as part of an organization? He was independent, and from now on he could indulge his quirks without interference from anyone.

As soon as George Westinghouse began to commercialize the new invention, a fierce battle between the Edison Electric and the Westinghouse Company ensued. This rivalry became known as "the war of the currents."[27] What was involved was the question of whether it was to be Edison's direct current or Westinghouse's alternating current that was to be adopted for industrial development and eventually for home use. One way to fight alternating current was to discredit it as extremely dangerous. This is just what Edison did. His pronouncement was: "Just as certain as death Westinghouse will kill a customer within six months after he puts in a system of any size.... It will never be free from danger."[28]

When it became known that the state of New York planned to install alternating current for use in the death house at Sing Sing, the Edison forces were jubilant. They had no objection to its being used for killing. It bore out the master's pronouncement that alternating current was the right current for electrocution. But for every day use? No! Edison even offered his laboratory and supplied experimental animals to bolster his claim that because alternating current was so right for killing, it was too dangerous to be used for any other purpose.[29]

In this battle for the acceptance of alternating current Westinghouse found himself in such a tight squeeze that he was forced to seek outside financial backing. (Edison had succeeded in securing the financing of J. P. Morgan's organization.) When the bankers reviewed Westinghouse's contract with Tesla, they balked at the royalty clause. Declaring it to be excessive, they confronted him with the ultimatum that unless the inventor could be made to drop his demand for the royalty, they would not furnish the needed capital.

Although Westinghouse claimed to have been unwilling to abrogate the arrangement he had agreed to, he went to Tesla and made known the bankers' terms. Tesla realized immediately that the only hope for the acceptance of alternating current was for Westinghouse to remain solvent. What purpose would the royalty clause serve if Westinghouse were ruined? Besides, he appreciated the faith Westinghouse had shown by purchasing his invention. He made a quick decision. Though he knew that the royalties represented a fortune, it was more important to him to insure the adaptation of his system than to become rich quickly. He tore up his contract. In relieving the Westinghouse Company of its obligations to him, he released "the sleeping giant called electricity."[30] But he curtailed drastically his own power to develop the ideas that were proliferating in his mind. Later it became clear that he had sacrificed seven to twelve million dollars in royalties.[31]

V

He was too optimistic to worry about the income he had so magnanimously tossed away. The money he had received appeared to him to be a tremendous sum, sufficient to enable him to devote his entire time to pure research. Besides, he felt that if he had earned a million once, he could do it again. He never stopped believing that he was bound to make more money than he could ever use.

In his gratitude to Westinghouse for his confidence in alternating current, Tesla was willing to give him all the help he could by demonstrating on himself that alternating current was harmless. In exhibitions to which the press was invited, he let thousands of volts go through his body, lighting lamps and bending melting wires with the current circulating through him. Attired in evening clothes for effect, with a tall silk hat which made him appear even taller than his six feet two and a half inches in height, he made himself glow from head to foot to the "ohs" and "ahs" of those witnessing his performance. In this manner he demonstrated the principle that underlies diathermy treatment—that it is not high voltage that inflicts damage, but high amperage—and that high-frequency current is safe if the amperage is kept low.

At the end of 1889, after five years of residence in America, he became a citizen of the United States. Now when he applied for patents, he could begin with the statement: "I, Nikola Tesla, a citizen of the United States..." instead of: "I, Nikola Tesla, a subject of..." In the five years his attitude to America had undergone a profound change. His first impression that America was "no land of dreams" did not differ from that of countless other immigrants whose expectations were much more modest than Tesla's. It was bitterness that made him say: "The genii had carried me from a world of dreams into one of realities; what I saw was machined, rough and unattractive." America seemed to him "more than one hundred years behind Europe in civilization."[32] Five years later he declared America to be "more than one hundred years AHEAD of Europe."

He now stood at the zenith of his career. He undertook a lecture tour through Europe, where he was showered with acclaim, returning to be present at the Chicago World's Fair of 1893, known as the Columbian Exposition. It was a triumph for him, for the Westinghouse Company had supplied all power and equipment, thus furnishing the first large-scale demonstration of what Tesla motors and dynamos using only alternating current could achieve.

In addition, Tesla had his own exhibition of a metal egg lying in a large velvet case, which, when current was turned on, began to move, then stood on end, and within seconds whirled around, while the inventor explained that a rotating magnetic field did the trick. It was considered one of the "stunning displays of the exposition."[33] He also demonstrated to the awed crowd the safety of alternating current by letting one million volts go through his body.[34]

The most spectacular triumph of his career came in 1895 when power was transmitted from Niagara to Buffalo for the first time. Westinghouse had received the initial contract to install three generating units of five-thousand horsepower with which to convert the hydraulic power of the falls into electric energy by means of alternating current. What must have given Tesla the greatest satisfaction was that Edison had sought and received the contract for building the transmission line to Buffalo, which he could do only under the alternating-current system.

A gigantic battle between the Edison and the Westinghouse forces had preceded the decision to use alternating current. Lord Kelvin, chairman of the International Niagara Commission, had favored direct current, but when it was realized that direct current could not even furnish sufficient power to Buffalo, only twenty-two miles distant, whereas alternating current could not only accomplish it with ease, but would probably be able to deliver current to New York City,[35] Edison lost the battle. The thrill Tesla must have felt that the prophecy he had made as a youngster had come to pass was undoubtedly compounded by the fact that Edison had been forced to lease from Westinghouse the right to use the polyphase alternating-current system in order to fulfill the contract for the transmission lines.

This dramatic superiority of alternating over direct current ended "the war of the currents." Later, Lord Kelvin admitted: "Tesla has contributed more to electrical science than any man of his time."[36] Today the electric-power system of New York is connected to the powerhouse of Niagara Falls. When the power failure of 1965 plunged the whole Northeast into darkness, the trouble was traced to failure there. What Tesla had demonstrated at Niagara Falls was a whole series of integrated inventions consisting of the first practical alternating-current motor, dynamos for generating current, a variety of motors for converting the currents into power, a system of polyphase transformers for raising and lowering voltages, and economic methods for transmitting electrical power for long distances.[37]

VI

The years between 1890 and 1895 were years of fame and good fortune. Tesla gloried in being financially independent and in being able to indulge his whims. His talent for showmanship was in proportion to his genius. Considered a handsome man (and as such typical of the Slavs), he was very tall, slim, and dark-haired, with an extremely narrow face in which light blue eyes gleamed sharply. He was wont to explain that they had become lighter from extreme concentration. He was a conspicuous figure in his tails and high silk hat as he entertained friends in a sumptuous style at Delmonico's and at the Waldorf-Astoria Hotel, where he plied them with the best wines and foods and surrounded them with all the accoutrements of luxury.

Afterwards he would take them to his laboratory for fantastic exihibitions during which he transformed himself into a modern Magus who permitted tremendous voltages to go through his body. He encouraged his hardier friends to submit to similar experiments. One of those who liked being a guinea pig was Robert Underwood Johnson, editor of *Century Magazine.* Another was Mark Twain, who became Tesla's "fascinated admirer." Johnson tells that Tesla would produce lightning flashes fifteen feet long and that at these demonstrations he would make photographs from fluorescent lighting as souvenirs. Even when he conducted a private experiment he was apt to don his full-dress outfit, which was an indication to his assistant that the experiment was an important one. The panache with which he surrounded himself hints of a need for self-glorification in the Renaissance magical tradition.

While the polyphase system was proving itself, Tesla was

experimenting on the transmission of energy without the use of wires, which he called his "wireless." He was constantly perfecting new ideas that possessed startling potentialities. During those years he worked out a system of radio broadcasting which he presented in lectures before the Franklin Institute in Philadelphia, thus indicating that he was aware of the principles of modern radio.

But his period of good luck was coming to an end; misfortune was lurking in the wings waiting to pounce on him. He had built a transmitting and receiving station and was continuing to test and improve it before scheduling a full-scale demonstration of his wireless system when a fire broke out in his laboratory and destroyed it completely. All his machinery, in which he had invested a fortune, was lost. He carried no insurance. A phrase from the German, which he spoke well, expresses what he must have felt: "Es war so schön gewesen,/ Es hät nicht sollen sein." ("It was so beautiful,/ But it was not to be.")

The only income Tesla had came from royalties on patents in Germany, but it was not sufficient to maintain an experimental laboratory. At this juncture a member of the Morgan group who had participated in the Niagara Falls project came forward with a plan to finance a new company with a capital stock of half a million dollars that would enable the inventor to concentrate on pure research. His backer pledged himself personally to the extent of one hundred thousand dollars, of which he paid forty thousand immediately.[38] Tesla was in the process of setting up a new laboratory when even greater financial inducements were offered him, provided the son of the backer became a partner in the new enterprise. Tesla turned the offer down without giving any reason. In spurning the proposition, he turned down an alliance that would have relieved him of all financial responsibilities. The refusal was baffling. Was it because he was aware that he did not work well with others? Was it because he could brook no interference? Or because he wanted to remain a researcher? Or was it due to his prodigious optimism that millions were bound to fall into his lap, if only he held out long enough?

The forty thousand dollars that had been subscribed enabled him to continue for about three years. During that period he solved the problem of electrical communication without wires, in other words, modern radio. At the same time he experimented on an oscillator and on mechanical vibration. His neighbors and those who worked in factory buildings surrounding his laboratory were used to the crackling of electric current emanating from the site of his experiments. But when he began to make buildings tremble and windows vibrate, the police had to rush in to stop him. The effect of his oscillator was so powerful that he was convinced he might have reduced the Empire State Building to a tangled mass of wreckage in a very short time.[39]

In 1898 Tesla was ready to present his "wireless system." John Hays Hammond advanced ten thousand dollars that he might demonstrate it in a week-long display at Madison Square Garden.[40] To make the exhibit more spectacular, he combined two of his inventions, the "wireless" as well as the "robot" who would do his bidding through "wireless" control. A huge tank had been constructed that was filled with water in which was placed a metal-covered boat several feet long, equipped with electric lights. Inside the boat was a radio receiving set. The boat was equipped with two motors, one to propel it along, and the other to act as the mechanical brain which would receive the orders from the wireless set and carry them out. Every command of the inventor and of members of the audience who wished to participate was carried out upon pressure of the proper key.

Because the patents included specifications for a torpedo boat to be operated without a crew, it offered startling possibilities for naval warfare. Tesla also foresaw that an airplane could be launched from it and to have a certain approximate course imposed on it at a distance of many hundred miles. He offered this invention to the government, but as he related it fifteen years later, the official to whom he spoke "burst out in laughter." No one thought that there was "the faintest prospect of perfecting such a device."[41] The twentieth century, however, was to prove him right.

VII

In 1899 Tesla had run out of money. Also, he wanted a laboratory in the open spaces where he could conduct experiments that might prove dangerous in congested areas. The donation of thirty thousand dollars from John Jacob Astor and smaller gifts from other individuals made it possible to plan the building of a new laboratory. Having been offered land and electric power by the Colorado Springs Electric Company he decided to make Colorado, where the abundance of static electricity made tremendous lightning storms a frequent occurrence, the site for his experiments.[42]

In a fantastic-looking structure with masts and towers he constructed a giant oscillator. What he wanted to determine was whether the earth was electrically charged and whether it could be set into electrical vibrations. He found the earth to be literally alive with electrical vibrations, as he reported in an article in *Century Magazine* in June 1900.[43] In a spectacular experiment during which he was able to produce artificial lightning, the generator of the Colorado Springs Electric Company was knocked out. He had made the earth oscillate as if it were a piece of laboratory apparatus.

The fact that he was again in the grip of severe money troubles may have been one of the reasons why he made no record of his experiments in Colorado. Another explanation is that he was in the habit of trusting his memory to store facts so accurately that he could resume the work at any time he wanted to. But he never went back to it, and the results of his experiments in Colorado were completely lost to future research.

Upon his return to New York in 1899, he was broke again. J. P. Morgan himself came to his rescue. Tesla's article in *Century* had caught his attention. He gave Tesla one hundred and fifty thousand dollars to start a new laboratory. One of Tesla's biographers, James J. O'Neill, who was science editor of the *New York Herald Tribune,* says, "There were no strings attached."[44] Another states that Morgan demanded fifty-one percent of all the patents present and future, pertaining to wireless telegraphy and electric lighting and that Tesla accepted the conditions.[45]

Tesla's next project was to create a "world broadcasting system" in Suffolk County, Long Island, on a two-hundred-acre tract, donated by a real-estate operator, James S. Warden. It was to be named the "Wardenclyff Laboratory." Warden was another who had allowed Tesla's genius to beguile him. What he envisioned was a community of thousands of people, all connected with the project, who would be potential home buyers. Tesla's scheme was intended to fulfill the following purposes in addition to others: 1. Interconnection of the existing telegraph exchanges all over the world; 2. Establishment of a secret and non-interferable government telegraph service; 3. Interconnection of all present telephone exchanges or offices all over the globe; 4. Universal distribution of general news by telegraph, or telephone, in connection with the press; 5. Establishment of a World System of intelligence transmission for exclusive private use; 6. A universal marine service enabling navigators of all ships to steer perfectly without compass, to determine the exact location, hour, and speed, to prevent collisions and disasters, etc.[46] He also planned a world power station at Niagara Falls, intended to light the lamps of the Paris Exposition with power wirelessly transmitted from Niagara. That plant was never started because of lack of money.

By the end of two years a brick laboratory and a powerhouse had been built, which was dominated by a tower one hundred and eighty-seven feet high with a spherical terminal about sixty feet in diameter.[47] Since the equipment alone was estimated to have cost two hundred thousand dollars, Tesla was again in financial difficulties.

The most humiliating period of his life followed. At first J. P. Morgan responded to the pleas for additional capital. Tesla was being hounded by creditors as far away as Colorado and was threatened with law suits. His Colorado property was sold under the hammer. Tesla begged, cajoled, and reproached Morgan. He humbled himself by writing to him: "Since a year, Mr. Morgan, there has hardly been a night when my pillow has not been bathed in tears."[48] It was useless; Morgan could not be softened. Though Tesla received contributions from other wealthy men—H. O. Havemeyer, the sugar king, and Thomas F. Ryan, the traction magnate—they were like drops of water on a hot griddle. Substantial backers were scared off by the rumor that Morgan had withdrawn because of the impracticability of Tesla's scheme.[49] Tesla was forced to abandon the Wardenclyff laboratory before it was finished. Its grandiose tower remained as a reminder of his dream until in 1917 it was dynamited by the U. S. government in response to rumors that German spies were using it to convey information to the enemy.

Tesla was less than fifty when the Wardenclyff project collapsed, still young enough to go back to where he had left off. His idea was to build turbines that would be an improvement on existing models, but neither the Westinghouse nor the General Electric companies showed any curiosity in his demonstrations. When he finally aroused the interest of the Allis-Chalmers Manufacturing Company, he insisted on his own way to such a degree that he antagonized the engineering staff. Finally, he walked out on the tests at a crucial moment. During the twenties he explained that "they would not build the turbines as I wished."[50]

Good fortune continued to elude him. In 1912, according to one biographer[51] and in 1915, according to another,[52] an announcement appeared that the Nobel Prize in Physics had been offered to him and Edison jointly. One states that Tesla refused it—the only scientist to do so—and offered the explanation that he must have felt belittled by having to share it with Edison, whom he considered an "inventor" whereas he looked upon himself as a "discoverer." The conjecture is also advanced that he may have felt his recognition had been delayed too long. Another biographer (Miss Hunt) maintains that the prize had not been offered, or, that when the news broke prematurely, the committee withdrew it. She argues that if it had been offered he would have been happy to accept it, if for no other reason than that he desperately needed the twenty thousand dollars which would have been his share. O'Neill buttresses his contention that Tesla declined the prize by quoting that he had hesitated to accept the Edison Medal offered him by the American Institute for Electrical Engineers, and that in the end he did so only because he could not afford to antagonize his devoted friend, B. A. Behrend,[53] who had been instrumental in securing it for him.

From then on Tesla could only hint at what he was doing. Since he could not secure patents until he had working models, and since he could not make models because he had no money, the nature of his work remained a secret. The mystery with which he surrounded his activities caused many sly and belittling remarks to appear about him. Like all institutions, about which Emerson had remarked that they became bores at last, he became a bore too.

VIII

Tesla's later years were full of humiliation. He had lost the services of some of his most trusted associates. Though he maintained that he was working on discoveries from which he hoped to receive "a sum in eight figures (not counting cents, of course)," he was often so short of funds that he had to leave his hotel because of unpaid bills. He had been asked to move from the Waldorf, the St. Regis, the Governor Clinton. For the last ten years of his life he lived at the New Yorker. The hotels considered him an undesirable tenant for still another reason—he was a pigeon fancier who lured the birds to his windowsills. He would even coax them into his room, where they would perch on his desk.

Tesla never married. He was not known to have been interested in any woman save his mother and sister. His explanation was that an inventor should never marry, because women acted as a distraction. He also avoided close human relationships, because he felt an inventor must function in the way of a smoothly running machine. The only living things he cared for were pigeons, and he fed them daily. When he suffered a taxicab accident in 1937, he hired someone to attend to the daily rite of feeding pigeons for six months. He called them with his whistle and was known to tend sick pigeons in his room. He was particularly fond of a white dove with light gray wings of whom he spoke in the following way when John J. O'Neill and William L. Laurence, both science editors of New York dailies, interviewed him:

No matter where I was that pigeon would find me; when I wanted her I had only to wish and call her and she would come flying to me. She understood me and I understood her.

I loved that pigeon.

Yes, he replied to an unasked question. Yes, I loved that pigeon. I loved her as a man loves a woman, and she loved me. When she was ill I knew, and understood; she came to my room and I stayed beside her for days. I nursed her back to health. That pigeon was the joy of my life. If she needed me, nothing else mattered. As long as I had her, there was a purpose in my life.

When that pigeon died, something went out of my life. Up to that time I knew with a certainty that I would complete my work, no matter how ambitious my program, but when that something went out of my life, I knew my life's work was finished.[54]

Tesla was known to have had many phobias. He admitted in his autobiographical sketch[55] that looking at a pearl was apt to give him a "fever." A very frugal eater, he required a dozen napkins at one meal. All his eating utensils were picked up with a fresh napkin, which was then dropped to the floor until a mound of napkins grew beside his chair. He required as many as eighteen towels a day as a maid in his Colorado hotel reported.[56] He never used a handkerchief or a collar more than once; he was loath to shake hands with people. No one could use his washroom. O'Neill suggests that these idiosyncrasies may have been due to the fact that he had had cholera, a germ disease, twice in his life.

He was also vain, proud, extremely sensitive, and particular of his appearance. Wearing a derby, gray suede gloves, a four-in-hand tie (tie and gloves were discarded every week), and trailing a cane, he cut an impressive figure. In 1910, in the midst of serious financial troubles, he told a secretary that he considered himself the best-dressed man on Fifth Avenue and that he intended to keep up his standards.[57]

It may also have been due to vanity that in taking his first job in Budapest, Tesla refused to mention what his salary had been, and that the year he spent as a laborer is omitted from his autobiographical sketch. The assertion by his friend, Robert Underwood Johnson, that "he [Tesla] did not reap what he had sown; other inventors have taken his ideas to reinvent his apparatus for the purposes he foresaw," is the greatest understatement. Why did this genius find himself stymied in bringing his ideas to a successful conclusion? Whose fault was it that his genius remained thwarted?

The conclusion seems inescapable that Tesla was his own worst enemy. He was horrendously impractical and impervious to counsel. He could have eliminated money worries if he had turned over financial matters to a business manager who would have enforced payment on patented material, and if he had not brushed aside everything but his theoretical research as "small stuff, not worth bothering about." Opportunities that might have led to a steady income were ignored. He did not want to make money on his inventions, except to use it in pursuit of other inventions. In this he was in marked contrast to Edison, who is said never to have been unaware of the balance sheet.

One reason for his succession of setbacks was that Tesla lived before the time when subsidies from the federal government became available for pure research. Fifty years later he would have received extensive support from the United States government. According to old letters, Lenin was interested in his work and twice invited him to come to Russia, but he could not tear himself away from what he was doing at that time.[58] But whether he could have worked harmoniously in such an environment is open to question.

It was not blindness to his genius that was responsible for his failure to attract sufficient private subsidies to develop his ideas. To the practical American nabobs he may not have seemed sufficiently down-to-earth. Though he could concentrate on realistic problems such as improving the efficiency of basic electrical apparatus, it was only while he was required to prove his value that he was willing to occupy himself thus. Many people were sufficiently captivated by his vision to advance large sums of money, but they would not back him indefinitely. Also, Tesla did not work well with others. The practical businessman on whose backing he depended could not fail to conclude that he presented a great risk.

There is justification for the argument that a fatal flaw in his nature kept him from achieving success. What was the fatal flaw? Hubris? A Faustian striving to transcend human capacity? A tendency toward gigantism? Or did the vastness of American resources serve to inflate his imagination and to exacerbate a tendency towards profligacy?

Yet, it is undeniable that only in America could Tesla have found as much scope as he did. But if he had remained in Europe, would he have developed the tendency of thinking in "millions" and of anticipating that eventually they must tumble into his lap again? The expectation of earning millions is not characteristic of Europeans. If it was the American climate that inflated his extravagant hopes, it must follow that it did not serve him to the best advantage.

He was a very proud man. How painful it must have been to find himself balked, doubted, belittled, can be imagined. George Westinghouse, who bought Tesla's invention, was elected to the Hall of Fame. Tesla was not. Other scientists received the Nobel Prize for work based on his ideas. He never attained the American Olympus.

He would have fared worse in his old age if his native Yugoslavia had not come to his rescue. When he was close to eighty, the Society for the Foundation of the Tesla Institute in Belgrade, organized by scholars, friends of the inventor, and the government, established an endowment that brought him an income of $7,200 a year. But despite this regular income, he fell behind in his hotel bills. The reason was that he tried to repay debts and that he was too generous in dispensing gratuities he could ill afford. Also, he was unable to deny help to those who needed assistance.

In the last years of his life he suffered from heart disease, but would not consult a doctor. In January, 1943, when the new year had just begun, he was found dead in his hotel room by a chambermaid who had decided to enter against his express orders. He was eighty-seven years of age. After a funeral service at the Cathedral of St. John the Divine, during which his casket lay draped in an American flag, he was cremated and his ashes were returned to Yugoslavia.

The smallest tribute came to this discarded genius from the country in which he had lived and worked close to sixty years. He had held honorary degrees from Columbia, Yale, and the Sorbonne, and from other institutions in Prague, Bucharest, Grenoble, Poitiers, Graz, and Vienna. But the only place in America where his name is to be found is on a bronze plate of the first five-thousand horsepower alternators used at Niagara Falls. As far as his life in America is concerned, "his name was writ in water." He belongs to those of whom it may be said that they were "such stuff as dreams are made on."

ANTON JULIUS CARLSON
1875-1956

The Development of a Physiologist

The life of Anton Julius Carlson presents a clear-cut demonstration of the mutual advantage inherent in the relationship between America and its immigrants. In this newcomer, who proceeded from carpenter to minister to physiologist, the world gained a scientist whose researches brought him universal recognition, and America, an outstanding teacher who prepared thousands for careers in the field of medicine and medical research.

The Causes of Swedish Emigration

In the seventeenth century Sweden was an ambitious power. Her king, Gustavus Adolphus, had won much territory around the Baltic by conquest; but most of what he had acquired was lost during the eighteenth century. The very last acquisition, Finland, was wrested from Sweden at the turn of the nineteenth century by Czar Alexander I of Russia. Afraid of further depredations, Sweden offered the crown to Marshal Bernadotte, one of Napoleon's marshals. As a consequence Bernadotte refused to support Napoleon and, unlike Denmark (which remained loyal to Napoleon), joined his enemies. The reward was the transfer of Norway from Denmark to the king of Sweden. Norway did not succeed in breaking away from Sweden until 1905.

During the first part of the nineteenth century, Sweden remained divided into a landholding class and a dependent peasantry. Conservative and illiberal, the landholders strove to perpetuate aristocratic traditions. The peasantry lived in crushing poverty, depending for all their necessities upon the labor of their hands. They raised their food and spun their flax and wool into the clothes they wore. Constant subdivisions over generations had made the average peasant farm too small to yield enough food for subsistence. In Sweden the son who had inherited the father's farm was legally bound to house his parents and to provide for them as long as they lived.[1] An additional difficulty was that Swedish peasant lands were apt to be stony, hence unproductive. Between the 1750's and the 1880's there were several famine years due to crop failures. The result was a large increase in sharecroppers and landless farm laborers.

Until past the mid-nineteenth-century mark the country was ruled by a medieval Diet. What helped to liberalize Sweden was the character of its natural resources, of which iron ore, lumber, and water power were dominant. These assets encouraged industrial and scientific development, which led inevitably to the strengthening of the middle classes and urban workers. In 1866 a parliament was established, but high property qualifications denied widespread participation to the electorate. Not until 1909 did the people of Sweden achieve universal manhood suffrage. The rule of the conservative elements having been broken, a new order consisting of Liberals and Social Democrats came into the saddle.

The exodus from Sweden began in the 1840's and increased in momentum until its reached its crest in the 1880's, when almost a hundred thousand abandoned their homeland for America. It was such a large number for a small country that some provinces, particularly in the southern parts, lost every tenth person. From some villages one-half of the population emigrated. The reason for this flight was mainly poverty, but such factors as compulsory military training and the hostility of the state church to the evangelistic sects—Mormons, Baptists, Methodists—were contributory causes. Though the strongest attraction was free land, and the availability of work at wages that seemed high to people into whose hands money came rarely, the fact that in America education was not restricted to the upper classes also proved a powerful allurement to those still young enough to hope that the direction of their lives could be changed.

An important element in promoting emigration were the letters from America to those who had been left behind. The favorable reports were responsible for spreading the "America fever." But underneath the exaggerations there was a basis of truth. For instance, when a man wrote that in America even the hogs eat their fill of raisins and dates,[2] one is reminded that in the late seventeenth century a Dutch visitor to Manhattan, marveling over the abundance of luscious peaches, was told that even the hogs had had enough of peaches and would not eat them.[3]

Though some letters were undoubtedly critical of America, they made little impression on people to whom the dream of a lordly estate of one hundred and sixty acres was akin to the longing of a parched traveler in the desert for the sight of an oasis. The hundred-and-sixty-acre homestead was not a mirage; nor was the expectation of being able to find work at what was considered good wages. These twin magnets were so powerful that people sold their farms and, placing their possessions in their "America chests," set off for that long journey that would end for some at the edge of the frontier and for others in some of the large cities. A carpenter's job in Chicago was to be the starting point of Anton Carlson's career.

The American Setting

Despite her small size and limited population, Sweden was among the first of the European powers to seek a toehold in the New World. In 1638, eight years after the establishment of the Massachusetts Bay Colony, a Swedish plantation was started along the Delaware River. The warrior king, Gustavus Adolphus, was dead, but Swedish ambitions were kept alive under the reign of his daughter, the mannish Queen Christina. After having been fired as governor of the Dutch colony, Nieuw Amsterdam, Peter Minuit, under the aegis of Sweden, conveyed several small groups of colonists to "New Sweden." The colony remained small because reinforcements, which were an absolute necessity for growth, became scant. In 1655 the colony fell prey to the ambitions of Peter Stuyvesant, who annexed New Sweden to Nieuw Amsterdam. When James, Duke of York, conquered the Dutch colony in 1664, the erstwhile Swedish settlement merged with the English, eventually adopting English customs, speech, and religion.

By the end of the eighteenth century the number of descendants of the original Swedish settlers numbered over twenty thousand, and they had spread to Pennsylvania, Maryland, and New Jersey. There was no additional influx of sizable proportions from Sweden until the 1840's, when the Rev. Gustav Unonius led a group to Pine Lake, Wisconsin, which became known as "New Upsala." From then on the increase was constant. A great number of Swedish newcomers gravitated to the upper Mississippi Valley. Settling in Illinois and Minnesota first, they turned Minnesota into a Swedish colony, then overflowed into Iowa, Michigan, Wisconsin, and the Far West. It is estimated that they cleared twelve million acres of land in America.[4]

Those who remained in the cities found work as carpenters, mechanics, machinists, woodworkers, etc. A city to which Swedish people swarmed was Chicago. It is claimed that Chicago has more people of Swedish descent than any city except Stockholm. Unskilled workers could find employment on the railroads or in lumber camps. Swedish workers and settlers were considered so desirable that companies and railroads advertised in Sweden's newspapers and sent representatives to Europe to shepherd immigrants across the Atlantic and across the American continent to their destination. One of these agents was Hans Mattson,[5] whom Jay Cooke, backer of the Northern Pacific, employed to bring thousands to America.

The great majority of Swedish newcomers consisted of humble folk. They had great respect for education. Even among the poorest crofters the rate of illiteracy was very low. One reason for this was that in order to be confirmed it was necessary for one to be able to read the Bible. This is reminiscent of the Puritans in Massachusetts, who established compulsory school attendance in the 1640's, so that their own children might escape the clutches of "the deluder, Satan," by being able to read the Scriptures. Many immigrant children who were taught reading in a sodhouse by the light of homemade candles later found their way to the colleges and universities of America.[6]

These new settlers were so eager to provide education for their young that in 1860, before Swedish immigration had reached its peak, Augustana Academy and College in Rock Island, Illinois, was established by the Augustana Synod for both Swedish and Norwegian Lutherans. A decade later the Norwegians, equally ambitious for their children and at the same time anxious that their ancient traditions survive, separated to found their own Augustana College at Sioux Falls, South Dakota. It was said of Augustana College at Rock Island that it was "designed to convert 'hired men' into ministers in three years."[7] Before the end of the century there were a half dozen more colleges for Swedish and Norwegian youths, many of whom went out to preach the word of God to their people in remote regions of the Northwest; others showed a leaning towards engineering and the sciences. Anton Julius Carlson followed both paths—as preacher first, then as scientist for the rest of his life.

I

Carlson was one of the tens of thousands who in 1891 were streaming out of all corners of Europe to form a mighty caravan bound for America. Sixteen years of age, he had lost his father at the age of seven and had only "a country-school-general-education." He brought with him a hunger for knowledge and a specific curiosity about the physical world. Another asset was the training his mother had given him. Since the age of four he had been taught that "those who don't work will not eat."

He was seven when he began to work during the summer months as a goatherd. Like Michael Pupin,[8] who says that he became aware of the way sound is carried as a herdsboy in his native Serbia, Anton Carlson, watching his animals and climbing after them, pondered why some rocks were so smooth that they seemed polished and why others were rough to his bare feet. He also speculated on who might have carried seashells two or three hundred feet above sea level. His mother and his teachers told him that the answers to these questions could be found only in education. But how was a poor Swedish boy to acquire education?

America gave him education and the chance to follow the career he chose. In 1950, during a speech on the occasion of his seventy-fifth birthday, when former students, colleagues, and friends gathered to pay him homage, he said: "I take it that what I have been able to do is primarily due to this great country giving me the opportunity to work." By then Dr. Carlson spoke as a physiologist of world renown, whose researches were admittedly of the greatest significance to medicine. In addition, he had taught some eight thousand medical students, and perhaps fifty to sixty thousand undergraduate students. The physiologists he had trained to carry on in his tradition were giving him, as one of his colleagues observed in a testimonial letter, children, grandchildren, and great-grandchildren to continue his work. A Swedish colleague spoke of him as "the best gift of Swedish culture and spirit to you Americans"; another referred to him as "a great Norse medical pine."

II

Carlson's parents were poor Swedish farm folk who had to work hard to wrest a living from the land for six children and themselves. When the father died in his prime, the farm was lost, and the burden of directing the family fell upon his mother. The older girls went into household service; the older boys found work on neighboring farms. In the winter Anton went to school two miles away, but in the summer he could help out by herding sheep for neighbors. In the evening he helped his mother with her chores, including knitting the garments he wore.

At sixteen, when the problem of his future had become worrisome, opportunity in the shape of a letter suddenly crooked a beckoning finger. It was a letter from his brother in America, and it opened an unexpected vista. His brother, who had started as a sailor, had become a carpenter in Chicago. Not only did he enclose money for the fare across the ocean and to Chicago, but he promised Carlson a job with the same carpenter for whom he worked. That his brother had acquired a wife, a rented house (though it was on the south side of Chicago), and had money enough to be able to give a younger brother a helping hand, confirmed that the wonders he had heard about America were true. If nothing else, in America one could find a living and, possibly, one could achieve much more. He made a rapid decision to accept his brother's offer. Though the idea of parting from his mother must have been painful to both, she made no effort to dissuade him. He never saw her again.

Years later Carlson told an interviewer that he knew at the

time three words in English. They were "Yes," "No," and as for the third, he said: "Well, you wouldn't print it anyway."⁹

The famous Dr. Andrew C. Ivy, who was his student and became a co-worker and close friend, tells a story about the young immigrant's arrival in New York, which Carlson had related to him after living in America for thirty-five years:

... as a boy in Sweden he had heard about an apple. He had read about the apple; he had seen paintings of bright red apples. He had longed for and dreamt about an apple. He said to himself "when I get to America and land in New York City, the first thing I am going to do is to get an apple and eat it." So, when he landed in New York, he saw on a stand bright red fruit. He walked to the stand, spent his last pennies for one of these bright red "fruits" and quickly bit into it. Immediately his face was covered with juice. It was a tomato, not an apple. ... He said that he had never been so mad and at the same time so shocked and disappointed before or since this incident in his life.¹⁰

This story of an immigrant's disillusionment has several variations. Other newcomers have told of the unpleasant surprise of biting into a banana with the skin on, to the great merriment of onlookers. On the symbolic level it expresses the sharp disappointment that was bound to assert itself after the expulsion from the European womb, and on the other hand, the extravagant expectations with which so many immigrants faced life in America.

Michael Pupin experienced a similarly sharp sense of disenchantment when he spent half of his entire fortune of ten cents on what loked like a tempting prune pie and found that the taste was nothing like the anticipation. But in some of the more important respects Carlson had no reason to feel disappointed. His brother met him at the station in Chicago, took him to his home, and on the next day to a job as carpenter's helper that was waiting for him. The wage was one dollar and twenty-five cents a day for ten hours' work. He kept the job for two years. By 1893 he had not only paid back the money his brother had advanced, but had saved three hundred dollars besides. He had also acquired some English.

He had also joined the Lutheran Church. Recognizing the young man's mettle, the minister, undoubtedly on the lookout for immigrants of promise, pointed out to him the surest way to advancement—Augustana College! It had been founded for just that purpose—helping immigrants to rise in the American world, often beyond what they had thought of as their limits of expectation. The fact that he lacked preparation was not a serious drawback. Many of the western colleges provided the necessary training for those whose education had stopped at the grade-school level.

In this respect it was no more difficult for foreigners than for young natives. Many young men were compelled to interrupt their schooling in order to earn the money before they could think of continuing their education. Many colleges had preparatory departments where students could make up for a missed secondary education. Augustana Academy prepared young men for entrance into Augustana College. Carlson plunged into his studies with unusual zest. His plan was to prepare himself for the ministry, "to become a missionary to the heathens," which to Swedish immigrants represented the highest in prestige. Within five years he earned the Bachelor of Arts degree, and a year later, in 1899, a Master of Arts degree in philosophy.

III

But religious skepticism had begun to invade his mind. During his sophomore year he happened to read a book called *Physiologische Psychologie*, and it made a deep impression on him. Also, he found himself mysteriously drawn to one of the men teaching geology. An anecdote is told which illustrates his turn of mind and, at the same time, foreshadows a personality trait for which he was to become famous among his students and co-workers. It was that of shocking a listener into an instant realization of what was illogical and therefore ridiculous. In a classroom discussion during his senior year about the effectiveness of prayer for rain, Carlson suggested that since the United States Weather Bureau kept accurate records of the amount of rainfall in the various states, it was only necessary to compare these figures with any changes that might be effected through a concentrated bout of praying. It was an example of *quod erat demonstrandum* as well as *reductio ad absurdum*. Because his suggestion smacked of levity, if not outright impiety, he was barred from serving as valedictorian, to which he had been chosen by his classmates.[11]

Nevertheless, he took a pulpit as substitute minister in the Swedish Lutheran Church in Anaconda, Montana. During the year he served as minister, he preached in the Swedish language and taught science and philosophy to the young people. A story that is told indicates that at this particular time his attitude did not differ from the ultraconservative view which was characteristic of the transplanted Swedish church in America.

At one of the socials of the local Good Templars Lodge he was asked to deliver a lecture on the uplifting subject of ethics and religion. The young minister obliged. But when he discovered that his talk was to be followed by dancing, he expostulated that dancing was sinful and that he had been inveigled into taking part in a disgraceful party.[12]

Condemning dancing was not enough. In addition, Carlson distributed a statement in Swedish to his congregation and to the members of the Good Templars Lodge. The following excerpt, containing eight "don'ts," reveals on the one hand a narrow viewpoint and on the other that his mind had taken on a physiological coloration.

Dancing from a Physiological and Ethical Viewpoint

Cicero: No sober person dances, except possibly a lunatic.

(1) Dancing, that is rhythmic movements of the body, which express or increase feelings of joy or sorrow can be followed in folk customs as far back as the dawn of history. . . .

(5) Dance movements stimulate the feelings. The music increases the enjoyment, but due to the influence of liquor and the close bodily contact of the dancers, the aesthetic feelings are transformed into illicit sensual passion. . . .

(8) Even if not all the dancing parties for youngsters and other persons in this and other cities bear the bitterest fruits, yet one can hardly expect good fruits from the seed of dancing. These parties bring us, as private citizens and as a people, little blessing and small honor. . . .[13]

IV

Within that year Carlson realized that a career in a field in which one had to accept the "nonobservable" and the "non-experimental" did not suit him. He wanted to be a physiologist. But in order to embark on a new field of study, he needed money. The offer of a loan by his friend, Charles Dragstedt, proved sufficient for him to abandon the ministry and to go off to Stanford University to study physiology. Stanford had been founded in 1885 by Leland Stanford, one of the railroad magnates (some would call him one of the robber barons), in memory of his only son. Thus began what Andrew C. Ivy calls his long and passionate love affair with science. At Stanford Carlson conceived a lifelong admiration for its president, David Starr Jordan. It did not take long for his scientific talents to come to the surface. The problem assigned to him was to study the rate of conduction in the motor nerves of invertebrate animals. He chose a snaillike organism, capable of a retractile process. In comparing the response when in its elongated state with the response when its size was reduced, he realized that in its elongated state the response was slower. This led him to conclude that "the conductible substance in the nerve fiber must be liquid rather than solid."[14] It was to prove a seminal work.

After receiving the Ph.D. in physiology in 1902, Carlson went to the Carnegie Institute of Technology as a research associate, remaining in this post for two years. There he tackled a long-debated problem in regard to cardiac impulse by setting out to determine whether the inhibitory or the accelerator nerves to the heart appeared first in evolution. He chose to conduct his research on the lower marine animals, a project which could best be undertaken at the Marine Biological Station at Woods Hole in Massachusetts.

There he worked on the Limulus, or the horseshoe crab, on whose heart the cardiac nerves spread in ganglion form. Cutting communication between the cardiac nerves, he found that this rupture caused the transmission of the cardiac impulse (heartbeat) to be interrupted, and concluded therefrom that in the horseshoe crab the heartbeat is stimulated by the cardiac nerves.[15] Later research provided the information that in the embryo of the Limulus the heart begins to beat before the appearance of nerve fibers. These findings led him to deduce that, though the heart muscle may be in control of heart action in the beginning, the cardiac nerves take over as soon as they are fully developed. The article setting forth his theory in the *American Journal of Physiology* created a stir. As a consequence, Carlson was asked in 1904 to the Department of Physiology at the University of Chicago.

He remained there until his death fifty-two years later. The explanation offered by his friends for his refusal ever to leave the University of Chicago was his admiration for William Rainey Harper, its first president, and the high regard he had for many of the scientists of the university. What he thought of Dr. Harper is clear from a speech he made on the occasion of the testimonial dinner honoring Carlson's seventy-fifth birthday. In his usual electrifying manner he remarked: "The four University of Chicago presidents who followed Harper didn't even reach up to his knees." In 1914 he became chairman of the department and, though he retired officially in 1940, he remained active in research and lecturing at the university.

V

Carlson's reputation would have been awesome even if he had confined himself either to teaching or research. He performed brilliantly and made an extraordinary contribution in both fields. Written testimonials indicate that his gifts as a teacher were unique. Though his main function as a teacher was to train graduate students in physiology and to teach physiology to medical students, he also gave orientation lectures to freshmen in the natural sciences as part of a series called "Nature of the World and Man."[16] The same magic quality that made science students flock to him was evident in his relation with non-science students. It is said that they did not cut any of his classes. Also, he did not disdain "private teaching," as when he appeared before Clarence Darrow's "Biology Club" of seventy-five members, who boasted that they wanted their facts straight.[17]

The precepts Carlson urged on others he followed himself. One of his oft repeated slogans was: "Work, work, work from diapers till death." Though some of his lectures began at seven in the morning, according to the reports of eyewitnesses he had a hundred percent attendance. After that he continued to work in classrooms or in his laboratory all day, and in addition he worked three or four evenings a week. He always made time for conferences with students, and would listen quietly, puffing on his corncob pipe until as it frequently happened, the student stumbled on the solution to his problem by himself. As a classroom lecturer he acquired a legendary reputation for his wit, his peppery statements, and, above all, the inevitable question: "Vot iss de effidence?"

Another characteristic remark was: "Let's not waste any more time; let's get to work." There are pictures of him that show a large man with a crew cut, a quizzical look in his eyes, standing with an immobile face before a class filled to capacity with young men and women, all dissolved in laughter. But it was the question: "Vot iss de effidence?" that became the identifying feature of the man and the one for which he is most remembered. This question was aimed not only at students, but also at scientists, young and old. It was like the knell of doom for those reporting the results of a faulty experiment, because it implied that the evidence to insure its acceptance was lacking. It was as a teacher that Carlson became known as "Ajax," after the legendary Greek hero who prayed to Zeus to be delivered from darkness. Though the origin of the nickname may have been suggested by the initials "A. J.," someone must have realized that this doughty man resembled the heroic Greek in his indefatigable and unconquerable spirit.

VI

While some of his students may have feared his caustic wit, he was loved and venerated. Sentiments of affection and respect are repeated in testimonials years after students had achieved recognition as physicians and scientists. To many he was "Papa Carlson," who scolded and criticized but was always willing to help. Many expressed the sentiments of Dr. Dragstedt, who stated: "He was my friend and teacher and the greatest influence on my scientific career."[18] The words appear again and again in an extraordinary conflation of letters by former students and colleagues in the form of a "*Festschrift*"[19] presented to him on his seventy-fifth birthday, a volume containing three hundred sixty-four letters from physicians and physiologists working in American institutions and abroad, which abound in the kind of tribute few teachers have been privileged to receive. The phrases that stand out are "master experimentalist," "wise counsellor," "Viking of science," "champion of integrity," "tower of strength," "shining example," and others. The word "friend" appears innumerable times. One said: "The world is indeed a much better place in which to live because you have passed this way"; another: "Thank you for living among us."

The legend that has grown up around the man is based on his ability to get to the heart of a scientific problem, as well as on his extraordinary personality. He was capable of amazing patience in listening to what was "hopeless twaddle." He could be blunt, he could be severe, but the look in his piercing blue eyes was not unkind and he rarely meant to hurt. As Ivy declared: "He meant to hurt only the bluffer, the sophisticated, the ostentatious."[20] While it was not unusual to hear him exclaim: "Ach, how can anybotty be such a Gott-damned fool?" he could also admit ruefully: "When I see the same mistake made year after year, I get discouraged; I forget it is a *different* freshman making the *same* mistake." A remark would be no less caustic for being amusing, as when he said to a girl student trying to stimulate a frog muscle in a salt solution with an electric wire: "Vake up! You might as well try to stick your electrode in the Atlantic Ocean and stimulate Ireland."[21]

Carlson was just as likely to administer a dressing down to scientists of reputation. He is quoted as having said to a visiting dignitary: "You have said dot vunce; sit down."[22] At another meeting he announced: "Now that the flatitudes are over, let's discuss the paper."

He did not hesitate to unleash the same bluntness when disagreeing with Robert Maynard Hutchins, president of the University of Chicago, whose proposal that one hundred great books be the basis of a liberal education made perennial headlines. Carlson did not hesitate to characterize Hutchins' preference for "dead poets" instead of for live science as "yust ignorant." This view was shared by Hanz Zinsser, who, though more tactful than Carlson, wrote: "No greater misfortune could happen to American universities than if Mr. Hutchins' views were to be adopted and research were relegated to a minor position."[23] Once, when the president proposed that academic tenure be eliminated because it would keep all professors on their toes, Carlson replied: "Mr. President, you made a mistake. Vot you mean is dot it will keep dem on der knees."[24]

He was a master of the ex cathedra statement, and the pungency of his remarks gave to any point an extra fillip of effectiveness. For instance, overeating and obesity were his special detestations. But Carlson would not limit himself to a statement on the dangers of overeating. Instead he authorized the following comment in the *Chicago Sun* (now defunct), which was reprinted in the magazine of the University of Chicago:

Dr. Anton J. Carlson, professor of physiology at the University of Chicago, suggests a tax on fat people who try to get fatter, and on those who aid and abet them. . . . The remedy he suggests is a tax of $20 for every pound the citizen weighs which is over the normal weight for his or her size and years.[25]

He was apt to make no less startling assertions in his everyday conversations. Dr. Dragstedt reports that after being told about a well-known scientist who had left his position at the university because he had fallen in love with another man's wife and the divorce that followed it had caused unfavorable comment, Carlson remarked: "I yust can't understand. Vy there isn't twenty-five cents worth of difference between one woman and another."

Another characteristic of the man was his fearlessness in making a fight for what he believed was right. An issue that was close to his heart was to counteract the opposition of antivivisectionists to using anesthetized dogs in medical research. It seemed ridiculous to him to deprive researchers of experimental animals when the city pound was catching and killing forty thousand dogs every year by asphyxiation. His argument was: "If man isn't worth more than a dog, then our effort to improve man is an error." He was successful in securing a city ordinance to make dogs available to medical investigators. In order to promote unhampered research, he founded and organized the "National Society for Medical Research." When the serum against infantile paralysis was developed, he pointed triumphantly to the fact that without animal experimentation it would not have been possible.

VII

Whether his achievements as a scientific investigator were of greater significance than his contributions as a teacher is a question that members of his own profession would hesitate to answer. For having changed many physiological concepts, Carlson is considered a trailblazer in medical research. He has been called "the common man's scientist," and "a scientist's scientist," which was the caption accompanying his picture on the cover of *Time*, for February 10, 1941. Among his most important researches are studies of the stomach, the endocrines, the visceral nervous system, and the lung. The book that gave him immortality among scientists is entitled, *The Control of Hunger in Health and Disease*, published in 1916. It is considered a classic of its kind. In it he questioned Pavlov's theory of the "conditioned reflex." Pavlov's thesis was that the glands secreting gastric juices are inactive when the stomach is empty. But Carlson had gathered evidence that proved Pavlov in error. Hunger is automatic, said Carlson, basing his deductions on what he had verified with his own eyes.

Previously, he had rigged up experiments on himself to measure his own pangs of hunger, in the time-honored way of researchers who make guinea pigs of themselves when no other means of verification is possible. He had learned to swallow a stomach tube with ease and made a movie of himself in the process of swallowing it in order to demonstrate how easy it was. He advised his graduate students to learn the trick of how to do it and shamed them into trying it until they mastered the procedure. In the late 1940's he conducted experiments on the effect of 3.2 alcohol by making blood tests on himself and students. In his hunger experiments he inserted a balloon attached to a tube into his stomach. By connecting the tube with an instrument which recorded pressure, he could measure his hunger pangs. But, of course, he could not see what was going on.

Suddenly, a providential opportunity to observe the workings of the stomach presented itself. A Czech student brought to the laboratory someone who as a child had swallowed a dose of caustic potash in his father's saloon in Prague. As a result of injury to his esophagus, he could take nourishment only through an opening in his abdomen that the surgeons had provided. It was the second time an American was able to observe with his own eyes the workings of the human stomach. In 1822 an army doctor, William Beaumont, observed through an open hole the flow of gastric juices and the effects of stimulants such as tea, coffee, and alcohol. His report, *Experiments and Observations on the Gastric Juices and the Physiologie of Digestion,* laid the foundation for the physiology of digestion.[26] What Carlson discovered was that the stomach juices flow periodically, even during periods of fasting. He deduced therefore that hunger is automatic and that it is independent of appetite, which is conditioned by smell, sight, and taste.

One of the effects of this experiment was that the rigid views of physicians on infant feeding were softened. The implied lesson in Carlson's findings was that a baby should be fed when it is hungry, which it indicates by crying. His theory also revolutionized the treatment and the feeding schedules of people suffering from ulcer. When insulin was discovered and it was claimed that an overdose of insulin produces hypoglycemia (a condition characterized by a decreased amount of sugar in the blood), and consequently that insulin stimulates hunger, Carlson proved by experiments on dogs that insulin hypoglycemia induces hunger pains only if the vagus nerve is intact. This discovery provided important information for surgeons performing vagatomies (the severing of the vagus nerve) in their treatment of duodenal ulcer.

Dr. Carlson was not a physician. His M.D. is an honorary degree. (Honorary degrees in medicine are almost unheard of.) For all his professionalism, this man who understood and dealt with the great mysteries of life did not confine his interests to science alone. He was a member of the Chicago Literary Society and an "enthusiastic participant" who attended Monday evening meetings for many years.[27]

VIII

During World War I Carlson enlisted in the newly organized Sanitary Corps. Assigned to reorganizing the diet of fighting soldiers, he was responsible for increasing their dietary allotments. At the end of the war he was transferred to the Hoover Commission, where he was in charge of food relief for the starving people of Europe. He returned as a recognized authority on nutrition. One consequence of his war experience was hatred of war, and another, a new interest in the welfare of children. It led him to participate in the effort to secure free lunches for poor children in the public schools and to take an active part in the National Society for the Study of Infantile Paralysis.

Though his official connection with the university terminated when he became sixty-five, Carlson did not stop working. Retirement enabled him to give more attention to the problem of alcoholism and to become, in 1937, one of the founders of the Research Council on Problems of Alcohol.

Carlson regarded alcoholics as sick people and not as social lepers, and alcoholism as a problem that called for far more basic research than it was receiving. His insistence that the answer to the problem of alcoholism did not lie solely in the understanding of individual factors such as the culture pattern of which an individual was the product, or the personality of the drinker, or the function of the body, or the amount of liquor consumed, but rather in the understanding of all these factors combined, aroused widespread agreement. His satisfaction came when twenty-six states adopted a program of which he approved for the treatment of alcoholics.[28]

In his observations on the problems of aging, Carlson was undoubtedly influenced by his own reactions to retirement. He regarded the philosophy of "security from the womb to the tomb" as unbiological. He considered work "the biggest factor in happiness and longevity." The solution he offered was that older people should work few hours, at less pay, but that those able to work should continue—not to "work like he--" but as long and as hard as they felt they could.

During World War II, though officially retired, Carlson acted as consultant to the United States Army, advising them on the K ration and improving it after trying it on himself. Among other organizations he served were the United States Public Health Service, the United States Food and Drug Administration, for which he acted as expert witness in violations of the Pure Food Law, and the National Research Council.

His passionate defense of civil rights was misunderstood by Senator Jenner, who was suspicious of some of his statements before organizations held suspect by the FBI. In June, 1953, when he was seventy-eight and had served the United States in various capacities for years, Carlson was summoned to a secret hearing before Senator Jenner and asked if he was a communist. Carlson's response was to request a public hearing, so that he "could face the evidence, if any, against me." It was denied.[29] Upon leaving the committee room, he gave a statement to the press which was criticized by Senator Jenner as "violating the spirit of the session."[30] To Dr. Ivy, Carlson was the "antithesis of a Communist."[31]

Dr. Carlson died in 1956 at the age of eighty-one of cancer. At the end of his life, this man who knew so much about the human body learned something new about the human condition. During his long and painful illness, he remarked to the wife of Dr. Ivy, who had come to visit him: "I didn't know it was so hard to die."[32] These words are the opposite of Carl Schurz's last utterance: *"Es ist so einfach zu sterben."* ("It is so easy to die.") Death intensified the legends that have grown around this great scientist and teacher, who was a dramatic showman to boot. The veneration of those who knew him remains undiminished. No one familiar with his work would dispute the statement contained in the *Festschrift* assembled for his seventy-fifth birthday—that the heritage he left "will live as long as physiology survives."[33]

OLE EDVART RÖLVAAG
1876-1931

From Hired Hand to Author

He is the creator of the novel Giants in the Earth, *in which he immortalized one of the most dramatic episodes in the growth of our nation. It is the conquest of the Northwest by groups of intrepid pioneers, many of whom were recently arrived immigrants from Scandinavia. They were men and women of Brobdingnagian strength and courage. Neither participant nor spectator himself, he based his chronicle on the testimony of those who had shared the pioneering experience. In recreating a story of men and women contending with nature for mastery of their environment, and winning the contest, he has given to the American people a legacy that neither time nor changing customs can diminish.*

The Norwegians Leave Their Homeland

Tales of the abundance of the blessings to be found in America, among which unlimited land and lack of interference could not fail to strike a rural people as being the greatest good, began to trickle into Norway at the beginning of the nineteenth century. Norway had been united with Denmark until 1814, when the victorious coalition against Napoleon attached Norway to Sweden in what was called a "personal union." The king of Sweden became king of Norway. The reason for depriving Denmark was that Denmark had supported Napoleon and Sweden had not. The transfer was a reward to Sweden and its new king, Charles XIV, who had been Marshal Bernadotte and one of Napoleon's generals, for turning against him.

The Norwegians resented being treated as pawns, but they were helpless. All they could accomplish was to force Sweden to grant them their own constitution, which vested authority in a Norwegian parliament, called the Storthing. Unlike Sweden, where control rested in the hands of large, politically conservative landholders, the peasant owners of Norway demanded more extensive democratic measures than the king would grant. During the rest of the nineteenth century the Norwegians continued to press for greater political reforms. In 1898 they won universal manhood suffrage and in 1905 the Storthing finally forced separation from Sweden.

Economic conditions in Norway were stringent. The bulk of the populace consisted of small farmers, fishermen, mariners, merchants, bureaucrats, and a small but highly respected intellectual class. The majority was poor, depending for subsistence upon the soil and the sea. Because of continued subdivision of peasant lands among successive generations, the yield of the individual peasant farm frequently fell below subsistence levels. In consequence, there was a growing number of crofters and landless laborers. It was not surprising that the imagination of people whose farms were too impoverished to supply the necessities of life should be stirred by visions of unlimited land in America, waiting only for labor to make it fruitful. As for those who wrested their living from the sea— fishing, especially around the Lofoten fishing grounds, was a hazardous and uncertain occupation.

The primary motive for the emigration of Norwegians was therefore economic, though religious harassment was also a factor in forcing Protestant dissenters to seek a more permissive climate in which to practice their religious beliefs without hindrance. The first group of dissenters, who reached New York State in 1825, included a group of Quakers. In the late 1830's, Ole Rynning, who had trained for the ministry, led a group of his countrymen to the Midwest. They settled in Illinois, where they purchased a tract of land which proved swampy and therefore insalubrious. There, at the age of twenty-nine, Ole Rynning died of the ague and was buried on the prairie. After his death the survivors dispersed and some returned to Norway. Before Rynning died, he composed a tract on immigration[1] which went through several printings in Christiania. Soberly written, it portrayed America and Americans favorably, and offered a hopeful picture to future emigrants. Because of the large circulation the pamphlet achieved, it was held to have given a strong spur to emigration, thus augmenting the effect of "America Letters," wherein Norwegians who had left earlier praised life in the new country extravagantly and not always truthfully. But the most important stimulus was supplied by a series of social crises in Norway during which, in the 1840's and 1850's, crop failures, poor fishing, and illegitimacy, crime, and jail sentences increased.

Approximately eight hundred thousand Norwegians emigrated during the hundred-year period between 1836 and 1936. A conspicuous characteristic of Norwegians was their hardihood and their capacity for enduring isolation. Another was that illiteracy was all but unknown among them. The reason was that the ability to read was essential for confirmation in the Norwegian Lutheran Church. Until the advent of school, children learned to read and write when their parents found time to teach them—in Norwegian, of course.[2]

The American Setting

Settlement of the West was no less the accomplishment of European immigrants than of American pioneers. Natives who moved from the older states into the territories and beyond, where government surveyors had not even entered, were the first to begin pushing the frontier back. After clearing the land and erecting a place to live these native homesteaders were not averse to selling their holdings and moving farther into unexplored country as if life in the bosom of nature represented the nearest approximation to the Garden of Eden. While Americans were pioneers by inclination, many immigrant groups whose destination was the West—Germans, Swiss, Dutch, English, among others—preferred land that had already been cleared and on which a place fit for habitation, however rude, had been erected.

Among the settlers who seemed unafraid of wilderness living were the Norwegians. As they were used to seclusion and hardship, life at the edge of the frontier, if not in the very heart of the prairie, presented no real obstacle to these sturdy people. Their hope was to create homes for themselves in the amplitude of the prairie, where they could revel in acres and acres of their own land. Before the appearance of the railroad they proceeded to their destination via a string of canalboats; during the latter part of the century, the crude, jolting immigrant trains were an unavoidable part of their travel experiences. If on arrival at their destination they lacked the means to buy the essentials for setting themselves up, such as a team of draft animals, a cow, and the necessary staples of food, they hired themselves out to others until the needed amount was accumulated, in the meantime sharing another family's dugout or sodhouse.[3]

It was the Homestead Act, passed in 1862 when many of the foreign-born had already taken up arms in defense of the Union, which lured agricultural settlers to the Northwest. Under this legislation a quarter section (160 acres) was available to any native or foreigner who would "come and get it." Land-hungry immigrants looked upon 160 acres as a princely gift and upon the Great Plains as the "land of Canaan." Upon the penetration of Scandinavians and other pioneers, the prairie became dotted with sodhouses that appeared like anthills in the vast flatness of the prairie. But within a few years they were replaced by frame houses, and within much less than a decade general stores, churches, schools, and granges were very much in evidence.

The heaviest exodus from Norway occurred between the Civil War and the 1880's. The "America fever" was so strong that by the end of the nineteenth century the crofter class had almost entirely disappeared from Norway.[4] It was a commonplace to find photographs of distant sons decorating practically every peasant home in Norway. At first the movement to America was predominantly from rural areas. By 1850 Norwegians were thinly scattered over Illinois and had penetrated some of the northern states, particularly northern Iowa and southern Minnesota. In the 1870's they began to overflow into the Dakotas and from there into Montana, Washington, and Oregon.

But emigrants from the artisan and laboring classes also began to swell the exodus at the end of the nineteenth century. These Norwegians gravitated more to the towns of America. With the exception of New York City, Chicago, Minneapolis, and

Seattle, where there are large numbers of Norwegians, the smaller cities proved more attractive to them than the large urban centers.

During the eighties all agricultural elements prospered. The grasshopper plagues which, beginning with 1873, occurred annually during the seventies, did not repeat themselves during the eighties. Beginning with the 1860's Norwegians established religious schools and colleges in more than fifty communities, which were intended to keep old world traditions alive. The colleges that became the best known were Luther College in Decorah, Iowa (the first American establishment), Saint Olaf College in Northfield, Minnesota, Concordia College in Moorhead, Minnesota, and Augustana College in Sioux Falls, South Dakota. Many immigrants and, later, their children, received their start in these schools. One of them was Ole Edvart Rölvaag.

These sturdy newcomers made the West grow in more than one way. During slack periods on their farms they helped to extend the railroad. Settlers and railroads depended on one another. The railroads needed settlers in order to dispose of the land the federal government had given them as an incentive to undertaking the building of transcontinentals. Only homesteaders could grow the grains on which freight charges could be collected. The settlers needed the railroads to inject life into the region and to transport what they raised to marketing centers. Together, railroads and pioneers made the West bloom. Later, when the railroads openly exploited farmers, clamor and implacable enmity was the result.

The most important contribution of the Norwegians was to help in pushing back the frontier. These newcomers built an enduring life for themselves and their children on lar.d they had wrested from the wilderness. But today the names of many of their descendants may also be found, as is Rölvaag's son, among governors and congressmen of the Midwest, as well as among the engineers, scientists, and teachers of America. Also, because Norwegian immigrants developed the maritime and fishing industries on both coasts, some of their names may be seen inscribed on hulls of ships plying the waterways of the world under the American flag.

I

It was almost a full generation after the crest of pioneering among Norwegians had passed that Ole Edvart Rölvaag, a twenty-year-old, untutored immigrant, disembarked in New York. The year was 1896. Entraining immediately for South Dakota, the Mecca of Norwegians, he expected to join an uncle who was an agricultural laborer. No one, including himself, expected that he would develop into an intellectual, a writer who was destined to be considered one of the best-known Norwegians in America.

He achieved this distinction as the author of *Giants in the Earth*, which authenticates the experiences of pioneers who undertook the task of turning uncultivated lands into homes. Like others among the foreign-born who became writers out of a compulsion to offer their version of the immigrant experience, he was stirred by a vision of the struggles of those who undertook to penetrate into territory no white man had entered. Speaking through his characters, Rölvaag likened this hegira in search of a new Canaan to "the Crossing of the Red Sea." The reader is a fascinated witness to the awful struggle that must ensue between man and nature before shelter and the necessities of life can be wrested from the harsh environment. By subjecting his characters to the hardships pioneers encountered and surmounted, Rölvaag has made graphic an experience in our history of which it might be said, in the words of Thomas Paine, that it was sufficient "to try men's souls."

This epic theme of man's victory over the forces of nature kindled the imagination of several Scandinavian writers who were aware of the role their countrymen had played to make the Northwest habitable. One was Johann Bojer,[5] a Norwegian writer and contemporary of Rölvaag; another was the Swedish novelist, Vilhelm Moberg,[6] whose trilogy on the development of Minnesota by immigrants from Sweden was not completed until the 1960's. Both Bojer and Moberg came to America to familiarize themselves with the American scene—Bojer during the early decades of the twentieth century and Moberg during midcentury. But when they felt that they had absorbed enough of the American atmosphere, they returned to their natal countries.

Though they recorded the transition of Europeans into Americans, they wrote as Europeans and as onlookers.

Rölvaag, however, wrote from a deep personal awareness of what the process of Americanization entailed. Though he never forgot that he was a native of Norway and passionately preached that no Norwegian should, he is one with the characters whose existence is tied to the land they are laboring to make their own. The aspiration to blend their lives with the American future was theirs and his as well. He had married a young woman of Norwegian parentage, whose father had come into South Dakota from Minnesota along the route followed by Per Hansa, the main character of *Giants*. He must have visualized his father-in-law in those pioneers and his wife in the pioneer children. When he expressed for his characters the thrilling realization that a newborn child was eligible to become governor of the state, and perhaps even president, it may have been an expression of hope that his own sons might achieve this distinction. By his own admission these children belonged to America and America was irrevocably theirs. One of Rölvaag's several children, his son Karl Fritjof, became governor of Minnesota in 1963.[7]

II

Ole Edvart Rölvaag was born in 1876 into a humble home on the island of Donna, close to the Arctic Circle, where sea and mountains come together to form a spectacle he would never be able to forget. There he attended school until he was confirmed at fourteen. His people were fisherfolk, but several members of his family—a brother, a sister, and an uncle—possessed more than average mental endowment. Because he was not considered a promising student, the severe sacrifices required of those who wished to continue at school did not seem justified. The family was poor, they made their own lines and nets; they wove their own yarn, which they turned into the clothing they wore. He wore homemade garments until, at fourteen, he began to go on fishing trips to the Lofoten fishing grounds. He was a handsome youth with the good looks characteristic of the Norwegians. He was also moody, sensitive, romantic, and introverted. He was aware that his moodiness was a trait of his personality and he described it as "something strangely double in my nature, a great life joy and a heavy melancholy."[8] As a boy, he was such an avid reader that he is supposed to have taken a journey of fourteen miles, on foot, lasting two days, to get a copy of *Ivanhoe*. He read not only Scandinavian literature, but also translations of French, English, and American books, and among the latter, the novels of James Fenimore Cooper.[9] Lincoln Colcord, the translator of *Giants in the Earth*, who had the opportunity to hear of many incidents of Rölvaag's life from his own lips, tells of a walk the young boy took with his mother, to whom he was deeply attached. She asked him what he wanted to be when he grew up. A poet, he replied. Whereupon she chuckled, as if amused at an ambition for which she considered him ill-suited. Apparently, the urge to write started early, for one day when he was about twelve the older brother, with whom he shared a room, surprised him at his scribbling. His brother tried to snatch the paper from him, tearing it in the scuffle.[10] His next creative eruption did not occur until fifteen years later, when he was a senior in an American college. It was an attempt at a novel, which he abandoned when he could not find a Norwegian publisher.

At the age of eighteen Rölvaag decided to ask an uncle in South Dakota to send him a steamship ticket. By then he had made several annual fishing trips. He was to remain passionately fond of the experiences connected with fishing expeditions; during his later visits to Norway he would go back to his "old trade" and write to his wife of the satisfaction it gave him to do the "harpooning" himself. It took his uncle two years to send the steamship ticket he had requested. It arrived just as the owner of a new and beautiful boat promised it to him, provided he first worked off its cost. Though he was tempted, he chose America.

The foreword to *Giants* discloses how the twenty-year-old youth reached his destination in South Dakota. When he was put on the train by immigration officials he owned a Norwegian coin and an American dime. Penniless immigrants were not unheard of. Twenty-five years before Rölvaag Michael Pupin,[11] destined to become one of America's outstanding foreign-born scientists, possessed only five cents when he landed on American soil. Although it was required of immigrants that they possess a sum of money deemed sufficient for the interval between arrival and finding work, neither Rölvaag nor Pupin was barred from entry, but the sixteen-year-old Michael Pupin (who had neither relatives nor friends in America) was counseled to accept the first suitable job that would be offered to him in Castle Garden. (He did.)

Rölvaag had only a loaf of bread throughout the whole trip of three days and three nights, but he made sure of having tobacco for his pipe. Due to a misunderstanding, his uncle was not at the station when the train pulled in. Though he knew not a word of English and undoubtedly felt hungry and forlorn, he set out on foot to find the farm where his uncle worked. The fact that he must have asked directions and must have received information in Norwegian is reminiscent of what Henry Villard, a German immigrant of the 1850's, observed in Belleville, Illinois. Villard remarked: "I hardly heard a word of English, for there was not a single American there."[12] After walking eight miles and getting lost in the darkness, Rölvaag found his uncle.

III

In South Dakota, Rölvaag was thrust into farm work, tending horses and pigs and cleaning stables. For one used to the sea such work was distasteful enough to make him think of returning to his homeland. Norwegians, accustomed to spectacular scenery, considered South Dakota a "flat country." To a homesick youth who was susceptible to the fascination of an endlessly moving seascape it would seem monotonous. Before leaving Norway he had begun a diary which became the repository for his thoughts and disappointments, and which he kept up for five years. Though he lost no time in starting to study English, he made very slow progress. To his diary he confided that he was unhappy and "drifting in a sea of emotion."

Homesickness was a natural reaction in one who cherished the remembrance of "the mighty peaks and shining fjords" of his birthplace. Though he is said to have been fascinated by the prairie, the ocean retained the strongest pull over his imagination. He saw the ocean in the waving wheatfields and in the haze created by distance, even if the prairie lacked the sound of the sea. Years later, on one of his visits to Norway, he wrote to his wife that when he could not sleep he would conjure up visions of the fishing fleet coming into the harbor at sunrise. Even after more than two decades of living in the Northwest the ocean remained a potent memory, for *Giants* is filled with ocean imagery. The vista the prairie presented to the group trudging to their destination in the wilderness was that of an "unknown lifeless sea," and the "broad expanse of the prairie stretching away endlessly in every direction, seemed almost like the ocean." Johann Bojer, too, when describing the prairie in his novel, *The Emigrants*, likened it to "an ocean of earth." Rölvaag, who loved music, also imagined musical sounds in the rustle of grain and the sound of crickets.

After two years Rölvaag had paid back his debt to his uncle and he decided to enter Augustana Academy, a secondary school, operated by a Norwegian-American church body. A boarding school, it had an enrollment of a hundred and forty-eight students. He was still doubtful of his abilities as a student, for he wrote to his father:

You say that the Lord has not given me talents. I grant that you may be right, but how can you be so sure of it? Of course I know that I am not as gifted as either you or my brother. . . . I heard that so many times during my boyhood that I have not forgotten it. But let me ask you in all sincerity: How do you know that books and learning are not for me?[13]

At the end of the first year his funds were exhausted. He followed a pattern established by countless immigrants of all backgrounds to whom the securing of an education represented the greatest good offered by the American system—he worked as he studied, as a farm laborer and book agent during summers and as a handyman and chimney sweep at school. It pleased and surprised him to take note of the fact that "everyone is so democratic—both teachers and students. . . . Any class distinction other than that which talents and superior intelligence can give, we do not know of."[14]

IV

When he graduated in 1901, Rölvaag was qualified to enter Saint Olaf College in Northfield, Minnesota. (His son would also study at Saint Olaf.) Founded in 1874 during the peak of Norwegian immigration, it added a college department in 1886. By then Rölvaag was committed to the philosophy that the immigrant heritage must be preserved. It was a conviction from which he would not depart and which would lead him into various activities to preserve the ties between the old and the new way of life. In his later years he helped to form the Norwegian-American Historical Association and despite ill health he remained its secretary until his death. His first intention was to prepare himself for the ministry, for Norwegians as for Swedes the most prestigious profession. His knowledge of the Bible was thorough, and religion had great power over him; but dogma and ritual did not.[15] Though he soon gave up the idea of the ministry, he remained deeply religious and convinced of the efficacy of prayer, interpreting recovery from illness as the Lord's answer to his entreaties.

A college graduate at twenty-seven, Rölvaag was still straddling two worlds. He had been living in America nine years, but he could neither relinquish the Old World nor yet fully commit himself to the American world. During his senior year he had begun a novel on Norwegian-American life. His intention was "to do something for Norwegian-Americans on a large scale . . . through his authorship."[16] But the publisher in Christiania who would later accept *Giants* turned him down and Rölvaag dropped the project. It was a painful blow. Consequently, the hope of becoming a teacher seemed a very desirable goal, though he was by no means certain of achieving it. He borrowed five hundred dollars from one of his teachers and departed for his homeland for further study. (His son would in his own time also spend a year as a student at the University of Oslo.)°

As the first student from Saint Olaf, Rölvaag was anxious to make a good impression. A letter he wrote to his fiancée indicates that he regarded himself as a representative from America as well as from his alma mater. He put it this way: ". . . I was an American, and the big fellows in Christiania have not much faith in us. Perhaps my examen may do a little to strengthen it." Because he wanted to teach the supercilious scholars of Norway respect for American students, he worked so hard that he made himself ill and was forbidden to study for more than a few hours

---

° Christiania became Oslo after 1925.

a day. "Only three hours a day!" he lamented. "I have an awful fear." But instead of flunking he passed his "examen philosophicum" with the highest marks. However, his physical condition was so poor that he was forced to recuperate at the home of his parents in Donna. He was still unable to dispense wholehearted hymns of praise to America, for he declared in a speech before a gathering:

Culture demands nuance, perspective, contrast. . . . Poor little old-fashioned Europe, where people are not free, and of which the Yankee has passed many a taunting remark, nevertheless has something which all the money in the world cannot buy. It has an indescribable flavor of mellowed culture; there is romantic charm in the many forms that have come down from the ages past. . . . What an abundance of originality in a small land like Norway![17]

These are sentiments some of our native writers have expressed, including Nathaniel Hawthorne and Henry James. Both complained that America lacked many of the inspirations valuable to writers, which Europe offers in plenty, particularly the "mellowed" culture—castles, churches, old universities, etc.

Though he must have known that many doors were now open to him in Norway, which would have remained closed if not for the education America had made possible, Rölvaag returned to the United States. It must have been hard for him to turn his back on the land that was to him "of all things on earth the most beautiful." One reason he was drawn back was undoubtedly because he had a fiancée waiting for him. Another may have been a reaction Johann Bojer described as typical of returning Norwegians: "If you come back, you wanted to leave again; if you went away you longed to come back. You had one home over there and one over here."[18] Evidently America had begun to exercise a pull no less potent that that of Norway.

V

He returned to begin a teaching career at Saint Olaf. It was a welcome appointment, for he had accumulated debts which had to be paid back. He would not be able to marry his fiancée, who had been waiting patiently, for another two years. When he married at thirty-two he had already begun to feel intimations of serious ill health, which may have been the beginning of the angina pectoris to which he would succumb at fifty-five.

Though he rose in the academic world, Rölvaag was a teacher by necessity rather than by choice. If he could have followed his inclinations, he would have devoted himself entirely to writing. It was through creative work that he could make known his thoughts on the assimilation of foreigners into the American way of life. He saw clearly that if the old values were to be lost before new values could be fully absorbed it would be disastrous, not only for the deracinated newcomers who would be losing their ethnic identity before they could consider themselves Americans, but also for the evolving culture of America. He considered it essential that the old traditions be made part of the new life lest the American people become "gamblers in foreign goods."

He admitted that immigrants gained "great things" in America, but he stressed that by the same token they lost "great things." Immigrants were America's "adopted children," who had "traded their fatherland for a new and untried existence." This was to him a loss of great consequence. He realized that the American-born children of the foreign-born could expect to play more significant roles in American society than their parents, but he wanted them to retain the knowledge of and respect for their ancient customs. In that way, he felt, the value of the immigrant contribution would become enhanced. To him, those who discarded their racial heritage during the period when they were not yet Americans were "international vagrants belonging nowhere."

It was a view many of the foreign-born of different nationalities—German, Slavic, Italian—corroborated fully. For instance, the Italian-born Leonard Covello, who played a significant role in the educational system of New York City, put it this way: "The source of cultural strength for any immigrant must be the country of his birth. Until the immigrant can assimilate to a point where he can begin to draw power from American sources, he must look backward into the past."[19]

The first time Rölvaag expressed this view publicly was in an oration upon graduation from Augustana Academy. He was to restate it in different words throughout his life. After a decade in America he declared:

Perhaps some will say we are all Americans. We need no other history and no other language than the American. But was it our kin who fought for the War for Independence? Was it our fathers who struggled heroically in the Sixties to preserve the Union? Are Washington, Lincoln, Franklin, Hamilton, Lee and Grant of our stock? No, our past in the building of America has been done here in the Northwest in comparatively recent years. We are Americans, but our people have not been in this country from the beginning. We cannot truthfully sing, "Land where my fathers died." For good or for bad, this is the truth.[20]

This sense of embarrassment over saying the words, "Land where my fathers died," afflicted individuals of other nationalities. Abraham Rihbany,* a Syrian, who became the minister of the Church of the Disciples in Boston (founded in 1840 by the Transcendentalist minister, James Freeman Clarke), admitted that the lines "stuck in his throat" until he came to feel that though he was born in Syria, he had been "reborn" in America and that the fathers of his "new and higher self did live and die in America."

Consonant with his convictions, the first work Rölvaag created was a compilation of English and Norwegian material for use in the classroom. But his creative instinct could not be downed. His first attempt at fiction was clearly autobiographical. Called *Letters From America (Amerika Breve)*, it was composed of twenty-three letters in which he discussed an immigrant's experience and his relationship to his new country and his place of origin. It was published under a pen name, because the letters were of a "personal" nature. In choosing the epistolary method he may have been following the example of Kierkegaard, with whose writings he was thoroughly familiar.[21] Also, the letter form for stating certain beliefs was then very popular. Since the beginning of the nineteenth century many of the northern European countries had been flooded with "America Letters," which not infrequently contained brash and exaggerated accounts of the New World. These extravagant tales praising life in America, which appeared in newspapers of the home countries, were often intended to demean life in the Old World. It is not unlikely that by choosing the same form as the detrac-

---

* Abraham Mitrie Rihbany, *A Far Journey* (Boston, 1913).

tors of the European homelands, Rölvaag meant to counteract prevailing impressions.

Again he sent the manuscript to the most prominent publishing house in Norway, and though it was not accepted, it was not rejected, for the publisher suggested that the book be rewritten and shortened. However, a religious publishing house in Minneapolis—the Augsburg Publishing House—accepted it immediately. Rölvaag was launched on his career as a novelist.

But Norwegians in America were less inclined than prospective immigrants to be interested in the recital of experiences with which they were only too familiar. His own brother wrote that when he received a copy of the book his first impression was that of annoyance that instead of a work by the "incomparable M. Twain," he should be receiving such "confounded Norwegian-American rot."[22] But after reading it, he realized it was "the genuine stuff." The message of the book was not intended to encourage the Norwegians to become Americans as rapidly as possible, but to stress what many were deliberately ignoring—the need to preserve the immigrant heritage. Instead of praising American life, Rölvaag likened it to the "Babylonian captivity."[23] He was discouraged by the fact that the book was being received with indifference and that the financial returns were very small.

His next literary attempt, *On Forgotten Paths,* again published by the same church publication in Minneapolis, appeared two years later. Set in a purely American locale, it was a novel which concerned itself with the effect of the prairie on a Norwegian family. In this novel the American environment received much greater emphasis than the Old World. Rölvaag was clearly responding to the effect of the new environment. In portraying life on the prairie as destructive of human beings and their happiness, there is a foreshadowing of the path he would follow in *Giants.* He was to make several more attempts at fiction before he produced the novel that was to make him famous in Norway as well as in America.

VI

By 1896, the time of Rölvaag's arrival in America, North and South Dakota were well settled. Both had met population requirements in 1889 and had been admitted to the Union. The frontier was declared to have come to an end in 1890, but there were still many thinly populated areas, where a man could find solitude, as Rölvaag did when in 1923 he began the actual writing of *Giants*. The pioneer experience had receded into the memories of those who in the 1870's had made the migration into the Great Plains with family and the most essential household goods—a plough, tools, pots, sometimes a chicken and rooster, a pig—all piled into a prairie schooner drawn by oxen, the cow trudging behind, wife and children marching along, at least part of the time, except for the very young or infirm.

The first years had been hazardous, but the hardy and patient pioneers had borne with fortitude such occurrences as illness and death, drought, grasshopper plagues, and snowstorms so fierce and unexpected that a man could lose his way between home and barn. Native pioneers who came on the scene later to find the best lands preempted were apt to become so disheartened over repeated drought and other setbacks that they were likely to depart in high dudgeon. The sight of caravans bearing signs such as: "Fifty miles from water, / Hundred miles from wood, / To Hell with South Dakota, / We're leaving you for good,"[24] were not uncommon. It was reminiscent of earlier years when returning wagons displayed the announcement: "Busted, by God."

By the 1920's these farms, originally carved out when the prairie was an unbroken sea of grass swaying in the breeze, were in the hands of the third generation of Norwegians, Swedes, Germans, Bohemians, and natives. Rölvaag had to depend for his data on "hearsay," specifically the reminiscences of his father-in-law, Andrew Berdahl, who had been one of South Dakota's earliest settlers.

The theme of the effect of the pioneer existence on people who were used to civilized life and yet were unafraid of isolation had already been brewing in his head when he read in a Norwegian newspaper that Johann Bojer was planning a trip to America to gather material for a pioneer novel. Rölvaag realized that unless he could finish his novel before Bojer's was ready for publication, his would be considered an imitation. He did not tarry. He requested and received a leave of absence and withdrew to his summer cottage at Big Island, Minnesota, alone, in order to saturate himself with the kind of solitude the pioneers had experienced. While his wife and children spent the winter at the home of his father-in-law in Sioux Falls in South Dakota, he was writing at fever pitch, sometimes six thousand words a day.[25] Though he depended on information which his wife secured from her father and forwarded to him, his literary influences were the Bible, the Norwegian sagas, and the Scandinavian writers Ibsen, Björnson, and Jonas Lie. Something told him that his writing possessed power. Before he finished he departed for Oslo, there to complete his novel and to find a publisher. When Aschehoug Publishers accepted his book, he wrote to his wife:

This is the greatest day of my life. . . . Here I stand a poor Norwegian immigrant, with a greater literary work than has hitherto been produced by any of our people in the United States. The finest and most critical publisher in Norway has accepted it. I am neither proud nor humble, but a peculiar feeling runs through me.[26]

A *cri de coeur* which reveals how much recognition of his accomplishment meant to him.

He beat Bojer in the race to the printer; but Bojer, too, managed to complete his book so that he could not be accused of having plagiarized from the American writer. Rölvaag need not have worried about being unfavorably compared to this much better known writer, for Bojer's treatment of the same theme—man's confrontation with nature—is trite and pallid in comparison with the high sense of genuine drama that pervades *Giants*. It presents the nearest approximation to "felt" experience. Not until Vilhelm Moberg's version of the settlement of Minnesota by the Swedes was this subject again presented with such power. This observation suggests that *Giants* may have been the inspiration for all later books (some by American descendants of immigrant pioneers) in which the subject is the turning of the wilderness into civilization. Rölvaag's identification with his characters is proof of his acceptance that his destiny, no less than theirs, was in the American land.

VII

Issued in 1924, the book appeared in Norway in two volumes under the titles, *I de Dage (In Those Days)* and *Rikets Grund-*

lagge (*The Founding of the Kingdom*), and met with immediate success. In America it encountered some criticism by the clergy and pious laymen who felt "it gave evidence of little faith." This bears out the contention that immigrants in America were apt to be more conservative than the people from whom they had come.[27] The Norwegians in America were much less enthusiastic about *Giants* than the people of Norway, causing Rölvaag to write in 1924: "If only my countrymen *here* would read it too."[28]

Even as he was writing the book in the Norwegian tongue, it occurred to Rölvaag that it might have validity for Americans as well and that it should be translated into English. It was offered to the publishing house of Alfred A. Knopf, which would not undertake publication in English for the reason that it could not handle the translation. The publicity that ensued attracted the attention of Lincoln Colcord, a writer of fiction connected with Harper Brothers, who undertook to do the translation. It is conceded that the translation heightened the impact of the story. Eugene Saxton of Harper Brothers suggested the English title, which affirms the author's religious views and strengthens the spiritual overtones of the book.[29] Colcord received one-third of the royalties. The book became a "Book of the Month" selection.

The first of a trilogy, *Giants* is the most powerful of the three. Quintessentially, the theme is the magnitude of what man is able to achieve if he possesses courage and determination. The author indicates that puny as man is he can triumph even over nature, provided he is willing to pay the cost in suffering. The novel is also a superb character study of several men and women who accomplish the miracle of bending nature to man's will. Though two characters occupy the center, each member of the cast possesses tremendous vitality. There is not a single character that can be considered a stereotype. All are raised to heroic stature as they perform herculean labors, stand by one another, share hardships, and face heartbreaking setbacks together. All—men and women—possess superhuman fortitude, but in one, the sensitive, introverted wife of the main character, it is latent at first. She was Rölvaag's favorite character.[30] Her strength comes to the surface after a series of trials culminating in the death of her husband, the Viking Per Hansa.

VIII

The story is this: Three Norwegian couples set out together in the spring of 1873 to take up homesteads in the heart of the prairie. The dominant character is Per Hansa. A fearless, ambitious conqueror, he has a superhuman zest for work. He is on fire with the vision of "the royal kingdom" he will make his own and the "mansion" he will build for his family. Beret, his wife, is in conspicuous contrast to him. Through her the author expresses the cost imposed on pioneers, particularly the women. In being presented as the "conserver" of the old-world values which meant so much to Rölvaag she becomes symbolic of Norwegian virtues. By nature timid and superstitious, she is obsessed by fears of the vastness, the emptiness, and the deep silence that surround her. She is repelled by the fact that there are no birds on the prairie, no insects (save mosquitoes), and that there is "not a thing to hide behind." The other women in the group are a contrast to the quaking, fearful type of person she represents. As Beret's thoughts turn more and more inward, she scans her former life for sins and transgressions she may have committed, for which God's punishment, she believes, has now descended upon her.

She is certain she will not survive the birth of the third child she is expecting in midwinter, and she is so terrified of being buried on the prairie that she exacts a promise from her husband that he will bury her in her stout "America chest," which she feels will withstand the assault of prairie animals. By the time her delivery draws near her mind has become clouded. On Christmas, after a severe and protracted labor during which she actually does come close to losing her life, her child is born and is named by the jubilant father, "Peder Victorious," a name which seems sacrilegious to her. She lives, but her mind remains affected until an unexpected visit from an itinerant preacher produces the miracle of dispelling the fog which has enveloped her mind. From then on she becomes unremittingly and fanatically pious.

As the years pass, the settlement grows. Despite the annual appearance of locusts during the decade of the seventies, and other hazards to crops and livestock, the people prosper, especially Per Hansa. During a fierce winter their closest friend, neighbor, and ally, a man of great body and prodigious strength, is caught in a severe snowstorm and develops pneumonia. As the whole region is covered by huge snowbanks, it is impossible to bring a doctor to him. During a vigil at the bedside of the desperately ill man, Beret convinces him that it is a minister he needs rather than a doctor. On her insistence that it is imperative to make the attempt to fetch a minister, Per Hansa, although suspecting that he is going to his death, finally dons his skis and departs in a wild whirl of snow. He does not return. The sick man dies and is placed in the deep snow to await burial in the spring. When the snows melt the cadaver of Per Hansa is discovered not far from home, sitting on a stump, his skis beside him, looking toward the West—the "sunset land" of his hopes and ambitions. Beret's fearsome piety has sent him to his death.

IX

In the second book of the trilogy, *Peder Victorious*, the sense of involvement into which the reader has been coerced has diminished. Now that Per Hansa is dead, what is there to care about? Beret? Yet, one is curious about her. She has developed courage and has hardened into a self-sufficient pioneer woman. She is mistress of her home and of her farm, which continues to thrive. The community has acquired a school, a church, a minister, and neighbors of various ancestry. Her children, with the exception of her youngest, have become alienated from her. Peder Victorious, her only American-born child, whom she has dedicated to the service of her Protestant God, is drawn to a girl of Irish parentage who is a Catholic. Beret has accepted that the scrambling of various strains is inevitable in the American environment. Though she disapproves, she does not voice her protest. Rather than lose her son, she accepts a Catholic daughter-in-law.

The third book, *Their Fathers' God*, again involves the reader in some suspense. Will the marriage of these two people, each nurtured in a different belief, endure? Will the effect of the American environment succeed in neutralizing the pull of conflicting traditions? No, the marriage turns out to be a rocky one. Neither husband nor wife is able to overcome the divisive influences. The author's message is still the same: It cannot be done. The young couple seem to be in the grip of rival gods and rival dogmas. Their offspring is baptized by the grandmother in the Protestant faith and by the mother in the Catholic faith. Though Rölvaag seemed to have realized that the separation of different religious groups is not possible in the American environment, his attitude was not that of Hector St. John de Crèvecoeur, an eighteenth-century newcomer from France who observed approvingly: "I could point to a family whose grandfather was an Englishman, whose wife was Dutch, whose son married a Frenchwoman and whose present four sons have now four wives of different nations."[31] With messianic zeal the author restated the doctrines to which he had committed himself thirty years before:

You have been entrusted with a rich inheritance, an inheritance built up through the ages. Isn't it your irrevocable duty to see how much of it you can preserve and hand down to those coming after you? A people that has lost its traditions is doomed.[32]

X

Rölvaag's triumph in becoming a successful writer was dimmed by his steadily deteriorating health. The discovery that he had tubercular scars on his lungs confirmed the fear he had always felt, that like his brother and sister he would not escape the dread disease of tuberculosis. When he started the sequel to *Giants* he knew he had not much time left. He completed it in 1929, and in 1931 the third volume of the trilogy.

The second book made him a celebrity. He was overwhelmed by requests for lectures and speaking engagements, including a series of lectures at the University of Chicago. In 1929 he received an honorary degree from the University of Wisconsin, for his books had brought immortality to the pioneers of the Northwest. The Norwegian government also took note of his accomplishments. He was invited to be the guest of the Norwegian government at the commemoration of Ibsen's birth. He used the opportunity to give a series of talks on the "Vikings of the Western Prairies."[33]

But his heart was failing rapidly. He died in the fall of 1931, outliving his father by only a few months. Had his father, he remarked in a letter to his brother, found more "elbowroom" in Norway, he would have been a man of "greater consequence." America gave Ole Edvart Rölvaag the "elbowroom" he would not have had in Norway. In America he acquired an education, which was the *sine qua non* for success as a writer. In the magnitude of the American experience he found the theme that would engage his writer's imagination to the fullest.

SELMAN ABRAHAM WAKSMAN
1888-

A World Benefactor

He is the discoverer of a series of wonder drugs that he himself designated "antibiotics." The best known of them is streptomycin, which opened the way to the treatment of many infections resistant to penicillin and sulfa therapy, notably tuberculosis.

As the director of the Institute of Microbiology at Rutgers University, which was built and equipped with funds from royalties on streptomycin and other antibiotics that he and his students isolated, he continued at the Institute until the age of eighty to direct research in the field of microbiology.

The European Setting

At the turn of the century the mass of immigrants from Russia were Jews. The heavy exodus was caused by a series of pogroms that began in 1881 and continued into the twentieth century. Thousands of the young and the old were slaughtered and their homes were destroyed. The causes of the pogroms were embedded in the socioeconomic cultural pattern of czarist Russia. The bulk of the Russian people consisted of a peasant class, numerically the largest, a landholding group, most of whom were members of the nobility, and a subgroup of town laborers, artisans, and middlemen. Peasant huts dotted the vast expanse of Russia, which struck travelers as being composed of interminable stretches of fields, forests, and rivers. In this seemingly illimitable landscape towns appeared to be relatively scarce.

The Jews generally huddled in certain areas of villages and towns of old Russia, which were known as the "Pale." Not being permitted to own land, they sometimes rented small sections of land, or they eked out a living as artisans, small merchants, or town laborers. The landholding class, when not residing in their town houses or abroad, lived on their country estates in old-fashioned splendor reminiscent of bygone eras. But the peasants, who had been freed from serfdom in 1861, were abysmally poor. Not only were individual farms too small to yield a sufficient livelihood, but there was also a large peasant proletariat who owned no land at all and were forced to subsist as paupers and mendicants. Illiterate, backward, and driven by horrendous superstitions, they let their rage and misery spill over into murderous attacks on the Jews. In order to deflect the wrath into channels that did not threaten the government, the authorities deliberately encouraged the peasants to vent their fury thus. For instance, in describing the pogrom of 1903 the daughter of the Yiddish writer, Sholom Aleichem, says: "The pogrom was instigated by the Czarist government to 'drown the revolution in Jewish blood,' with the local police looking on and five thousand troops in their barracks."[1]

Most of the Jews were not much better off than the peasants. Theirs was a hand-to-mouth existence. But they were sustained by their religious faith and the ethical traditions which were part of their ancient heritage as well as by cultural strivings which town life encouraged. These factors set the Jews apart from the peasants and stamped them as irreversibly alien. Yet, the peasants and the Jews were dependent upon one another. The Jews acted as middlemen, buying the produce from the peasants and supplying them with their necessities. In the towns were to be found the intellectuals and the socialists, who agitated for political change and fanned the spirit of rebellion. Though between Jews and peasants there frequently existed genuine fondness, the Jews found their existence to be one of constant dread. As Selman Waksman explains:

One of the most despicable tricks of the old Russian government was to use the Jews as cat's paws for diverting from it the anger of the city and village population. When it appeared that violence was about to break out against government agencies, either among the workers or the peasants, intensive propaganda was started at once through the government subsidized press, or through some other devious and insidious channels, to the effect that the Jews were all socialists and revolutionaries and were largely responsible for the major hardships that had befallen the country.[2]

What added to the hopelessness of the situation in which the Jews found themselves was the stifling lack of opportunity for Jewish children. The number permitted to attend secondary schools was extremely low because of a very stiff *"numerus clausus"* (quota) and distance from the centers where such schools were located. Admission to the universities was even more difficult, the quota being two to three percent.[3] The only path to education open to Jewish students was to become non-matriculated students or "externs." Educated by private tutors, "externs" could present themselves annually, upon payment of stipulated fees, at any gymnasium for a formal examination. If they passed the final tests they received a matriculation certificate, but it was hard for "externs" to be admitted to universities because they lacked grades by which their scholastic abilities could be judged. Competition invariably favored those who were fortified with high grades and gold and silver medals, which were awarded only to matriculated students. To enroll in foreign universities, as many were forced to do, was an unsatisfactory solution, for it meant that after returning to Russia they would encounter the same prejudice in employment.

Thus, while for many who sought entrance to the United States the primary motive for the flight from Russia was the fear of bloody persecution, an ancillary spur was undoubtedly the expectation of being able to improve their economic condition. But there were also those who were drawn to America by still another magnet—the dream of self-improvement and education without the discrimination practiced in Russia.

This was the ambition that brought the twenty-two-year-old student, Selman Abraham Waksman, to America in 1910.

The American Setting

During the first decade of the twentieth century America too was seething with demands for reform. But the changes for which the American people agitated were of a different kind from those that were desperately required in autocratic Russia. The reforms demanded by the "muckrakers," so dubbed by President Theodore Roosevelt, were the regulation of "Big Business," which appeared to have become too powerful in controlling American life, the elimination of graft and political abuse on all government levels, and measures to improve the common welfare.

Strident and preoccupied with its own affairs, America in 1910 was basking in the deceptive security of the nineteenth century. There seemed to be no threatening clouds on the horizon. America had sent a diplomatic note to the czar's government protesting the pogroms, but Europe and particularly Russia seemed worlds away. However, the outbreak of World War I, with its immediate clamor for munitions and subsidies, brought the awareness that the oceans separating the American land-mass from the European and Asiatic continents did not constitute a sufficient bulwark against foreign involvements. Another effect of the war, even before we became embroiled in it, was to put an end to the domestic reforms intended to improve the quality of life for Americans. The war also spawned a hydra-headed progeny in releasing a spirit of illiberalism that manifested itself among other things in intensified demands to curtail free immigration, in "Red-baiting," and in increased hostility to labor.

The first assault on free immigration had been made at the end of the nineteenth century with an attempt to impose a literacy test on incoming immigrants. Vetoed initially by President Cleveland, later by President Taft, and twice by President Wilson, it was finally repassed in 1917 over Wilson's veto.

However, the enactment of a literacy test proved itself an insufficient bar to containing the continuing flood of immigration. In 1921 and again in 1924 more restrictive anti-immigration acts were passed, and 1929 brought the enforcement of permanent quotas on the basis of "national origin." A direct legacy of the war was the Great Depression. It achieved what lawmakers had not been able to bring about through legislation: a change in the pattern of immigration. For the first time in the history of the nation the number of people who left the United States exceeded those seeking admission.

Thus, by a succession of events, some of which "the fathers" of our country had specifically warned against, America entered the period referred to as "reaching maturity." This revealed itself in the acceptance of new and unaccustomed responsibilities, among other things, as well as in mounting achievements in the cultural and scientific fields. The progress in pure science during the early decades of the twentieth century was spectacular and disproved the belittling opinions that American scientists (among whom were to be counted an increasing number of the foreign-born) were incapable of achievements greater than the putting to use of discoveries made by Europeans.

The promotion of the practical aspects of science had received its initial encouragement in the second half of the nineteenth century through the enactment of the Morrill Act of 1862, which had granted land subsidies to colleges that would teach subjects relating to "Agriculture and the Mechanic Arts" (in addition to humanistic studies). There was in existence also a Bureau of Animal Studies in Washington, where, in the 1890's, Theobald Smith, acknowledged to be the first of the microbe hunters in the United States, tracked down the cause of "Texas fever" in cattle.[4] By the end of the century several scientists had reached distinguished positions in the various fields of pure science. Outstanding among them were Joseph Henry, physicist and director of the Smithsonian Institution, Benjamin Silliman, professor of chemistry at Yale University, and Josiah Willard Gibbs, professor of mathematical physics at Yale.

It is claimed that "America came of age earlier in zoology and botany than in physics and chemistry."[5] Some of the most startling scientific developments of the twentieth century affected the fields of chemistry and physics, as well as biology, medicine, nutrition, and public health. All branches of science began to find encouragement and aid in various government-sponsored agencies—the United States Public Health Service, established in 1912, the Science Advisory Board, created in 1933, the National Science Foundation of 1950—as well as through grants and subsidies amounting to billions of dollars.

Among the microbe hunters of the twentieth century none played a more conspicuous part in the advancement of the "life sciences" than Selman Waksman, an immigrant from Russia.

I

His birthplace was a small town near Kiev in the steppes of the Ukraine "down where the Dnieper flows." The Ukraine was the granary of Russia and of much of Europe and a place of great charm. Celebrated by Russian poets for the beauty of the countryside, the softness of the air, and the song of the nightingale, in Keats's words singing "of summer in full-throated ease," it was a place to remember.

He was born in 1888, at a time when the Jews of Russia felt they were living under the sword of Damocles. His pious Jewish family was governed by matriarchal women. But the dominance of women did not denote a culture of poverty, as it does in the Negro and Puerto Rican matrifocal households of today. His mother had a small business of her own, as her mother had had before her. The home in which the family lived had been built by his mother out of what she earned in her store while her husband was serving in the Russian army. These women managed their homes, bore children, and cared for their little enterprises, while many of their husbands spent their days and nights studying the Hebrew commentaries. Nor did these female breadwinners hold their husbands in low esteem. On the contrary, because the desire to immerse oneself in Talmudic studies denoted an intellectual bent, it was highly respected.

The governance of women was due to the fact that they were energetic and competent. Waksman's grandmother, who had been a widow since the age of thirty, had raised eight daughters while managing her commission business without benefit of reading, writing, or arithmetic, keeping her accounts in chalk marks intelligible only to herself. On her earnings she had married off her eight daughters, a not inconsiderable achievement in countries where dowries were an essential requirement for marriage. The boy's mother followed the precept of her own mother in becoming the financial mainstay of her family and exercising a strong influence in her home.

Waksman was an only son and, after the death of a younger sister, an only child. The loss of his sister, who died because a shipment of diphtheria antitoxin arrived too late, served to make him aware before the age of ten of the lifesaving aspects of science. He was taught privately, at first the daily prayers and rudiments of the Bible, and later the more advanced Jewish lore. Aware of the demands of the outside world, his mother engaged tutors for him who supplemented religious education with instruction in the Russian language, in history, geography, and mathematics. He was also an avid reader, he tells us, not only of the Russian writers, but also of foreign classics in translation.

Influenced by the example of his mother, who never refused to help the poorer members of the family, or the poor of the town, he began while still in his teens to teach free of charge other boys who were not receiving a secular education. In this project he enlisted the help of other boys who were being privately taught, and he tells us it was the responsibility of all to collect money for such expenses as books, paper, pencils, and also in order to have some cash with which to bribe the police when they came to raid the "school" as an unauthorized establishment. The experience of teaching others was to prove valuable to him, for as he progressed in his education he was able to tutor Russian children for entrance to various schools. Later, as a college student in America, he instructed foreigners in the English language and prepared some for admission to college.

As soon as he was old enough to leave home, Waksman became a nonmatriculated student—an "extern." Under the supervision of a tutor he prepared for the annual examinations given at the local gymnasium. These examinations were an ordeal, for the examining teachers were more likely than not to indulge in spiteful chicanery. Isaac Babel, a promising Soviet writer who was liquidated during the Stalin purges, expatiates on this phase of his youth by stating: "The teachers used to put cunning questions to Jewish boys; no one else was asked such devilish questions."[6] Waksman, however, passed his final examination and received a certificate that he possessed the necessary preparation for entering a university.

But admission to a Russian university was even more severely limited to Jewish students than the secondary schools. This and the fact that his mother had died made him think seriously of America. Urged by relatives who had emigrated before him, he decided to cut the ties to his birthplace. It was 1910 and he was twenty-two. Only sons, he tells us, were sometimes exempted from military service. As one who had received exemption, he was able to depart in broad daylight, instead of being smuggled across the border in the dead of night, which was the usual experience of young Russian males subject to military call-up. He was accompanied by four childhood friends, one of whom was the brother of the girl he planned to marry. This future brother-in-law had not been able to pass his final examination as an "extern," which made it more difficult for him to succeed in America than for Selman Waksman. After the outbreak of the revolution in Russia his brother-in-law permitted himself to be lured back to the country of his birth, a decision he regretted bitterly when the Bolsheviks came to power. As the train was crossing the German border, Waksman tells us, they broke out into a tumultuous chant: "We have shaken the shackles off our feet, / We are entering upon a new world." On the way to freedom all could afford to be optimistic, for the future was unknown to them.

II

A newly arrived immigrant was a helpless person. What could he do but allow himself to be carried along by the direction supplied by relatives or friends? In Waksman's case a cousin helped him in finding his bearings in the new environment, thus determining the course of his life.

The cousin owned a poultry and vegetable farm a few miles from Rutgers University in New Brunswick. He was passionately interested in scientific farming and husbandry. This environment suited the newcomer, whose memories of a rural life were still vivid and who was drawn to scientific exploration. Because it was November, he could not enter college until the following autumn. While he worked around the farm learning essential facts about seed germination, plant growth, decomposition of plant and animal residues, he applied at the College of Physicians and Surgeons at Columbia University and was accepted. Throughout the nineteenth century and the first decade of the twentieth, discrimination in American colleges and universities against foreigners who had the requisite preparation for higher training was nonexistent. Hence, the immigrant who was strongly motivated to improve his position through education encountered no stumbling blocks. Education was one of the chief avenues through which newcomers were able to achieve spectacular successes in the American environment.

Under the tutelage of his cousin Waksman found himself more drawn to the "underlying reactions" which govern the growth of plants and animals under specific conditions. He became so engrossed in the problem of chemical reactions as they affect living matter that he began to doubt whether the study of medicine was the best field for him. Consultation with Dr. Jacob G. Lipman, a Russian who was the head of the Department of Bacteriology at Rutgers University, convinced him that experimentation with plant genetics and soil conditions would offer him a fuller outlet for his interests. When he was granted a state scholarship, the die was cast. He dropped his intention of studying medicine. What he wished to study about was:

the numerous chemical and microbiological processes that go on in the soil and that result in the liberation of a continuous stream of nutrients which make possible the continuity of life and which serve to complete that chain of living reactions in nature. It was to the soil, therefore, that I decided to go for an answer to the many problems that had begun to puzzle me about the cycle of life in nature. This gradually led me to the study of the microscopic population of the soil, its role in soil processes, and the biochemical activities of microorganisms, problems that were to become the crowning glory of my research career.[7]

For a year and a half he commuted to college from his cousin's farm, but at the end of the sophomore year he realized it was essential for him to be able to spend more time at the laboratory and in the library. He also found it necessary to earn money, which was not possible at the home of his cousin. Living at the College Farm grounds provided several sources for earning sufficient money for his upkeep. One was to teach English to foreigners living in New Brunswick.

By the end of the junior year Waksman had accumulated all the credits required for graduation, and he was able to devote most of his time during the senior year to research. His assignment was to study different groups of microorganisms occurring in the soil. As the only student majoring in soil bacteriology, he was placed with a group of graduate students. He was surprised to find growing on the agar plates that he had prepared from water suspensions of soil, in addition to bacterial and fungus colonies, other organisms which looked under the microscope like fungi, but were the size of bacteria. In discussing it with more expert researchers, it was decided they were a type of microbe, perhaps a group of "Higher Bacteria," named *Actinomyces*, about which little was known. He had no intimation that *Actinomyces* would become the major preoccupation of his life, but from then on he never lost interest in them.

At graduation he was elected to Phi Beta Kappa. One of his teachers, Byron Halstead, a Quaker, whose assistant he had been, gave him the key as a graduation present. Waksman developed such an admiration for him that when his son was born (Halstead was dead by then) the child was named after him. Dr. Halstead was not the only one among his teachers who helped him in his transition from being a foreigner into being an American. In addition to Dr. Lipman, whom he considered a special friend and benefactor (later naming a laboratory after him), Waksman mentions in his memoirs several others who took more than a perfunctory interest in his progress. He remarks of one: "He took infinite pains in teaching me the proper enunciation and diction." Of another he says: "Dr. North [professor of General Chemistry] took special interest in me personally and encouraged me in various ways to come to him with my questions and problems."

Waksman is not an isolated example of those who benefit by the American educational system. Many other immigrants found in American teachers a constant source of encouragement that exceeded the demands of duty. Teachers were wont to hearten and guide them, to correct their speech and manners, to lend money, and to aid them in the solution of personal problems. The paths of many immigrants were eased tremendously by the understanding shown them by their American teachers. School, whether primary or professional, often (though not always) proved an oasis in the rigor of the immigrant existence, offering the only means of acquiring experience without hurt to the ego.

III

A college graduate! What next? The decision that confronted Waksman was whether to get a job or to continue with his studies. If the latter, where? At Rutgers University, where he could pursue the research he had begun, or at another school, where he could obtain more advanced training? He accepted Dr. Lipman's offer to remain as a research assistant in soil bacteriology at the New Jersey Agricultural Experiment Station. Continuing to devote himself to the soil's "microbiological population"—the soil fungi and actinomycetes—he worked with such absorption from the early morning hours until late at night as to cause people to question him whether he worked through the night as well. During that year he became a citizen, achieved publication of his first scientific paper in the *Journal of Bacteriology*, and at the end of the year received a Master's degree and several offers of fellowships to continue doctoral studies. He chose the University of California at Berkeley on the basis of its reputation and the monetary value of the fellowship offered him. The head of his department was a biochemist who had been a student of the famous Dr. Jacques Loeb. Waksman's intention was to explore the study of biochemistry, but he took along various cultures of actinomycetes and fungi he had developed at the laboratories at Rutgers.

The trip to California became a honeymoon trip. Before setting out Waksman married the sister of his friend who had emigrated with him. She had followed her brother shortly after his departure from Russia. On borrowed money the young couple set out for California, intending to see America from one end to the other. Traveling by night and sightseeing by day, they traversed the continent, stopping like so many honeymooners of that day at Niagara Falls and, because he wanted to meet some scientists of whose work he knew, at Chicago, and at the more famous landmarks of the West.

His stay of two years at Berkeley culminated in the acquisition of the Doctor's degree. Not having been assigned a specific research project in biochemistry, he continued to devote himself to the soil microbes. Had he been given a research problem in biochemistry, he explains, it would have led him into the field of pure biochemistry. He would then have been deflected from the study of the organisms that was to bring to mankind benefits of such magnitude and to him undreamed-of fame. He was finished before the allotted period, and while he waited to receive his degree he accepted a position in a commercial laboratory producing antitoxins, serums, and vaccines. It was valuable experience, for it prepared him for a more responsible job in an industrial laboratory when after his return to Rutgers he found it imperative to supplement his income.

IV

A Ph.D.! Again the important decision of what to turn to next. Waksman had a choice between a full-time job in a commercial laboratory and several teaching positions, including an offer from Dr. Lipman at Rutgers University. Though it was the least remunerative, it was the position he accepted, and until his salary at the college was sufficient for his needs he supplemented it with earnings from a job in an industrial laboratory.

At that time he was following what he calls the "soil approach" in microbiology. This line of research kept him from studying any aspect of the problem not directly connected with the nature of the chemical reactions brought about by microbes in the soil and their role in soil fertility. Like Sir Alexander Fleming, the discoverer of penicillin, who observed the first mold in 1919, but did not perceive its significance until 1940 when penicillin was "rediscovered," Waksman was not ready to regard the actinomycetes from the point of view of their possible function as growth-inhibitors upon other microbes. The discovery of streptomycin in 1943 came about after he had switched in the late 1930's to the "biological approach," which riveted his attention on the possibility that the soil microbes might have a function in the treatment of human and animal diseases. He admits that until then he "barely thought of the problems concerned with causation of disease."[8]

During the years that followed, Waksman built up the Department of Soil Microbiology and traveled extensively to European scientific centers where experimentation in the field of microbiology was conducted. He also wrote several textbooks. A steady increase in the number of graduate students and visiting foreign investigators in his department helped to center attention on the work he and his students were doing. Foreign students came from all the countries of Western Europe as well as from the Orient. During the ten-year period between 1929 and 1939, which he calls his "humus" period, Waksman extended his researches to the study of marine bacteria and peat formations and traveled extensively in the United States, Europe, and the Holy Land for the purpose of studying the nature of peat and bog formations. The year 1939 marked the beginning of a new period characterized by his determination to study soil microbes from a totally different point of view.

V

Among the foreign students who came to Rutgers to do advanced work in his laboratories was René Dubos, a Frenchman. After he received the Ph.D. from Rutgers, Waksman recommended Dubos to the Rockefeller Institute. There in the early 1930's Dubos isolated an organism which produced an antibacterial substance, tyrothricin. It proved itself effective in attacking the pneumococcus bacillus.

By Waksman's own admission, the proof supplied by René Dubos that bacteria could be used to inhibit disease-producing bacteria influenced him tremendously.[9] Another important factor was that war would bring new diseases and epidemics. (World War I had brought influenza.) In 1939, Waksman reveals, he recommended to the director of the experiment station that he and his group of students investigate the possibilities of using the soil microbes for the control of infectious diseases. The project was approved, and all the members of the staff were set to working on his problem. Within a year, in 1940, the first "antibiotic" was isolated from a culture of an actinomycete. It was called actinomycin.

This was the beginning of a cycle of developments that culminated in the discovery of streptomycin, the drug that demonstrated its effectiveness in the treatment of diseases resistant to penicillin and the sulfa drugs. It proved the "first chemo-therapeutic means" (salvarsan was the "first true chemo-therapeutic agent")[10] by which tuberculosis, notably tubercular meningitis, intestinal infections, typhoid, typhus, leprosy, and syphilis could be successfully treated. At the request of an editor of a journal, Waksman coined the word "antibiotic." He explains the functions of antibiotics as follows:

They are products of microbial growth. They have the peculiar property of inhibiting the growth or even of destroying other microbes. More important, they are active not only in the test tube, but also in the human and animal body. They also have a selective action upon different bacteria and other microbes, and may thus be destructive to some organisms and not to others, be injurious to pathogenic organisms and not to cell tissues. . . . Although efforts had been made to utilize antibiotics for combating infectious diseases prior to 1939, it was on the eve of the second World War that this phase of microbiology, which was to revolutionize medical science, took a new lease on life.[11]

The first product, actinomycin, proved too toxic and had to be set aside, though years later, Waksman asserts, it was claimed to be effective against Hodgkin's disease.[12] Intensive teamwork produced a succession of products that were less toxic, but not entirely satisfactory, until the appearance of streptomycin. It was an outgrowth of research done on an organism called *Streptomyces griseus,* which was first isolated by Waksman and a coworker at Rutgers in 1915. It had not been tested for antibacterial properties then, because at that time the interest of the two researchers did not center on antibiotics.

V

In the development of streptomycin Waksman received financial help from several philanthropic organizations, notably the Commonwealth Fund and the Lasker Foundation, as well as the support of Merck and Company and later the clinical assistance of the Mayo Clinic. Merck and Company had established a fellowship in 1938, and later they increased their participation in the program by providing chemical assistance, experimental animals, and chemical equipment. In return, they received the rights to processes that were patentable, for which they were to pay the university a royalty of two and a half percent on patents that would prove valuable. The patents for streptomycin bore the names of Waksman and one of his collaborators.

Streptomycin was thus developed without any governmental assistance, in contrast to penicillin, on which the American government is said to have spent about six hundred million dollars.[13] In 1946, when it became evident that the possibilities of streptomycin were immense, Merck and Company, on the suggestion of Dr. Waksman, voluntarily relinquished the rights to exclusive manufacture and reassigned the patents to the university.

It was then the trustees of Rutgers University decided to establish the Rutgers Research and Endowment Corporation for the specific purpose of handling patent rights as well as the income from royalties. It was a way of shielding the university from criticism over relinquishing to commercial exploitation a process intended to save human lives. The purpose of patenting the process, Waksman explains, was to insure uniform standards of production. Commercial competition was the cause for the huge drop in price from twenty-five dollars a gram in 1946 to a few cents in 1962.[14]

Production of the drug began in 1945, and from the very beginning output and, consequently, royalties, climbed steadily. By the 1950's nearly twenty million grams per month were being produced. In addition to eight American companies, two in England, four in Japan, one in Sweden, and two in Italy were engaged in the manufacture of streptomycin. In the United States alone the output amounted to hundreds of millions of dollars a year. The funds collected in royalties enabled the university to plan for the establishment of the Institute for Microbiology with extensive facilities for research. It was opened in 1954, with Dr. Waksman as its first director.

In 1946, when Merck and Company reassigned the patents to Rutgers Research Foundation, the trustees offered Waksman twenty percent as compensation for the additional duties he would be assuming in looking after license arrangements and the coordination of other practical details. He accepted the compensation, he says, so that he would be enabled to dispose of some of the funds in establishing fellowships and in promoting research in other institutions. When the royalties proved higher than he expected, he cut his share voluntarily to ten percent and turned over the other half for distribution to all his students and associates who were active in the development of the antibiotic program. Later, he again assigned half of his ten percent to a foundation for microbiology[15] to promote the study of the science throughout the world.

The consequences of fame soon began to make themselves felt. As testimonials praising the efficacy of the drug poured in,

Waksman found himself overwhelmed with honors and awards from scientific centers and universities all over the world. Requests to deliver lectures and to outline research programs poured in. He attended medical congresses and scientific councils and visited hospitals, where doctors brought out patients his discovery had saved from certain death. His lectures in Russia were published in book form by the publishing house of the Russian Academy of Science. Governments and scientific institutions clamored for his presence. He found himself famous all over the world.

VI

This "era of good feelings" was soon interrupted. In March, 1950, a student who had helped in isolating streptomycin returned from a stay in the army and brought a suit against Waksman and against the Rutgers Research Foundation for a share of the royalties, and also to enjoin Waksman to forgo claiming to be the sole discoverer of the antibiotic. His collaborator's name had appeared on the patent. After enduring what he calls a "nightmare existence," Waksman recommended that his former student be paid a hundred and twenty-five thousand dollars and three percent of the royalties. He was also legally and scientifically recognized as the coinventor. Waksman explains that he capitulated on the advice of friends and interested persons who feared that long litigation would postpone the plans for the Institute for Microbiology, which was to be the crown of his scientific efforts.

The suit brought against him resulted in his decision that all his coworkers in the laboratory where streptomycin had been developed should receive some financial compensation for their efforts. He suggested that the original half of his share which he had returned to the Rutgers Research Foundation be distributed among all of the twenty-six students and assistants who had participated in the program. He explains:

After all, there would have been no streptomycin had it not been preceded by streptothricin; there would have been no streptothricin were it not for actinomycin. Furthermore, if a student or assistant who streaks out a bacterial plate, or inoculates a flask, or makes a chemical determination is entitled to scientific consideration, the assistant who washes the dishes, or makes up the medium, or prepares the chemicals has also made a contribution toward a solution of a scientific problem, even if his name does not appear in the scientific report. A great scientific contribution is like a beautiful mosaic made up of many stones, or like a marvelous symphony to which many musicians contribute their share, but no one of which constitutes the mosaic or the symphony itself.

The apogee in Waksman's career came in 1952, when he received the Nobel Prize. Receptions and celebrations awaited him wherever he went. Parents brought to him children, otherwise doomed, whom streptomycin had brought back to life.

In addition, the building which was to be the Institute for Microbiology was nearing completion. Waksman looked upon it as "the climax of my lifetime association with microbes and the study of their role in the cycle of life in nature and in human welfare." Through his work, microbiology, hitherto considered one of the "borderline sciences," was raised to new importance.

In 1963 Waksman was stricken by peritonitis following a rupture of the appendix during a lecture tour through South America. His life was saved by antibiotics, but he was warned to curtail his activities. At the age of eighty he was still active in research at the Institute and as a trustee of the Oceanographic Institute at Woods Hole in Massachusetts.

Waksman concludes his autobiography with this paragraph:

Let, therefore, this humble story of the life of one who has devoted himself to the study of nature and natural processes serve to remind those who chance to read these lines that truth is universal, that man is more than a mere collector of facts or fancies, that the human spirit is continuous and universal, that the lowest abodes may hide treasures as promising as the great palaces, that man, if given the opportunity, will identify himself with the spiritual and cultural values which have made him what he is and which distinguish him from other creatures of nature.[18]

DAVID DUBINSKY
1892-

The Genesis of a Labor Leader

The name of David Dubinsky is inextricably interwoven with the International Ladies' Garment Workers Union. He did not create the union, but he remade it at a time when its existence was threatened. He resuscitated it after it had fallen into a state of dangerous weakness through internal dissension. After nursing it back to health, he guided it so competently that it was never threatened again. Under his management the workers achieved economic security and a host of personal benefits. The union became one of the most forward-looking organizations in the labor movement and a bulwark in the preservation of democratic principles.

The European Setting

Among the immigrant groups that caused a tremendous swelling in immigration between 1880 and 1914 were the Jews, whose desperate need to escape from various Eastern European countries was due to the twin scourges of persecution and stifling poverty. From 1900 to 1914 alone approximately a hundred thousand were added annually to the population of the United States.[1] The heaviest exodus was from White Russia, the Ukraine, and that part of Poland which Russia annexed after the partition of the country. Most newcomers were chiefly laborers, but there were among them some skilled workers, shopkeepers, and middlemen.

In Austria-Hungary, which also contributed heavily to the increase in our population during that period by sending us large numbers of Jews and other minority groups (of whom she had more than any other European nation), the treatment of the Jews was less harsh than in Russia. The daughter of the celebrated Jewish writer Sholom Aleichem asserts: "They [Jews in Austria] suffered no official discrimination—there were no specific anti-Jewish laws on the statute books. All the educational institutions were open to them...."[2] Though Jews were permitted to enter government service and the professions, advancement was limited and slow at best, unless they converted to Roman Catholicism, a practice that was prevalent before World War I. The position of the Jews was incomparably worse in Rumania, where persecution was frequent and vicious.[3] The worst conditions existed in the dominions of the czar. The Jews lived in such dread of the Cossacks that even after years of life in the United States immigrants remembered "the Cossack's whip with undimmed horror."[4]

In Russia most Jews had no alternative but to accept a fate of a hopeless, abject, hand-to-mouth existence for themselves and their progeny. The American writer, Harold Frederic, who represented the *New York Times* in London at the turn of the century, showed himself to be unusually sympathetic to the plight of the Jews in Russia. After traveling through Russia and observing the conditions under which they lived, he wrote: "I have never seen anywhere in Europe, not even in the poorer part of Ireland which I know well, a more terrible poverty than is the rule of their lives."[5]

Later, when Jewish immigration to the United States was in full swing, the Jews found another sympathizer in Lincoln Steffens, who was fascinated with the Jews of New York's East Side and their lore. He admits he was "almost a Jew" and explains:

I had become as infatuated with the Ghetto as Eastern boys were with the wild west and nailed a mazuza [a receptacle containing the ten commandments which orthodox Jews place on the entrance to their doors] on my office door; on Yom Kippur I spent the whole twenty-four hours fasting and going from one synagogue to another.... My friends laughed at me; especially the Jews among them scoffed. "You are more Jewish than us Jews," they said.... But there were some respecters of my respect.[6]

What finally initiated the flight of Jews from Russia were outbreaks of "pogroms" which began in the 1880's. The number of Jews who fled between April, 1881, and June, 1882 alone is given as two hundred and twenty-five thousand. The exodus continued for the rest of the nineteenth century and received a fresh impetus from the pogroms of Kishinev in 1903, when a desperate peasantry was deliberately encouraged to vent their wrath upon the Jews by burning and looting their homes and butchering young and old, while the police and soldiers stood by unconcerned. The idea was "Kill Jews and Save Russia."[7]

The Jews were not the only group in Russia who were in the grip of despair. The intelligentsia had long smoldered with resentment over the repressions imposed by the autocratic regimes of the czars. Reforms had been fitfully introduced since the reign of Alexander II, who had freed the serfs in 1861, but they were insufficient and were frequently extinguished after a short trial period. By the end of the nineteenth century the Industrial Revolution had taken firm hold in Russia and had created a working class that longed for Western liberties and, in their absence, listened avidly to socialist doctrines. The discontent of the Russian people came to a head during the Russo-Japanese War, when the reverses suffered by the Russian military forces provided the impetus for the uprising of 1905. Forced by circumstances Nicholas II granted in the October Manifesto a national parliament—the Duma—and promised many individual liberties on the Western model. One of these was a decree permitting the formation of labor unions.

These concessions were accepted with general rejoicing by all but the revolutionary groups, who preferred a clean sweep. Such measures were palliatives to them—"capitalist reformism" —which would only delay the revolution they considered necessary for the common good and for which they plotted with fanatical zeal. The Jewish workers embraced the Jewish Workers' Union, or the "Bund," as it was called, with jubilation. But before long Nicholas II experienced misgivings and began to whittle away at the privileges he had granted. Union organizers found themselves persecuted, imprisoned, and banished to Siberia. Among them were two teen-age youths—David Dubinsky and Sidney Hillman—who were destined to play important roles in the growth of the American labor movement.

It was fear mostly that made the Jews of the Pale more and more susceptible to the siren song of America. Harold Frederic, who seems to have had an intuitive foreknowledge of the role these newcomers were destined to play in America, prophesied:

The woebegone outcast in cap and caftan, wandering forth dismayed into exile, will take heart again. His children's children may shape a nation's finance, or give law to literature or sway a Parliament. At least they will be abreast of their fellows, they will be a living part of their generation; they will be freemen, fearing neither famine nor the knout.[8]

Most Jewish immigrants left Russia by stealth. Men subject to military service were not permitted to emigrate. Conveyed to the edge of the border in peasant carts, covered by a load of hay or other produce, and quaking with fear as they listened to an exchange of banter between their guides and police stationed at various checkpoints, most emigrants were smuggled out of Russia, or escaped in the dead of night. The story told by Vladimir Horowitz, that when he left Russia by train in 1925 he was reminded respectfully: "Do not please forget the motherland,"[9] was not the experience of the average Russian emigrant. Horowitz had a proper passport, but for most Jews wishing to leave the country passports were unobtainable. Instead, they had to run for their lives in the predawn hours, across bramble and stones or through the deep snow of winter until they stood on German soil. From there they made the journey by rail to where immigrant ships awaited their human cargo in Hamburg or Rotterdam to take them into freedom, if not into riches. As soon as they reached America and secured some kind of work, they began to scrimp and save pennies for purchase of steamship tickets for younger brothers and sisters, for relatives and friends, thus keeping up a one-way traffic to the "Golden Land" until the guns of World War I brought it to a halt.

The American Setting

At the end of the nineteenth century America was fully in the grip of industrial capitalism. During the decades following the Civil War the economic power of "Big Business" grew so enormously that in 1890 Congress found itself compelled to pass the Sherman Anti-Trust Act banning monopolies or combinations in restraint of trade. But adequate machinery to enforce the law was not provided. Though President Theodore Roosevelt (1901-1909) brought some prosecutions under the Anti-Trust Act, and his successor, William Howard Taft (1909-1913), pursued an even more vigorous antitrust policy, the growth of these giants went on unimpeded.

These gigantic combines in steel, coal, oil, meatpacking, railroad-building, absorbed thousands upon thousands of recent immigrants—Yugoslavs, Poles, Italians, as well as a continuing stream from the countries that had contributed to our population since the beginning of the Amercian experiment. In addition to the industrial behemoths, hosts of smaller entrepreneurs depended upon immigrant labor. All exploited immigrants by paying as little as they could and by extorting the utmost in effort. Richard Hofstadter describes the fret and fever that accompanied American industrial development: "With its rapid expansion, its exploitative methods, its desperate competition, post-bellum America was like a vast human caricature of the Darwinian struggle for existence and survival of the fittest."[10]

Among the enterprises depending upon immigrant labor were the manufacturers of clothing for men and women. The women's ready-to-wear business, in particular, was an offspring of the post-Civil War era. During the antebellum period prosperous American women wore custom-made clothes and their poorer sisters, homemade apparel. As for their outer wear, women wrapped themselves in shawls until the first clothing manufacturers, German businessmen, introduced cloaks for women. Their output was not very large; by 1880 it did not exceed thirty-two million dollars.[11]

After 1880 and the arrival of multitudes of Eastern European Jews, the needle trades grew with great rapidity. Of the Jews who went to work in shops and factories, three-fourths turned to the needle trades. By 1890 the number of shops had increased from 562 to 1224[12] and the output more than doubled to sixty-eight million dollars.[13] Not all factories were housed in "inside" shops or lofts under the direct supervision of the manufacturers. It became economically desirable to parcel out the work to contractors and subcontractors who turned out men's, women's, and children's wear in their living quarters on rented sewing machines, at prices that were lower only by pennies from those of their competitors.

To these places flocked thousands of recent Jewish immigrants. They were the most exploited of workers. As pieceworkers their wages were so meager that it was necessary to work twelve hours or more for mere subsistence. The price of needles, thread, and electric power was deducted from their miserable earnings. Their contractors, who differed from them only in that they had come to America somewhat earlier, could not succeed unless they "sweated" their workers. In the Darwinian world they learned very quickly that one who would be a victor could not afford to be softhearted, and no one strove more desperately to be a "victor" than a new immigrant.

From such conditions grew the movement to create a union for garment workers. Some newcomers were familiar with the benefits to be expected from union membership; those whose experiences in Europe had been remote from factory work learned fast in the atmosphere of misery and exploitation. The first attempts to enlist workers in a union were made in the late 1880's when the United Hebrew Trades was formed under socialist leadership.[14] Within two years the enrollment was six thousand. The first general strike occurred in 1890 and was led by one of the most beloved leaders in the needle trades, Joseph Barondess. The International Ladies' Garment Workers Union (I.L.G.W.U.) came into existence in 1900 and was immediately chartered by the American Federation of Labor. Established in 1881, the A.F. of L. was in 1900 far from being a powerful labor organization. A turbulent decade followed, during which bloody conflicts between police and strikers or scabs were everyday occurrences. Lincoln Steffens describes an "especially wretched case" that he observed in police headquarters while he held a job as labor reporter for the *New York Evening Post*:

an old Jew, who plainly had been hit many times with the long night sticks; across the nose and eyes, on the side of the head, on his right hand, left arm or shoulders, and his back. He was crying and shrank from the slightest touch. It was pitiful.[15]

Three major strikes occurring in 1910 marked the beginning of the growth of the unions for garment workers. The first strike, in which twenty thousand shirtwaist makers, mostly women, participated, lasted three months; the second, coming a few months later, was called by fifty-five thousand cloakmakers, who were men. A third strike, involving workers on men's wear in the Chicago factories of Hart, Schaffner and Marx, brought Sidney Hillman to the fore. All three strikes were marked by violence, injunctions, arrests, and bloodshed which shocked the public. The "Uprising of Twenty Thousand," as the strike of the shirtwaist makers was called, created such a vivid impression that it inspired three novels: *Nine-Tenths,* by James Oppenheim in 1911; *The Children of Light,* by Florence Converse in 1912; and *Comrade Yetta,* by Arthur Bullard in 1913.[16]

All three strikes resulted in sizable gains. Through the first strike, the I.L.G.W.U. gained a fifty-two-hour week, free electricity, free needles and thread for workers, and recognition of shop committees to deal with employers. The cloakmakers' strike ended in the "Protocols of Peace," which was engineered by Louis D. Brandeis (before his nomination to the Supreme Court) and Louis Marshall. It brought to the union full recognition and established the first machinery for conciliation and arbitration of disputes and grievances.[17]

Many changes and vicissitudes of fortune lay ahead of the I.L.G.W.U. It had to pass through the twin dangers of Communist infiltration and the Depression before it would become one of the most stable unions in American labor.

I

Like the lives of all the foreign-born who were old enough to have accumulated distinct recollections of the European homelands they left behind, David Dubinsky's life may be separated into two parts, the years before arrival in America and the period since. Differing in his experience from most newcomers, for whom life in America, at least in the beginning, was not unlike a slow groping through a dark and endless-seeming tunnel, he made a quick and fortunate decision that put him immediately on the path to a lifetime career. His life in the United States may itself be separated into two periods:

that between 1911 and 1932, which were years of maturing and preparation for the "big job," and the long stretch during which he remained at the helm of the I.L.G.W.U. He has been a member of the union, first as a worker and then as an executive during all his years in America, except for the first few months after his arrival. From a struggling, faction-ridden, quarreling organization of workers, it became under his direction a model union and an example of labor stability. His personal achievement and that of the union are identical. Though he has now retired from active management, his name and that of the I.L.G.W.U. have remained permanently interchangeable.

The first formative years were over for the nineteen-year-old youth when he stepped off the immigrant ship in 1911. He had had more than the usual experiences of young Europeans of his age. He had been arrested twice, had been imprisoned, and had traveled to Siberia with a prison convoy from which he had managed to escape.

Born in 1892 in Brest Litovsk (where Trotsky was to sign an armistice with Germany in 1918), the youngest of six children, Dubinsky was taken as a small child to Lodz, then as now a squalid industrial town in what had been Poland. There his father installed a brick oven and set himself up as a baker. The boy began his working career by becoming his father's helper. He had received the equivalent of a primary-school education in a school conducted by a Zionist organization, and this made him the best-educated member of the family. He joined the Bakers' Union (which owed its existence to the reforms granted by the czar in 1905) while he was still in his early teens and was soon elected assistant secretary. The reason was that he knew how to read and write Russian, Polish, and Yiddish. He also knew how to keep books. These were important assets among the backward people of Eastern Europe.

While still in his teens, Dubinsky organized a bakers' strike, which was won. But despite the privileges granted under the October Manifesto, strikes were frowned upon and he was put under arrest, then released with the understanding that he would remove himself from Lodz. He did, but not for long. When he returned, he was arrested again for attending an illegal meeting. This time he was sentenced to be deported to Siberia as a troublemaker whose activities were considered hostile to the state. Because he was under age, he was kept in various prisons before he could be sent to Siberia.[18] While in jail he came under the influence of intellectual revolutionaries who were also serving prison sentences. They introduced him to Gogol, Dostoevsky, Bakunin, and the American Christian Socialist, Edward Bellamy, who utopian novel, *Looking Backward,* had penetrated into Russia.[19] But though the contact with trained minds awakened an intellectual response in him, it was not sufficient to turn him permanently into an intellectual. He seems always to have preferred the role of activist to that of student.

When the prison convoy reached Siberia, he decided to make a break for freedom. Attempts at escape were frequently successful, because the guards welcomed the opportunity of pocketing the allowance of dead or escaped prisoners. One of the Russian prisoners who succeded in escaping was Trotsky, and before him many anarchists, among whom were Prince Kropotkin and Mikhail Bakunin, had fled and made their way to various countries on the continent. Falling back on his trade as a baker, Dubinsky took the road back to Lodz. But his desire to be a revolutionary had evaporated. He wanted to make a new start where there was a chance of success—in America. Upon being asked what he had expected of America, he replied with a promptness that indicated it was not a question by which he was surprised: "Freedom, equality, the opportunity to express myself for or against."[20] A steamship ticket from his brother, who had emigrated before him, came as a welcome opportunity to break away from Russia. His arrival in January, 1911, occurred a few months after the victorious general strikes that had contributed immensely to the strengthening of the I.L.G.W.U. Ten weeks after he entered the United States—on March 25, 1911— occurred the shocking Triangle Fire, which cost the lives of one hundred and forty-six people, mostly young Jewish and Italian immigrant girls.[21] The disaster produced such shock and revulsion that the state of New York set up a Factory Investigating Committee under Frances Perkins to look into safety conditions for workers in factories. Miss Perkins had been trained by Mrs. Florence Kelley, whom Governor Altgeld of Illinois had appointed in 1892 as the first Chief Factory Inspector of the state. Miss Perkins tackled the assignment with such thoroughness that she impressed Alfred E. Smith and later Franklin D. Roosevelt, both of whom retained her when they were elected governors of New York State. It was this assignment to investigate the Triangle Fire and the ensuing legislation for which she was responsible that started her on the road to becoming the first woman cabinet member as President Franklin D. Roosevelt's secretary of labor.

Those were the days of the infamous sweatshops. Thousands of new immigrants found their first jobs in dank, crowded, unhygienic places that exposed them to a variety of health hazards and subjected them to unbelievable discomforts. The white plague—tuberculosis—was rampant among garment workers, particularly among pressers who found the constant inhalation of steam injurious. The following is a description of a place of work by a man who began as a manual worker and ended in the senate of New York State:

Then came the days when one went to work, when one was farmed out to an employer in a ramshackle building on Attorney Street. That was home and factory. There in three dark, miserable rooms lived the employer and his wife, with three children and three machines for making children's shoes. And foul-smelling leather and the dirt and grime and sweat of yesterday's work. Here one worked and one received $1.50 as pay for six days each week. Days which began at seven in the morning. Days which seldom ended before ten at night. Days in a room where meals were cooked and clothing was washed and dried. And children screamed.[22]

In such places—fetid with squalor—garments, trimmings, artificial flowers, and a variety of other articles were produced by people of whom many were infirm, old, or ill with communicable diseases. It was to change this situation that the I.L.G.W.U. undertook a long, uphill fight to force manufacturers to accept the responsibility for conditions in the working quarters of their contractors and subcontractors. "Jobber responsibility" remained an important issue between manufacturers and the union and was not resolved until the N.R.A. codes were accepted in 1935.[23]

II

On American soil Dubinsky rejected the idea of remaining in his old trade as a baker. (The conditions under which bakers then worked are known to have been appalling, but Dubinsky does not give this as his reason for deciding against going back to his trade.) It was during this early period that he toyed with the hope of becoming a student and, eventually, a physician. It was not an ambition that was impossible to achieve. At that time colleges still showed no special discrimination against foreigners, regardless of origin, provided educational require- ments were met. This attitude was soon to change for one of keeping "undesirable students out on the basis of origin and religion."[24] Nor did the immigrant who was determined to enter a profession find lack of money an insuperable obstacle. Money could be earned and no work was too onerous when the end result was the realization of a glorious dream that brought not only security, but also prestige. Though study was hard when one worked all day, the annals of immigrant life are filled with the names of countless immigrants who studied in the evening and became educators, lawyers, physicians, scientists, social workers, etc.

Like thousands of other newcomers, including Morris Hill- quit,[25] who began as a shirtmaker, David Dubinsky turned to the needle trades. It did not take any newcomer in New York a long time to find out about the I.L.G.W.U. Cutters, he was told, were the aristocrats among workers in the ready-to-wear industry. Besides earning considerably higher wages than other garment workers, they had the power to strangle any branch of the industry. When cutters refused to work, there was no work for anyone. Besides, the cutters' local was an English- speaking union, a clear indication that the union was composed of experienced workers. One could become a cutter only by being apprenticed to a practiced cutter and then by passing a test given by the union's examiners. If one passed the exam- ination, one became a union member automatically. But the union did not make membership easily accessible, especially to the newly arrived, who, in immigrant parlance, were "green- horns." It was to the interest of these superior craftsmen to limit membership to "a happy few."

After a quick apprenticeship the young man passed his test, received his union card, secured a job, and enrolled in high school. Also, he joined the Socialist party, a path Morris Hill- quit had taken more than twenty years before Dubinsky. But while Hillquit never wavered from socialism, Dubinsky eventually resigned from the Socialist party to become one of the founders of the Liberal party of New York. Hillquit was soon to become a warm friend of Dubinsky's and of the union, and his picture, that of a thoughtful, intellectual man, still hangs prominently on the wall of Dubinsky's office. At the end of his first year, Dubinsky recalls, he found himself accidentally making a speech in behalf of Meyer London. Also a former shopworker, who was running for Congress, Meyer London was the union's chief counsel and the idol of the cloakmakers. He was regarded as "their good shepherd for three decades, [whom] they elected . . . to Congress three times, turning their backs on Tammany to which these traditional socialists often paid the tribute of their vote."[26] Dubinsky made his first speech for him in Yiddish. He was thrilled to discover how much he liked speechmaking and political activity in behalf of social goals. With his "heart and soul" he threw himself into London's campaign.[27]

Thus, he was lost to medicine and to the professional community. His future, he had come to realize, lay in the labor movement. As he explained: "When you get into union work, you can't go to college."[28] The truth of this statement seems to to be borne out by the fact that in those days very few labor leaders, native or foreign-born, sought formal education. They simply could not find the time for it. Samuel Gompers was another who lacked time, rather than interest, in augmenting his education; for he stated that he suffered from "mental hunger . . . [that was] just as painful as physical hunger."[29] But it did not drive him into college. A man who worked and took union activities seriously had no time left for any other endeavors. Also, the labor movement supplied its own challenges and satisfactions, while at the same time it seemed to breed a suspicion of purely intellectual attitudes.

III

Though Dubinsky was a dedicated union member from the start, in the beginning he kept in the background during union meetings, possibly because he was sensitive about an insufficient command of the English language in the presence of English-speaking members. (Today he speaks a fluent, robust

English.) In 1914 he married a girl who worked in the shops. What Emma Dubinsky, a modest woman, thought of her husband is evident in the response she made to a request that she address a union meeting. Her speech consisted of a single comment. "You and I both got the best man," she informed them succinctly. All were delighted, including her husband, who, after thirty years, still chortles over the ability of his wife to convey so much in so few words.

It was not until 1918 that he was elected to the executive board of his local. After that he advanced rapidly. In 1919 he was vice-president of his local, in 1920 president, and in 1921 general manager. In accepting a remuneration as a union official smaller than what he could earn as a cutter, he was following in the footsteps of Samuel Gompers, who says that in 1895, when he was asked to return to the presidency of the A.F. of L. (1895 was the only year during which he was not president), it meant a salary lower than what he could earn as a cigar maker.[30] Nevertheless, he made the sacrifice, as Dubinsky would later. It was not until 1920 that Dubinsky made his first speech to the membership in English. He found union work so demanding that he "hardly had time to read a newspaper or a magazine without giving up some rest."[31] A recreation he always enjoyed was bicycling, in which he indulged with his granddaughter when she was young, or with a similarly minded crony.

John Dewey, whose interest in the I.L.G.W.U. began in 1908 when he started a dissertation at Columbia University on *The Women Garment Workers in New York,* remarked that "David Dubinsky is thought of by many people, and probably regards himself, as a doer rather than as a thinker or theoretician."[32]

This opinion has been widely endorsed. A magazine and newspaper reader, Dubinsky is considered knowledgeable without being intellectual.

It is recognized that most of his strength lies in an aptitude for steering as far as possible from situations that would make him appear partisan to one faction against another. If he cannot reconcile hostile groups, he strives not to incur the resentment of either. But he never masked his hostility to militant left-wingers and their tactics. During the 1920's the I.L.G.W.U. became the arena for a violent power struggle between right- and left-wing elements for control of the union. The Communists began the attempt to make their influence felt soon after 1918. For instance, they opposed Meyer London for his support of the Liberty Bond drives.[33] Although Dubinsky was then a member of the Socialist party, which repudiated the war and would do nothing to aid in the war effort, he felt that after America had entered the war it would be unpatriotic not to lend support.[34] It was this attitude that called the attention of the union's more conservative elements to him and during the twenties swung the support of the moderates to him.

He asserts he foresaw that "the disease of Communism" would spread to the American labor movement as the inevitable corollary of the success of the Russian Revolution. After a period of precarious jockeying during which infiltration by left-wing Socialists, anarchists, IWW's, and Communists could not be halted, the radical elements succeeded in 1926 in taking over the direction of a strike which proved to be a long and costly one and ended in a number of disastrous compromises.[35] When the strike was finally settled the union was in shambles. Three million five hundred thousand dollars had been squandered,[36] of which only five hundred thousand had been allotted for strike benefits. After the expulsion of three radical locals,[37] the left wing was finally curbed in 1928, but it was a pyrrhic victory. The membership had dropped from one hundred thousand to forty thousand.[38] Many members were in arrears and the union's financial assets had melted away. Only a loan of one hundred thousand dollars from Herbert Lehman, Felix Warburg, and Julius Rosenwald kept the union afloat.[39]

What was Dubinsky's role during the twenties while the union was shaken by ideological quarrels? The responsibility was not yet his. As general manager of Cutters' Local No. 10, he was giving his support to those who were true and tried unionists and who were bearing the brunt of the battle. He became so thoroughly identified with the centralist faction that during the McCarthy era the senator embarrassed him by suggesting that he help him in investigating the activities of Communists in the labor movement.[40]

In 1929, in his seventh year as vice-president of the I.L.G.W.U., he was elected as secretary-treasurer, a position which put him in control of the union's purse strings. It was tantamount to being president without the title and enabled the union to retain as president the experienced and devoted Benjamin Schlesinger, whom the radicals had attempted unsuccessfully to unsaddle. In 1929 Dubinsky became chairman of a strike committee that brought the forty-hour week, a wage raise, and an arbitration system with a full-time impartial chairman, innovations for which the union had clamored since 1910.[41] But on the horizon loomed a new danger—the effect of the crash of 1929. When the incumbent died in 1932, Dubinsky was asked to become president. Cynics saw in him "the undertaker" on whom would fall the job of burying the union. "All right," said the newly elected president, "if I have to, I will."[42]

IV

Two factors account for Dubinsky's skill in avoiding disaster: the man himself and the timely interference of historical factors. Of course, he was generously endowed with uncommon planning ability, vision, good sense, drive, unstinting energy, and devotion, as well as with a distinct individuality. An ingredient of his personality is a hearty chuckle that testifies to a larger than average capacity for enjoyment. He tells of a remark he overheard while he was being groomed for president: "This young man is a winner. He cannot lose. He smiles all the time."[43] A short, stocky man with ample hair confined in a crew cut, the expression of his face alternates between seriousness, when his blue eyes gleam shrewdly, and rollicking good fun. His infectious laugh shines out of a picture he took with President Franklin D. Roosevelt, surrounded by the cast of *Pins and Needles,* whom he had brought to the White House to perform for the president. This play, which had proved a smashing success, was produced by an amateur cast of garment workers and was staged by the union's own theater group. The famous quizzical smile of the president is pallid beside the exuberantly laughing face of Dubinsky.

In addition to a practical viewpoint, he brought to his job a talent for dealing with all kinds of people, for making necessary compromises, and for avoiding antagonism where it was possible. He has been called "a congenital conciliator." Like Henry Clay, "the Great Compromiser," Dubinsky possesses a winsome personality which is not untinged by a kind of cunning.

An example of his good sense was to reinstate those who wanted to return to the union after the defeat of the radicals. Two of them, Charles Zimmerman and Jay Lovestone, who had been leaders of the left-wingers, found no obstacles to their reinstatement once they convinced the leadership that they were not returning as troublemakers. Within three years Zimmerman was elected vice-president of the union. Jay Lovestone had been general secretary of the Communist party, but was purged by Stalin in 1929. He was taken back into the I.L.G.W.U. and eventually became director of the A.F. of L. C.I.O. International Relations Department.

But in the desperate days of the early thirties, when the whole economic system was tottering and manufacturers were panicky with fear, a stronger medicine was required than personality and good sense. A lifesaver was needed. This lifesaver was Franklin D. Roosevelt, and his lifesaving device was the N.R.A. (National Recovery Act).

V

The career of David Dubinsky after the onset of the Depression bears out the theory that the opportunity to create an impression on society is frequently provided by historical circumstances. While history may be shaped by uncommon individuals, the accidents of history have provided uncommon individuals with the chance to give to history a special turn. One of the great shapers of history in America was President Franklin D. Roosevelt, and David Dubinsky, and John L. Lewis as well, found their main chance through implementing the Rooseveltian policies. In making the most of the N.R.A. provisions, Dubinsky was able to bring far-reaching benefits to the I.L.G.W.U. and thus to make a permanent mark in the field of labor organization.

The N.R.A. not only strengthened the drive for unionization by making opposition to union membership illegal, and by outlawing company unions, but the codes, hammered out by both industry and labor, also brought gains for which the union had battled since its inception. For instance, the issue of "jobber responsibility" for conditions in the shops of those to which manufacturers farmed out their orders had never been fully accepted. Now this concession, which insured that working conditions would not fall below certain standards, fell to the membership like ripe fruit. They gained the thirty-five hour week. It also became possible to organize unions in various cities that held out for the "open shop." The upsurge in membership was so substantial that by 1934 it had increased from forty-five thousand to two hundred thousand.[44]

As a consequence, the debt of two million incurred through the Communist-led strike of 1926 was practically wiped out. The union's assets grew tremendously. After the invalidation of the N.R.A. the union was able to maintain the advantages it had secured with a Coat and Suit Industry Recovery Board Label, which was sewed into every garment. This was done with the cooperation of the various employer groups. In 1943 the income of the union had risen to eight million three hundred thousand.[45]

Unlike John L. Lewis, whose support for Roosevelt waxed and waned, Dubinsky never wavered in his admiration for the president. A bust of Roosevelt occupies a prominent place in his office, in which are also displayed busts of Lincoln and Kennedy. On the walls are photographs of men prominent in the labor field, including a signed photograph of Léon Blum, premier of France. The walls also bear evidence that Dubinsky is the recipient of several honorary degrees from various colleges and universities. He voted for Norman Thomas in 1932, but in 1936 he resigned from the Socialist party, to which he had belonged for twenty-five years, in order to be able to devote himself wholeheartedly to the reelection of President Roosevelt.

It is characteristic of Dubinsky to keep alive the memory of those who contributed to the union's welfare. Among the union's benefactors Morris Hillquit, who as a desperately ill man was flown to N.R.A. headquarters for the N.R.A. hearings, heads the list.[46] In 1938 Dubinsky was instrumental with nine I.L.G.W.U. affiliates in erecting Hillquit Memorial Hospital in the suburbs of Los Angeles.[47] The I.L.G.W.U. also endowed a chair at Brandeis University as a tribute to Hillquit. The memory of Franklin D. Roosevelt was perpetuated in the founding of the Franklin Delano Roosevelt School of Marine Trades at Mondello, near Palermo, Italy.[48] The union also honored Meyer London, Morris Hillquit, and the ex-presidents Morris Sigman and Benjamin Schlesinger by having four Liberty ships named after them. These ships were built with funds realized from the purchase of war bonds by union members.[49]

VI

The union's chronicler, Benjamin Stolberg, declares that Dubinsky looked upon the New Deal not only as "labor's greatest boon," but that he considered it an attempt to make capitalism work in terms of industrial democracy, to harness capitalism, so that "it won't run away with itself." Dubinsky is no foe of capitalism. In his opinion "trade unionism needs capitalism like a fish needs water . . . and it can live only in a democracy." He also believes that in America "socialistic measures" will not work. "They may be good for Britain, Scandinavia, Italy," he said, "but they are not good for this country." When asked for his reasons, he replied succinctly: "Too many cars."[50] In other words, the American worker has become accustomed to luxuries he would be unwilling to give up.

In order to safeguard the social gains of the New Deal and to cripple Tammany in its stronghold on New York politics, Dubinsky and other labor leaders founded the American Labor party in 1936. It was intended as a "social pressure group" and as an implementation of Dubinsky's conviction that "labor must be in social politics [but] not in party politics."[51] It was an attitude Gompers would have endorsed. But what happened was that the American Labor party became infiltrated by radical elements. Eventually they overwhelmed party machinery and seized control. The I.L.G.W.U. remained in the American Labor party until 1944, when Dubinsky helped to establish the Liberal party. Among the other founders of the party were Alex Rose (a high official of the millinery workers), George L. Childs, Adolph A. Berle, and George Counts. Left-wingers found in this event the ammunition to attack Dubinsky for being "a promoter of disunity."[52] The year 1944 marked Roosevelt's final successful attempt to capture the presidency. In polling three hundred and twenty-one thousand votes in New York, the Liberal party helped to secure this pivotal state for the incumbent president. In 1948 the Liberal party supported Harry S Truman because of his advocacy of the principles of the New Deal in his own Fair-Deal policies.

VII

Unlike most of the unions affiliated with the A.F. of L., the I.L.G.W.U. had always been organized on industrial rather than on craft lines. However, in many of the mass production industries union organization lagged because new groups could not easily be fitted into existing craft unions. In 1935, John L. Lewis, president of the United Mine Workers and, like Dubinsky, one of the members of the Executive Council of the A.F. of L., brought the issue to a head by demanding a change of policy in regard to industrial unionism. To encourage the formation of hitherto unorganized workers in the mass production industries into unions along industrial lines, Dubinsky joined Lewis and ten national unions in forming the Committee for Industrial Organization (C.I.O.). The intention was to promote the smooth functioning of the C.I.O. within the A.F. of L. without disrupting the A.F. of L. or encouraging dual unionism, the bane of all responsible unionists. It turned out differently than had been foreseen. Branding the C.I.O. as an attempt at dual unionism, the Executive Council of the A.F. of L. suspended the C.I.O. unions in 1936. As a consequence, the I.L.G.W.U. found itself out of the A.F. of L. and a member of the C.I.O.

But Dubinsky remained a centrist, and a permanent rift with the A.F. of L. was not what he favored. He wanted labor peace, but the obstacle was John L. Lewis. The phenomenal success of the C.I.O. during 1936 and 1937 in organizing automobiles, steel, rubber and textile workers had hardened Lewis's arrogance and had made him more unwilling than ever to return to the A.F. of L. Also, the Communists and fellow travelers, whom he had put into key positions, seemed to Dubinsky to be getting too powerful. When Lewis turned the Committee for Industrial Organization into the Congress of Industrial Organizations, thus setting up a permanent dual organization in the American labor movement, Dubinsky led the I.L.G.W.U. out of the C.I.O, thus furnishing the ammunition to left-wing critics who branded him a "betrayer of the C.I.O." The I.L.G.W.U. remained independent until in 1940 it rejoined the A.F. of L.

VIII

The accomplishments of this union leader may be said to lie in the benefits his judicious management has brought to the membership. The growth of the union has been tremendous. As he reported at the convention of 1956: "In 1932 we had fifty-two locals. Today, in 1956, we have five hundred thirty-three. . . . In 1932 we had twenty-four thousand members. . . . Today we have four hundred forty-five thousand—plus the three thousand in Puerto Rico. . . . In 1932 we spent ninety thousand dollars for organization work; now we spend two million annually."[53]

In the last thirty years the racial composition of the membership has changed significantly. Whereas in the beginning of the century the majority was composed of Jewish immigrants, in the middle fifties the Jewish workers numbered only twenty-three percent—about one hundred twenty-five thousand. The rest were eastern and southern Europeans, Puerto Ricans, and Negroes. In the middle fifties seventy-five thousand were Italians, forty-five thousand Puerto Ricans, and nearly twenty-eight thousand in New York were Negroes.[54]

The way in which Dubinsky viewed his role and that of the I.L.G.W.U. is best conveyed by his statement at the twenty-ninth convention in May, 1956, in Atlantic City. He said:

I am proud of the great service we have performed for America. When we banished the sweatshops, when we reduced the hours of work, when we increased wages, when we provided health centers, when we established Unity House, when we participated in community life, when we eliminated worry, suffering, hunger and starvation, we performed a service for the future of America.[55]

The union has moved far from the concept of pure bread-and-butter unionism, which dominated the aims of most of the early labor organizations. This simple conception of the function of unions seems as antiquated as pre-Civil War America appears in comparison with the highly industrialized society America has become. What are some of the specific benefits that the Dubinsky management has brought to the members of the I.L.G.W.U.? One of the greatest blessings came to union members through the extension of health benefits. The Union's present health center in New York City was begun in 1911 and until 1930 was maintained by a group of New York locals. It was then taken over by the General Executive Board and turned into a modern diagnostic clinic that in the fifties employed one hundred and seventy-six physicians, forty nurses and aids, thirty technicians, five pharmacists, two nutritionists, two social workers, and, in addition, a large clerical and administrative staff. Close to six hundred thousand medical services were performed.[56] The I.L.G.W.U. also operates sixteen more health centers, though on a smaller scale, in the major locations of the United States and Canada where women's apparel is produced. Originally maintained by allotments from membership dues, since 1945 health services, and retirement, vacation, and severance benefits as well, are financed by employer contributions, calculated on the basis of percentages on payrolls, as prescribed by union contracts.

The union also offers a variety of recreational and educational benefits. Chief among the recreational facilities is Unity House, the union's vacation center in the Poconos, where members are accommodated at very low rates. Begun in 1919 as a modest bungalow colony, it now has facilities for twelve hundred guests. In 1956 the union provided Unity House with a theater at a cost of five hundred thousand dollars.[57]

Dubinsky inherited the semi-monthly magazine *Justice*, which was printed in English, Italian, and Yiddish. A Spanish edition was added during his incumbency. In 1959, as a result of membership changes, publication of the Yiddish edition was suspended, while the Spanish edition was increased in size.[58] The emphasis is on union news and world news from the point of view of the labor movement. In regard to education for workers, Dubinsky learned by experimentation what type of education is of greatest value to union members. Ever since the first strikes were won in 1910 there has been a clamor for increased educational opportunities for workers and over the years various plans were initiated and scrapped. After much trial and error it became evident that a recreational-cultural program is of greater value to working people than one that is purely intellectual. It may be because Dubinsky himself is not an intellectual that he favors more practical means of enriching the lives of union members. It is his conviction that the union should "educate our people for service to unionism, not educate them out of the labor movement."[59]

As the union prospered, other projects were worked out under the Dubinsky banner. In 1955 the first I.L.G.W.U. cooperative housing units were erected on Franklin D. Roosevelt Drive.[60] In 1957 the union offered the funds for a housing project in Puerto Rico. In 1949 a group of American unions headed by the I.L.G.W.U., together with Nelson A. Rockefeller and Charles H. Silver, formed the Amun-Israeli Housing Corporation to finance low-cost housing in Israel. In addition to large contributions for charitable purposes, the union contributes to humanitarian projects the world over. These include gifts and loans to trade unions in Israel, to the United Jewish Appeal for the rehabilitation of European war victims, and support for an Italian hospital. Another is a training school for orphaned and displaced children near Paris under the auspices of "Ort," an organization providing technical and handicraft training to young people.

The word that is frequently used to describe David Dubinsky is "shrewd." Undoubtedly, it was due to his astuteness that the union was saved in 1932 and that in the years after it achieved power and prosperity. David Dubinsky, has been called "a public figure, because he is a labor leader."[61]

IX

He is now eighty years old. He retired from the presidency of the union in March, 1966, and was succeeded by Louis Stulberg. With an executive style that is soft-spoken yet insistent, cool rather than exuberant, the new president continues the I.L.G.W.U. on its traditional course toward higher standards, increased wages, and improved benefits. Dubinsky may still be found every day in his office as director of the Retired Service Department. The attitude of the union to its leader is clearly expressed in a birthday gift that was announced in January, 1967. Beginning with 1968, a fund of a million dollars became available from which grants ranging from five thousand to twenty-five thousand dollars were to be distributed annually for twelve years to various causes and institutions. In this manner, a proud and prosperous union honored the seventy-fifth birthday of the man who led a struggling group of workers to its present peak of prosperity. This birthday gift is no less an act of homage to America, where such success was possible, than it is a personal tribute to David Dubinsky.

HERMAN BADILLO
1929-

From Puerto Rico to the Congress
of the United States

An orphan in his pre-teens when brought to New York, he was accustomed to hunger and privation. He overcame his handicaps by his industry and unremitting efforts to secure an education. After graduating from the College of the City of New York he studied law and became a member of the Bar. Then he went from the legal profession into the field of politics.

He was the first Puerto Rican to win several high posts in the government of the City of New York and is the first Puerto Rican to have been elected to the House of Representatives.

Puerto Rico and Its Relationship to the United States

Among America's twentieth-century newcomers the Puerto Ricans are the most numerous. They differ from all other foreigners in that they are citizens of the United States by enactment of the Jones Law of 1917. They prefer to be called "migrants" because they feel that in coming north they are repeating the movement of other Americans across state lines. But in the fact that their language and their cultural patterns differ from those of the United States and that they must accustom themselves to an altered way of life they are no different than other newcomers and are just as vulnerable as any group of immigrants were or are.

Despite their American citizenship they are subject to that

sharp drop in equanimity which affected most immigrants, resulting in the loss of what Puerto Ricans so aptly call "*dignidad.*" It is not wholly a matter of language. Even immigrants from the British Isles were not exempt from feeling insecure, despite the swaggering assertions of some (one of whom was Samuel Gompers) that an individual of English birth could not feel alien in America. Puerto Ricans demonstrate that the possession of American citizenship does not automatically bestow a sense of self-assurance and that, *ipso facto*, it does not induce a feeling of belonging. Like the Europeans who were aliens in our country, the Puerto Ricans can acquire self-confidence only after they can feel that they have overcome the challenges of the new environment.

Puerto Rico was discovered by Christopher Columbus in 1493 on his second voyage to the New World. On the way to Hispaniola (official name of Haiti), where he had left a small group of colonizers the year before, he stopped to take on fresh water in what is now Puerto Rico. He named the island, which is as large as Long Island, but smaller than Cuba, Jamaica, or Hispaniola, San Juan Baptista, after St. John the Baptist. When he reached Hispaniola he found that the colony he had planted the year before had disappeared. His experience was one from which the British were not to be immune when they started their colonizing experiments in the southern portions of North America approximately one hundred years later.

Ponce de Leon was one of the men who accompanied Columbus. Fifteen years later, Ponce led an expedition of soldiers into what is now Puerto Rico with the intent of colonizing the island and searching for gold. He found a peaceful tribe, the Arawak or Boriquen Indians, who were easygoing and not hard to subdue. To the Spanish, they became the Boriqueños. Their gentleness has remained a trait of Puerto Ricans. The rigors of hard work under Spanish overseers decimated them. So many died that the conquistadores were compelled to import slaves from Africa. Slavery remained in existence until 1873. The first wave of conquistadores had taken no European women with them; they were brought in later. The first issue was Spanish-Indian; later generations were a mixture of Spanish, Indian, and Negro. Some Puerto Ricans are pure white; in some the Indian strain predominates; others combine the three racial strains.

It was a land to gladden the heart, an *"isla verde,"* but there was very little metal, precious or otherwise. Nor was there any indication of coal, iron, or oil. Ponce was soon deposed by the son of Christopher Columbus, to whom the Spanish monarchy had restored the privileges of his father. Compelled to seek his fortune elsewhere through another venture in exploration, Ponce turned his gaze toward the southern coast of North America. Joseph Monserrat, one of New York City's prominent Puerto Ricans, dubs Ponce the first immigrant from Puerto Rico to America. But the Indians of what is now Florida were not gentle and submissive like the Boriquens. They resisted, and Ponce was wounded. He withdrew to Cuba, where he died. His remains were returned to San Juan and were buried in the Cathedral of San Juan Baptista.

San Juan became the stopping place for vessels carrying gold from Mexico to Spain, thus providing Dutch, French, and English raiders with the temptation to attack the island throughout the next three centuries. Two fortresses were built which, surviving to this day, give to the harbor of San Juan a trace of "Old World" appearance. Spain's mercantile policy of limiting trade to Spanish vessels, and immigration to Spanish subjects, was not lifted until the beginning of the nineteenth century, when all of Latin America was seething with revolutionary ardor. In rising against the colonial powers, Spain and Portugal, the Latin-American colonies followed the example of the North American colonies who had successfully severed their ties with Great Britain. Only Cuba and Puerto Rico did not break away from the tottering Spanish Crown.

Puerto Rico remained a dependent colony until 1897, when it received autonomy from Spain. A year later, it was taken over by the United States as the result of the victorious outcome of the Spanish-American War. The most important assets of the island, which has no natural resources, were its strategic location and its scenic beauty. Puerto Rico became an "unincorporated territory" in contrast to the "incorporated territories," destined eventually for statehood.[1] The people remained citizens of Puerto Rico.

This small island had a population of nearly one million. Illiterate and poverty-stricken, the people appeared to be "beggars on Uncle Sam's doorstep."[2] Less than twenty percent of the people could read.[3] The public health service and the transport system were primitive. The economy was wholly agrarian: sugar was grown on the lowlands; tobacco on the lower mountain slopes; and coffee, of superior quality, in the upper regions. Coffee, the mainstay of the independent farmer, is particularly vulnerable to high winds, and Puerto Rico lies in the path of tropical hurricanes. In 1899 and again in 1928 the entire coffee crop was devastated. (Today the government of Puerto Rico provides crop insurance and builds homes for agricultural workers that are as hurricane-proof as it is possible to make them.) It is a serious economic handicap that the island must import sixty percent of the food it requires.[4]

The American military government which took over began by building schools and roads, and by installing a public health system. But universal suffrage, which Spain had at last granted in 1897, was abolished, and the vote for choosing municipal officers was confined to those who were over twenty-one and either property owners or literate. Thus, all but fifty thousand in a population of close to one million were disenfranchised.[5] The sugar plantations soon succeeded in attracting mainland capital, and sugar having been placed on the duty-free list, production increased. The economy began to expand, but the population leaped ahead so much more rapidly that by 1940 it had all but doubled.[6] Because of the island's small size, its swelling population—now about six hundred and seventy-two to the square mile, as compared with fifty-nine for the United States[7]—was to become Puerto Rico's most exigent problem, especially during the Depression, when sugar production was placed on a quota. Despite allocations for relief by the federal government, the Depression decade was for Puerto Ricans a period of hunger and great suffering. The outbreak of World War II brought a crop of new problems. After Pearl Harbor a blockade imposed by German submarines kept food and essential raw materials from reaching the island. Submarines frequently succeeded in sinking a ship a day, often within view of the islanders.[8] The war also brought an unprecedented demand for rum, due to a shortage of alcohol on the mainland. Because the federal government returns the excise tax on rum, revenues increased considerably. But while the rum industry brings in twenty million dollars in taxes, it employs comparatively few people, and consequently accomplishes little in alleviating the problem of unemployment.

Since the take-over by the United States the governing process of the island has undergone several changes. The first piece of legislation, the Foraker Act of 1901, signed by President McKinley, terminated the military government and replaced it with a civilian one. It provided for a governor, an eleven-member executive council, and five justices to serve on the island's supreme court, all appointed by the president. Puerto Ricans could elect their one-chamber legislature, but the bills it passed were subject to the governor's veto.[9] Though the law also contained a resolution making it illegal for one individual to hold more than five hundred acres of land, the sugar barons, many of them absentee owners, were not disturbed in their ownership. Not until the 1940's was an attempt made by Luis Muñoz Marín, to enforce the law. In this he had the support of Rexford Tugwell, the island's last appointed governor.

Another feature of the Foraker Law provided for an elected non-voting commissioner to sit in the House of Representatives in Washington as an observer. This was a continuation of the system in effect while the western territories were getting ready for statehood. The first commissioner was Luis Muñoz Rivera, the father of Luis Muñoz Marín. Having been Puerto Rico's representative in Madrid, he was the one who brought back the document granting autonomy to the island. His devoted representation in Washington gained for his people a new organic law, the Jones Law, which was of such far-reaching import to the people of Puerto Rico that he became known as "the George Washington of Puerto Rico."

It was the Jones Law, enacted in 1917 during the administration of Woodrow Wilson, that bestowed American citizenship on natives of Puerto Rico. Presidents Roosevelt and Taft had proposed the grant of citizenship earlier, but nothing had come of it. The Jones Law abolished the governor's executive council, creating instead a two-chamber legislature, both elected by the people. But governor and supreme court justices were still appointed by the president. Not until 1948, when the Jones Law was amended, were the Puerto Ricans able to elect their own governor. The first one was Luis Muñoz Marín.

Though he had received a completely American upbringing in the schools of Washington, Marín remained Puerto Rican in sympathy and identification. Tugwell wrote of him:

he spoke a full, flexible, meaty English without indication of origin, except perhaps a trace of New Yorkese in expression, though his tongue was altogether without an accent. I remember saying a word of appreciation for that once and having him tell me that his English was better than his Spanish. What was true, as he admitted, was that he was one of the few people who felt in two languages. He was the living proof that bilingualism is possible in men of great intelligence. But it may be that the proof was only that it was possible to men of great intelligence.[10]

During the years Luis Muñoz Marín lived in New York, he was a fiery rebel. He returned to Puerto Rico in 1926 and six years later was elected to a seat in the Puerto Rican senate. Passionately devoted to the interests of the poor peasants—the *jibaros*—he began to agitate in favor of implementing the Five Hundred Acre Law (limiting the size of agricultural holdings), thereby antagonizing the sugar interests and those allied with them. He also aligned himself with the faction in favor of complete independence from the United States. It was not because he was anti-American, but because he felt it was better for Puerto Rico to retain its own culture and not to become eventually another California.

Marín proved such an embarrassment to his party that in 1936 they expelled him. But contrary to expectations, this did not mean the finish of his political career. He returned to the political scene in 1938, built up a new party, the Popular Democratic party (*Populares*), dropped the issue of independence, and in 1940 was elected president of the Puerto Rican senate. His victory made him the island's most influential leader.

Muñoz received encouragement from Rexford Tugwell while the latter was governor of Puerto Rico (1942-1946). An embattled reformer, Tugwell was in favor of fully enforcing the Five Hundred Acre Law. However, the breaking up of large sugar estates was carried out with moderation. In the 1950's the government had taken over only about half of the total land which had been held by corporations in violation of the law.[11] The explanation for proceeding slowly is that the intention was to demonstrate the power of the government to acquire land when and if considered desirable. The program was so successful that by 1960 one-quarter of a million families were relocated on their own land,[12] yet mass production of sugar, which thrives on bigness, was not impaired.

Tugwell's liberalism did not endear him to conservative Puerto Ricans, or to the members of Congress who considered his attitude socialistic and a threat to southern agrarianism. Eventually, in 1946, the enmity of Congress and the vilification by hostile Puerto Rican elements forced Tugwell to resign. On his suggestion President Truman appointed a Puerto Rican as governor and in 1948 Muñoz Marín became the first elected native-born governor.

A further political change of great consequence occurred in 1950. It provided for the election of a constitutional assembly to draft a constitution for Puerto Rico which paved the way to complete self-government. In 1952 the Commonwealth of Puerto Rico—a free state associated with the United States— or an *Estado Libre Asociado,* came into being. Since then the Puerto Ricans have had local self-rule, but as American citizens they cannot pass laws which would violate the United States Constitution. Such laws can be struck out by the United States Supreme Court. Puerto Ricans are subject to military service, and during the Korean War ninety percent volunteered.[13] Puerto Ricans do not pay federal taxes. Customs duties collected on the island are returned to Puerto Rico. That incomes earned on the island are not subject to federal taxation is a tremendous advantage in inducing United States and foreign capital to start manufacturing enterprises in Puerto Rico, but only firms planning expansion through building subsidiaries in Puerto Rico are eligible for the benefits offered to business.[14]

Though Puerto Rico has advanced considerably under Commonwealth status, further changes in governmental structure have not been ruled out. President Eisenhower offered Puerto Rico "independence if they wanted it."[15] The island will be eligible to request statehood when the per capita income level reaches that of the poorest state within the United States, which is Mississippi. At present the income level of Puerto Rico is half that of Mississippi. Consequently, the possibility that Puerto Rico will become the fifty-first state is not something that is expected to take place in the near future.

San Juan, the capital, is as well known for the spectacular beauty of its beaches and its elegant tourist hotels, which add approximately fifty-five million dollars to the state's revenues,[16] as for its slums, which Tugwell described as of the kind that "would have revolted a Hottentot."[17] Named *"la Perla"* and *"el Fanguito"* ("the Little Mudhole"), the inference can be made that the Puerto Ricans possess a sardonic sense of humor. Housing programs for rural as well as urban dwellers have greatly reduced the slum areas. Many rural families acquired new homes through a "self-help" program, which encouraged prospective owners to build homes with their own hands under the direction and with the help of the government. Each home costs about four hundred dollars, and only twenty-five dollars is required at the start of the project. The owners pay two dollars and seventy-five cents a month for ten years to repay the government loan, which is interest-free. For urban dwellers there are low cost housing projects where the rent fits the income.[18]

Other achievements after the 1940's, when Muñoz began to dominate the political scene, include the generation and distribution of electric power, which made expanded industrialization possible and insures good lighting throughout the island. Also, through careful planning and a system of inducements, industry has grown so much that since 1956 industrial income has exceeded agricultural income. Puerta Rico has the highest per capita income in the Caribbean, with the exception of Venezuela.[19]

In the fields of public health and education the progress has been equally impressive. A sewage system, a purified water supply, the upgrading of dietary standards (schoolchildren are served nourishing lunches every day throughout the school year), have resulted in a startling drop in the death rate, thus increasing life expectancy from forty-eight to sixty-eight years. If President Franklin D. Roosevelt were alive, he could with impunity take that drink of water he said he expected to find in Puerto Rico.[20] Education receives one-third of the budget.[21] In 1960 there were over ten thousand urban and rural schools. Registration at the University of Puerto Rico, established in 1903 after the take-over by the United States, has more than trebled, and thousands are enrolled in vocational and trade schools.

Despite the phenomenal growth, the Puerto Rican economy is constantly struggling with unemployment. To absorb the young people entering the labor market every year, Puerto Rico must find employment for twenty-one thousand new applicants annually, and it costs as much as ten thousand dollars in terms of industrial investment in new enterpries to create a new job.[22] Because of two facts, one that Puerto Rico cannot at the present time absorb all the young people ready for employment, and the second that wages on the mainland are known to be higher, North America acts like a powerful magnet upon them. The word-of-mouth advertising, the letters, the money that is sent back to Puerto Rico, react upon the islanders in the same way as the glowing reports of high wages used to inflame Europeans who were considering emigration. Officially, the Puerto Rican government neither encourages nor discourages its people from going to the United States. Up to the start of the recent recession the number of migrants was high due to increase of unemployment in Puerto Rico; now the number is declining.

They leave their birthplace, it has been remarked, "in search of a job, food, a chance to succeed—just like everyone else."[23] It would be more accurate to say "like many of the other ethnic stocks," for among the huge throng of European immigrants who sought homes in the United States there were thousands upon thousands of people of all kinds of national origin whose prime reasons for leaving their homelands was to escape from the tyranny of political and religious oppression. From these scourges Puerto Ricans have remained free. But though their motives are mainly economic, "the chance to succeed" often involves spiritual goals that go beyond the search for bread. Without a doubt many of those embarking on that fateful (and not comfortable) airplane journey must yearn for more than physical comforts as they are swiftly borne to that fabled city—Nueva York.

The American Setting

Most of the Puerto Ricans who decide to exchange life on the island for an existence in America settle in New York City and its environs. The reason is not only that New York represents glamor and excitement, as it does to Americans from other states across the land, but also that it is the greatest labor market in North America. Because approximately nine hundred thousand Puerto Ricans live in New York and vicinity and only about one-quarter of that number are scattered throughout the United States, the emphasis here will be on their acclimatization in the "Big City."

In 1930, long before the start of the heavy influx, which is only a little more than twenty years old, the census reported the presence of Puerto Ricans in all forty-eight states. Since 1950, existing nuclei have been steadily expanding in New Jersey, New England, Philadelphia, and Chicago (where skilled workers have found employment in the field of electronics), and in Cleveland, Detroit, and Gary, where they work in steel mills, while new groups are being formed in other localities. Until recently, Puerto Ricans are said to have made a good adjustment outside of New York and to have encountered little if any perceptible prejudice,[24] but of late resentment against them has come to the surface. A considerable number of newcomers are seasonal workers who arrive here in mid-April, frequently under contracts arranged by the Migration Division, which the Commonwealth maintains for the benefit of newcomers. After helping to gather fruit and vegetable crops, they return to the island in the late autumn in time to harvest the sugar cane.

Although Puerto Ricans began to come to North America in the nineteenth century, the influx did not begin to accelerate sharply until 1940. The peak year was 1946, when the number of entrants reached fifty thousand.[25] A study made in the 1950's established that the influx was composed mainly of urban elements stemming from the two largest cities, San Juan and Ponce, that almost fifty percent were under twenty-one, and that there was a greater proportion of nonwhites.[26] The number of single women (divorced, deserted, widowed) is said to have exceeded that of males. Among the new arrivals the proportion of legally married couples to those living in consensual marriages was higher than on the island, which indicates an awareness of American attitudes towards marriage. The nonwhites among them were said to have had less education than the whites and the women less than the men.[27] The exodus was facilitated by inexpensive air travel from San Juan to New York.

Until recently, "Spanish Harlem," also known as *"el Barrio,"* an area comprising ninety acres from 96th Street to approximately 125th Street, and from Fifth Avenue to the East River, meant home to about two hundred thousand Puerto Ricans, but in the last decade the borough of Brooklyn has picked up many Manhattan residents. As a consequence, East Harlem has become more Negro.

In 1965 East Harlem had nine huge public housing developments, almost half of whose tenants are Negro, one in three Puerto Rican, and one in five other.[28] About one-quarter of a million Puerto Ricans live in the Morrisania section of the Bronx, among whom the proportion of whites is higher than it is in Harlem.[29] The "Puerto Rican jet"[30]—the Lexington Avenue subway—conveys thousands to and from work daily.

Other clusters are to be found on Manhattan's lower East Side near the Bowery and Second Avenue, originally the home of Eastern European immigrants, and another quarter of a million in Brooklyn.[31] Together they form nine and one-third percent of the city's population.[32] For those who can afford it, the next step up the ladder is Queens in Long Island, or New Jersey, where living conditions and schools are better than in Manhattan. It is harder for Negro types, estimated at one-third, to find homes outside of *"el Barrio."* To Piri Thomas, author of a vivid autobiography, "Long Island was a foreign country."[33]

What awaits the majority of Puerto Ricans in New York? A low economic status, housing conditions ranging from "poor" to utterly deteriorated, and a form of racial discrimination that is not always well concealed. In the 1960's, asserts Woody Klein, East Harlem still had fifty thousand "old-law tenements," all built before 1900, two-thirds of which are filled with Puerto Ricans. To many of them, he says, these slums are reminiscent of "*el Fanguito*," the notorious slum of San Juan.[34] An additional affliction are the vacant condemned buildings, which are inadequately sealed and give shelter to bums and heroin addicts. They who were accustomed to pure air, almost constant sunshine, and a climate that requires no more than light summer dress all year round, must adjust themselves to New York's severe winters and our enervating summers. The only heat of which tenants of dilapidated buildings are assured is the excessive heat of summer.

In the winter it is not unusual for tenement dwellers to freeze not only outside, but in their apartments as well. The gas jets are sometimes the only source of heat, and hot water is a luxury. An excerpt from the diary of a Puerto Rican woman, reprinted in 1965, presents this grim picture:

I don't wish nobody to live the way I live. Inside a house in this condition, no steam, no hot water, ceiling falling on you, running water from the ceiling, to go to the bathroom you have to use an umbrella, rats everywhere. . . . Children so cold they trembling. . . . It is really hard to believe that this happens here in the richest city in the world.[35]

The summer drives them into the streets, where they remain late into the night to escape the heat trapped in their airless rooms. While men argue and gamble on stoops and junkies prowl, alert for customers, children amuse themselves as best they can. This is Piri Thomas's description of Harlem streets in the summer:

All the blocks are alive with many-legged cats crawling with fleas. People are all over the place. Stoops are occupied like bleacher sections at a game and beer flows like there is nothing else to drink. The black musicians pound out gone beats on tin cans and conga drums and bongos. And kids are playing all over the place—on fire escapes, under cars, over cars, in alleys, backyards, hallways.[36]

Children become accustomed to dirt, rats, and vermin. They become brutalized by the sight of drunks "sleeping it off" in hallways and on stoops, junkies peddling their stuff in cellars and on roofs, by savage fights and the quick pull of a knife. Few are as softhearted as this sixth-grade boy who wrote:

I feel sorry for all the bums. They should have a house for them. . . . Sleeping out there, that's terrible. Then when it rains they catch a cold, and they don't hardly have coats or anything. . . .

My mother said that if she was rich that every bum she would see she would buy him clothes, you know, and she would buy a house and let them all live there.[37]

The crime and accident rate in *"el Barrio"* is high; incidents of minor violence occur all the time. Boys get their fixes (injections with a needle) in cellars or on roofs. Girls are "pushers" too. Not only garbage comes flying out of the windows, but more dangerous missiles as well. In 1961 a can was tossed from one of the five-story tenements at Assemblyman Lane who was seated in an open car next to Mrs. Franklin D. Roosevelt. He had to have four stitches. Fortunately, Mrs. Roosevelt was uninjured.[38]

The housing shortage is so serious that even slum apartments are at a premium. Hence, the rents are far in excess of what such apartments are worth. But lack of proper housing is not the only reason for unhappiness among Puerto Ricans. Another is the condition of schools in East Harlem. These schools are likely to be older than schools in other neighborhoods, there is a higher turnover of teachers and principals, and many are so overcrowded that children attend double sessions. An extremely high percentage of Puerto Rican high school students are dropouts and over forty percent of those who graduate from high school receive "general diplomas," which were admittedly "empty of any educational meaning."[39] The desire of Puerto Rican parents to have their children removed from neighborhood schools by busing is less strong than among Negroes.[40] They would prefer better schools and superior instruction in their neighborhood schools. The Puerto

Ricans are proud of their culture, and the fact that they are referred to as "culturally deprived," exacerbates their inferiority complex, to which the nonassertive are particularly prone. Puerto Ricans are inclined to be amiable, trusting, accepting, courteous, dignified, and capable of a great deal of human warmth. Their clannishness and dependence upon the family circle are reinforced by the denigration of their cultural and personal values.

Though the education of Puerto Ricans on the island has for some time now been geared to raising individual skills, most of them work in unskilled or semiskilled jobs, where earning capacity is low. Many flock to the service industries—restaurants and hotels; to shops manufacturing toys, plastic articles, and costume jewelry; and to the garment industry. Because they are willing to accept jobs that are looked upon as dreary, they have made themselves well-nigh indispensable to the economic life in New York. It has been freely admitted that if the present supply of workers were withdrawn and if the influx from Puerto Rico stopped, the garment industry and the restaurants and hotels of New York would be seriously affected.

In view of the tendency among Puerto Ricans to marry young, to have large families, and to buy on credit, they are apt sometimes to find themselves in the grip of economic difficulties. However, the impression that Puerto Ricans would rather accept assistance than work seems to be ill-founded, for the facts indicate that those forced to seek assistance get off the relief rolls "faster than any other group of people."[41] Piri Thomas recreates an interview between an investigator and a Puerto Rican woman whose child acts as an interpreter:

[Speaking of her husband] He's so proud, my God, he's so proud that even when he should be in bed he just gets up and staggers all over the place. . . . When he's well no man can stand up to him. . . . I do not ask for him, only for the kids and myself. I do not ask for him—he hates you all. He screams: "I'm gonna get me a gun—I ain't been born to beg—no goddam man was born to beg."[42]

A painful handicap from which European newcomers were exempt, but which reflects adversely on Puerto Ricans, is that the dark skinned among them are looked upon as Negroes. Though those living on the island are not entirely oblivious of color differences (even in Puerto Rico the more desirable jobs are held by the light skinned), it has never been as important an issue there as it is in America. "In our history of more than 450 years," writes Joseph Monserrat, "we have never had a broad scale of institutionalized discrimination de facto or de jure." He continues:

We are aware of the fact that we are seen by our neighbors as being "non-white." Since the question of color has not been a major theme in our experience or our history, we at first paid little attention to this designation. . . . We learned fast that in the States a new dimension has been added: the dimension of "color."

We therefore reject the designation of "non-white." We reject it not because those of us who are in fact non-white are in any way ashamed of being of color; we reject it because we reject the state of mind behind it, which in referring to us as "non-white" is really telling us that we are not equal to others —that we are "inferior."[43]

It has been suggested that this latest group of entrants are hindered in their efforts to make quick progress by the fact that social mobility is much more impeded than it was during earlier periods in our history. It would probably be impossible even for Andrew Carnegie, Henry Villard, and others like them to amass the huge fortunes they did in so short a space of time, even if they were alive today and actively participated in the economic life of the nation. But though the scope for spectacular successes may be more limited now than during the period one immigrant designated as "the American Middle Ages,"[44] the path through education is wider and much less thorny than it was for European immigrants a hundred, even fifty, years ago. To read of the difficulties with which immigrants grappled in search of an education (though a huge number achieved it) is to marvel at the strength of the human spirit. Institutions of higher learning are much more responsive today to the potentialities of the disadvantaged, and financial help is more readily available to promising students than it ever was. In former times there were no government loans at low interest available to students. There is not less but more need and appreciation for the physician, the social worker, the altruistic political aspirant. Can there be a doubt that professionally trained Puerto Ricans will be no less welcome than similarly trained people of other backgrounds?

It has been said of Puerto Ricans that they are apt to be "yearners" rather than "strivers" or "doers."[45] This pessimistic judgment is not borne out by today's evidence. There has been a significant increase not only in the number of teachers, physicians, engineers, lawyers, and social workers, but also in political aspirants. For instance, the *New York Times* reported that at the end of 1970 four Puerto Ricans were joining the New York State legislature as senators and assemblymen.[46] That Puerto Ricans are ready to fight for their interests can be seen in the following incident. When the president appointed Henry M. Ramirez, former director of the Spanish-American division of the United States Commission on Civil Rights, to a new post as chairman of the Cabinet Committee on Opportunities for Spanish-Speaking People, members of the Puerto Rican Association for National Affairs opposed the nomination because they felt that a Puerto Rican should have been appointed. They would not cease their protest until Ramirez promised he would include the names of Puerto Ricans for the second-highest position, that of executive director, an appointment only the president can make. As might have been expected, the members of the Puerto Rican Association for National Affairs were supported by Herman Badillo, the first Puerto Rican elected to the Congress of the United States.

A demonstration of the will to succeed may be clearly found in the career of Herman Badillo. He has taken it upon himself to carry out the Biblical command: "He shall be thy spokesman unto the people."

I

The best-known Puerto Rican in New York City, which is home to almost one million Puerto Ricans, is Herman Badillo. Since his election to Congress in 1970 as the first Puerto Rican in the House of Representatives, he is undoubtedly the most prominent Puerto Rican on the mainland of America. He is a slender man with a shock of dark hair and dark blue eyes, and he is very tall, so tall that in 1970 the *New York Post* declared him to be "tall enough to see beyond Bronx." His very contained manner hints of innate shyness. He listens with a lawyerlike concentration and intensity which convey that nothing escapes his attention and that very little, if anything, will need to be repeated.

Between January, 1970 and the end of that year his office was a large, well-furnished chamber that was part of an endless-seeming suite of rooms occupied by one of New York's prestigious law firms. On one wall of his office hung a crayon portrait of John F. Kennedy, whose election to the presidency sparked Mr. Badillo's entrance into politics. On the telephone he swings from English into Spanish. Despite a suggestion of accent, he conveys the impression that he is more American than Puerto Rican. There are so many characteristics about him that would be considered typically American that one wonders how it was possible for him to acquire them so thoroughly in so short a time.

II

In 1930, when the Depression was holding the United States and Puerto Rico as well in a relentless grip, Herman Badillo was a year old. The situation on the island was one of almost total paralysis and hunger. In addition, another scourge was rampant—an epidemic of tuberculosis, to which a large number of people succumbed. His father, who had been a teacher of English and was in the midst of compiling a Spanish-English dictionary, was one of those stricken. He died when his son was a year old.

The Badillo family had lived in Puerto Rico for four generations. On the paternal side all had come from Spain; his mother was of Spanish-Italian stock. His religious background was mixed, for his mother was Catholic; the father's family was Protestant. They had brought the first Protestant Bible into the island.

The whole decade of the thirties was for Puerto Rico a time of extreme need and privation. Public assistance, at first non-existent, became available after Franklin D. Roosevelt took office, but aid was exiguous and starvation remained prevalent.

Such necessities as shoes remained out of reach for most of the poor. The boy became accustomed to going barefoot and to having to go to bed without expecting an evening meal. In addition, there was his mother's illness for she, too, had contracted tuberculosis. At the age of five he became completely orphaned.

In the tradition of Puerto Rican families, the boy became the responsibility of an aunt, who was living apart from her husband and had the care of her own two children. Although she was unable to provide properly for them, she took her nephew into her home to share the poverty from which all suffered. He continued to go hungry most of the time. He was lucky, he explained, when there was something in the way of food to start the day with—a cup of black coffee for his breakfast. In those days, the policy of serving a warm lunch to all schoolchildren all over the island, initiated by Luis Muñoz Marín, had not yet come into existence. When he was released from school at noon he knew that most of the time there would be no lunch. He felt the pressure of poverty so keenly that at the age of eleven he began to seek employment so that he could contribute his pittance to the maintenance of the household. He found a job to clean seats in a motion-picture house.

Long before he was eleven his teachers and relatives had come to realize that he was a bookworm. His aunt had become used to hearing that if he could be given a chance to be educated he would have a bright future. But how to provide for an education when she could not even feed her children regularly? There was only one possible way—to take him to North America.

At last the discouragement over their situation and the insinuations of teachers and friends that the boy deserved a better chance than to remain in Puerto Rico, led her to the decision to make the break. With her son and nephew (the other child was left with relatives), she took the airplane that symbolized hope to those willing to leave their beautiful island for the slums of New York. The year was 1941, and Pearl Harbor was only a few months away. Herman was eleven and a half, and her own son was six months older. She hoped for the best for both boys, but she expected nothing spectacular from her own son, who, she was aware, did not possess the mental equipment of his cousin. The best her son would eventually achieve was to become a cook in the merchant marine; but her nephew would turn out to be the most outstanding Puerto Rican on the mainland.

Until his aunt could find work, Herman was sent to live with three or four different families in various slum tenements of *el Barrio*. When asked how New York struck him, he replied: "I thought I had come into Paradise. I had been starving for seven years and now I got three meals and could eat my fill. I had a pair of shoes. What made the greatest impression on me was that people did not seem to be hungry and instead of the widespread unemployment I saw all around me in Puerto Rico, most people seemed to have work. This alone was enough to impress me."

His aunt found it difficult to secure work in which she could earn enough to take care of a family, and so he was sent to one of his father's brothers in Chicago. But the uncle was poor, and in addition he was already burdened with several other newly arrived relatives; so after a few months the boy was again sent traveling, this time to another uncle in Burbank, California. This uncle, an aircraft worker at the Lockheed aircraft plant, was more affluent than the others, owning his home and a car, but he too had several relatives to look after. When asked how it felt to be shunted around from family to family, Mr. Badillo admitted:

> I was not happy about it. But I understand why they were not too friendly. Too much was expected of them; too many relatives were clamoring for help. It made me more determined than ever to take care of myself as much as I could and not to impose any more than I could help. That's why soon after I arrived in California, I began to think of a way in which I could earn some money. Before long I was mowing lawns and at the same time developing a newspaper route. I was twelve and a half and I didn't want to have to ask my uncle for any more money than was absolutely necessary.

Interrogator: Did you like Burbank?

Badillo: Yes, very much. The mountains and the climate reminded me of Puerto Rico. The dirty streets of New York and Chicago may not have caught my attention, but I couldn't help noticing the difference in Burbank. Even though I felt strange because there were no Spanish-speaking children in school, Burbank struck me as a fine place to live in. The kids were friendly and the teachers helpful. When it became obvious that I was learning English because I found it easier to talk to people and I was doing better in school I was thrilled. One reason learning didn't seem hard, because much of what we were being taught, I had already learned in Puerto Rico. I became a Boy Scout and I liked hiking, camping overnight and doing things out of doors. Life seemed pretty good.

But then after two years in California my aunt in New York wrote that she had a steady job and she asked me if I would come back to New York and be part of the family again. She was one of those to whom having a family meant a lot, because she also sent for her father from Puerto Rico. I didn't want to destroy the family feeling and though I liked living in California and knew I would miss it, I went back to *el Barrio*.

Interrogator: How did *el Barrio* strike you this time?

Badillo: It was such a contrast to California that I couldn't help seeing what was obvious. It *was* dirty and slummy. But it wasn't enough to overbalance the good feeling that I was back with my nearest kin who really wanted me. Maintaining family ties was more important than scenery and being a Boy Scout.

Interrogator: Isn't it a trait of Puerto Ricans to encourage close family ties?

Badillo: Yes, we care about one another and it's not only because here in America we are all strangers who need and depend upon each other, but we feel very much the same way in Puerto Rico, where we are all one kind. In Puerto Rico it is not unusual for several generations to like to live together. When I became a lawyer I would defend Puerto Ricans in criminal actions even when they couldn't pay. Those clients who paid my regular fees made it possible for me to defend poor Puerto Ricans. I would have liked to do more of that kind of work, but I had a living to make and it could not be done by concentrating on helping poor Puerto Ricans who got into trouble.

By the time he returned to New York he was ready for high school. But as a newcomer in America he lacked the kind of sophistication that would have cautioned him to be careful about the kind of high school in which to enroll. He landed at Haaren High School, which was a combination of an academic and a trade school. To the question whether he had decided on a high school that was not strictly academic because he wanted to learn a useful trade or craft, he replied:

> I went to Haaren because I knew no better. No one suggested that in an academic high school I might have a better chance. Perhaps it was because the school was located on the West Side and it was easy to reach. I was given no aptitude tests. When it was recommended to me that I take airplane mechanics, I was willing, but I wasn't thrilled about it. The way I felt was that if I became an airplane mechanic, it would not be a bad job as jobs go. By the fourth term I had learned to take an airplane engine apart and to put it together again. At about that time someone in school discovered that I liked to study and it was decided to give me a trial. I was put into the "high" classes that had an "H" after them and were for the above average students and at the end of the term I had the highest average in class. After that it was goodbye to airplane mechanics.

Interrogator: Did you work at the same time?

Badillo: Of course. It was absolutely essential that I earn money while going to school. I was a pin boy in a bowling alley at night and during weekends. Summers I worked as a delivery boy in fruit and vegetable stores, as an elevator operator, as a bus boy and a short order cook at Horn & Hardart. For me the best job was one that brought me the most money. For instance, when they made me manager of the bowling alley, I gave it up, because I could make more money as a pin boy. My height and long arms enabled me to work very fast and my customers appreciated it, which they showed by their tips. Honors at school meant a great deal to me, but at work what mattered most was the amount of money I could earn.

It was not his good luck to attract the attention of a teacher who would steer him into the right path by calling his attention to competitive tests or fellowships available to students of promise. Innumerable instances of such guidance by teachers are to be found in the autobiographies of the foreign-born, which prove that teachers were among the greatest benefactors to immigrant children, by spurring them on to attempt the seemingly impossible. Herman Badillo did not require a spur, but he might have benefited from proper counseling. What knowledge he acquired about colleges came from classmates to whom college meant the College of the City of New York, that breeding ground for some of New York's most prominent men—politicians, teachers, scientists, journalists, and even writers. (One of the last was Upton Sinclair, a native American.) All Herman Badillo needed to know was that City College was free and that he was eligible. He knew he could earn enough to maintain himself.

But he was also aware that he could not afford to spend four years at college without considering what work he would be fit for when he was finished. "So I entered as an engineering student," he explained. "But at City College there was counseling and after some testing they thought engineering was too specialized for me, that my tests indicated a broader range of interests. It was suggested that I consider business administration and I accepted the idea. The first two years I took academic courses and the last two years special courses in accountancy and business administration."

Interrogator: Did you like college?

Badillo: Yes, very much. I thought the teachers were very good. I liked the way they taught in conceptual terms. It represented a new approach which appealed to me. I also liked the boys. Many of them were real intellectuals. I had few very close friends in the neighborhood in which I lived, but I made friends at college.

Interrogator: Were you able to maintain high marks?

Badillo: Yes, I still got the highest marks in any class. I was happy studying and working and my family was happy about it too. My aunt especially could feel that she had helped in creating a better future for me. Towards the last years of college I began to train myself to become a C.P.A. [Certified Public Accountant] by working in offices during summers. I wanted as much practical experience as I could get in order to prepare myself for the examination in accountancy, for which a minimum of three years of experience is required.

By the time Badillo graduated from City College in 1951— magna cum laude—he had decided what his next step would be.

He would study law. He was aware that his experience in finance and taxes, which he was picking up in accountancy, would be a distinct advantage. Had a glimpse into the future been vouchsafed him, he would have expected to see his progress as a lawyer, but what would have surprised him would have been that he would practice law only from 1955 to 1962, then return to the law in 1970 only to become enmeshed in politics. Unlike innumerable young men who went into the law in the hope that it would lead to politics, at the time of his graduation from college he had no other ambition than to be a success in his chosen profession. In those days he asked for nothing more than to make his living as a counsellor-at-law.

Because he was working in the daytime as an accountant he could study only in the evening. Consequently, he registered at Brooklyn Law School, where hardworking young people were being given a legal education at night. He was able to get a book scholarship immediately, but in order to qualify for a general scholarship he had to wait until he could submit his grades as a law student. He received the Dean's Scholarship for his second and third years, and was also appointed editor of the *Law Review*, the highest distinction to which law students can aspire.

In 1955, at the end of three years, he attained his three goals simultaneously: he graduated cum laude as valedictorian of his class and received his law degree; he passed the Bar examination; and he passed the examination that entitled him to call himself a C.P.A.

III

There was no hesitancy in his mind about what to do next. Unlike many of the young law-school graduates whose aims are to become associated with prominent law firms or to secure promising jobs in government, Badillo had the intention of going into private practice with a classmate who had good real-estate connections through his father. As a married man, he looked forward to raising his earning capacity, but at the same time he hoped to be able to distinguish himself in some way in his chosen profession.

Between 1955 and 1962 he concentrated on building a practice, balancing his work in tax and real-estate law with criminal defense cases involving some of his more unfortunate country-men. He had joined the Caribe Democratic Club of East Harlem, which was under the leadership of Anthony Mendez, the first Puerto Rican political leader of the district, and he was also picking up political cases. But most importantly, he was being introduced into practical politics, and, as was usual with him, he was learning fast, though he could not expect that the study of political affairs would bring him academic honors.

In 1960, when the country was girding for the presidential election, Badillo, like the rest of the membership of the Caribe Democratic Club, was an enthusiastic supporter of Senator John F. Kennedy. But sensing that the normal political machinery would not succeed in getting Blacks and Puerto Ricans registered in sufficient numbers to influence the election, he decided to form a separate organization, with its own clubhouse, which he called the John F. Kennedy for President Committee, thus bringing all the emphasis to bear on the election of the presidential candidate rather than on the Democratic slate. It meant that he had to work directly through the Kennedy organization rather than through Anthony Mendez.

An intensive drive for registration conducted by Badillo's new organization resulted in an increase of forty-eight percent in registration. The presidential campaign not only made the whole Puerto Rican community conscious of Badillo, but it also alerted the politicians to the appearance of an ambitious new-comer on the political horizon. After the election he was sounded out about a job in Washington, but he turned it down because he wanted to remain in New York.

Having fully succumbed to the political virus, he immersed himself in the 1960 mayoralty campaign, in which Robert Wagner was running for the mayor's office against the regular Democratic candidate, Arthur Leavitt, who was being supported by De Sapio. Leavitt lost in the primary, and the organization Badillo had created swung behind Wagner in his campaign of 1961. Badillo made his first political bid by running for district leader against Alfred E. Santangelo, who was a strongly entrenched Democratic regular and a congressman to boot. Though Badillo lost by seventy-five votes, it was considered a great victory. As the election was judged to have been rigged, Badillo brought suit to force a new election. He won in a lower court, but the decision was reversed in the appellate court.

While he was awaiting the decision of the court of appeals Mayor Wagner appointed Badillo Deputy Commissioner of Real Estate and later set up a new department making him Commissioner for Housing and Relocation. In announcing the new position the *New York Times* remarked that "it was the highest appointment ever given a Puerto Rican and [that] it makes Mr. Badillo the youngest commissioner of New York. The job might well turn out one of the city's toughest."[47] A feature article accompanying the news recognized "the great intellectual capacity, a relentless drive to succeed and not a very secretly nutured (sic) ambition to run some day for high political office." To some politicians he appeared "too ambitious." This appointment marked the end of the first phase of his law career and the start of a new orientation.

As Commissioner of Housing and Relocation, Badillo brought innovations into what might have been a cut-and-dried procedure to find new living quarters for people who were to lose their homes through slum clearance. Of what did these innovations consist? As the *New York Times* reported: "It was planned that the program include not merely relocation, but also improved public information services, interim social case work by professional workers and tenant education." The most significant feature of the new program was "professional social service" which, because it was attached to the bureau, was made easily accessible to all who needed help. Badillo explained to this interrogator:

If we had simply moved people from old to new addresses without attempting to alleviate such ugly problems like drug abuse, delinquency, chronic illness, etc., we might have been helping to spread infection to new sites. But if some of these problems could be controlled, many of these people would take up their new homes with renewed hope for the future.

To the newspapers it presented a farsighted approach and they praised not only the new commission but the mayor as well for having chosen a commissioner of vision and social responsibility. But some members of the city administration were quick to assert that there was nothing new or unusual in providing social services to people who were in need of them. However, this kind of help had not been available in this kind of situation before. Badillo also had the satisfaction of seeing other communities adopt his approach. In terms of numbers, approximately five thousand families yearly were helped to make the move from old to new quarters. While he acted as Commissioner of Housing and Relocation he was placed on the Anti-Poverty Operations Board and later was appointed to New York City's Health and Hospitals Corporation.

As he explains, it was his having started on the same lowly plane as any of the poor and disadvantaged that enabled people on the lowest economic rung to feel it was not a vain endeavor to exert themselves to secure a better future. His rising importance enabled Pete Hamill of the *New York Post* to declare in 1970 that "he had done for the Puerto Ricans of New York what John Kennedy had done for Roman Catholics around the nation."[48] The extent to which he came to be looked upon as a leader among the Puerto Ricans became clear when the "Young Lords" caused a furore by taking over one of the churches of the neighborhood and a judge asked him to mediate the conflict.

In 1966 Badillo ran for borough president of the Bronx on a Democratic Reform ticket. He won, and though his opponent contested the election, he was declared the winner. The election proved that he was the choice of the general electorate, for the Puerto Rican vote, amounting to a little less than ten percent of the city's vote, would not have been enough to insure his victory.

Again he used the opportunity to introduce some innovations. Because the Bronx represents an agglomeration of fourteen planning boards with different problems, he established fourteen planning boards and held separate hearings in each of them, attending them personally, before taking recommendations to City Hall. Thus, he neutralized complaints that might have arisen that the needs of some areas were being overlooked in favor of special advantages to other sections. It was a technique of decentralization which Mayor Lindsay has attempted to implement in other branches of the city government.

Instead of seeking reelection as borough president of the Bronx, Badillo decided to compete for the mayoralty of New

York City. Mayor Wagner had assured him he would not be a candidate and had offered to support him.[49] But later Mayor Wagner changed his mind and turned against Badillo for becoming one of his opponents. It was a six-cornered primary in which the liberal strength was further diluted by Norman Mailer, who ran, in Badillo's words, on the "nonsense argument" that New York City would benefit from being detached from New York State. It is Badillo's contention that in the not-too-distant future it will be a distinct advantage to New York State to get rid of New York City's multiple liabilities. As a consequence of the many competing candidates, Badillo lost by a little over thirty thousand votes.

IV

After his defeat Badillo went back to the law only to become enmeshed in the congressional race of 1970. He was strongly backed by the *Times*, the *Post*, Governor Rockefeller, Mayor Lindsay, by many union groups, including the Amalgamated Clothing Workers, and by a group of educators. Representative Ottinger said of him: "He is a man who understands the cities," and Governor Rockefeller recognized that "he does not run as a Puerto Rican. He runs as a citizen of New York." Because he was opposed by another Puerto Rican and two Italians, he won the primary by the small majority of 587 votes. But he received the nomination of the Liberal party. Again a victory of his was contested, this one by Peter Vallone, one of the opposing candidates, who claimed voting irregularities. A lower court upheld Vallone, and the *Times* expressed regret in an editorial. But a higher court reversed the judgment, and its decision was widely applauded.

Just before the election Badillo was again given startling proof of his influence among the underprivileged. When some rioting prisoners at the house of detention asked for him (and congresswoman Shirley Chisholm) to help in the adjustment of their grievances, he spent, as the *New York Times* reported, "A tense all-night negotiating session."[50] Then he declared that "most of the inmates were held there only because they were poor," a recognition of the fact that they could not raise bail.

Badillo went to his new job as one of the nation's lawmakers with a confidence resulting from a solid victory. He had stressed several issues during the campaign which he promised to emphasize in Congress. The need of our cities appears to him to be the most exigent problem of the seventies, hence his main objective was to be an "Urban Strategy," in which, he said, "the voices of Irish, Italians, Greeks, Blacks, and Puerto Ricans would be heeded." What he proposed to do was to introduce legislation to give the cities a certain percentage of federal tax revenues. Not only has it never been questioned that he is motivated by consideration for all disadvantaged groups, be they black, Puerto Rican, or white, but it has also been recognized that he has displayed "remarkable skill in creating harmony between both minority groups and white New Yorkers."

Nor did he intend to limit himself to national issues. Because of his understanding of Latin America, Badillo is especially qualified to offer a solution to the thorny problem of how to gain and hold the trust of its republics. In his opinion, the surest way to make the "Good Neighbor Policy" work is to make Puerto Rico serve as a "bridge" between the United States and Latin America. During his campaign he promised to introduce legislation to abolish the policy of "matching funds" in Puerto Rico, which means that before Puerto Rico can receive two dollars of federal funds it must raise one dollar of its own. Because frequently they lack this matching sum, Puerto Ricans cannot get much federal money.

But his idea is to go further than merely to help Puerto Rico. This is how he explained it:

> Building up Puerto Rico is one way by which the United States could impress all of Latin America with its good will and sincerity. At present the Latin-American republics need only to point to Puerto Rico to make out a good case for not attaching too much importance to America's promises. The fact that seventy-two years under the American flag has not helped the Puerto Ricans to exceed a per capita income that is less than half of Mississippi, which holds the record for the lowest income of any state, proves to the world that the United States does not intend to exert itself to raise the standard of living in areas south of the American continent. If the United States allows discrimination in its attitude to Puerto Rico, which is its showcase in the Caribbean, how can the Latin-American republics be

expected to believe that promises to them would be taken more seriously?

Interrogator: Can you state what you mean by "discrimination in its attitude to Puerto Rico?"

Badillo: Yes. Take the proposed welfare legislation. It was drafted specifically to exclude Puerto Rico. Why? Surely not because the wealth of the people makes such support unnecessary. Why do highway programs not include Puerto Rico? Why not enlarge aid to small business and to disaster areas? If the United States extended that kind of help to Puerto Rico its standard of living would be bound to rise. Latin Americans could not fail to take notice. It would also make an impression on the so-called "uncommitted" nations of the world who are skeptical of the good intentions of the United States. This is why in my opinion Puerto Rico is in a position to serve as a bridge between North and South America, provided the United States were able to say to the world: "Look what I've done there!"

Sworn in as a new member of Congress, Badillo soon found an opportunity to assert himself. On February 7, 1971, barely a few weeks after assuming his duties, the *New York Times* reported under the rubric: "No Farmer He" that he had objected so strenuously to his assignment to the House Agricultural Committee to which liberal Democrats are often relegated, that he managed to be reassigned to the Education and Labor Committee, drawing from Wilbur Mills, chairman of the Committee on Committees the statement that "you can quote me in that I made a mistake."[51] The Education and Labor Committee handles the bulk of antipoverty legislation as well as labor and educational measures.

Mr. Badillo is proving that he has no intention to forget the underdogs of society. He has opened up a service center in the heart of the Puerto Rican district in Manhattan to help residents with their problems and has said he plans to open such coordinating service centers in the South Bronx and in Astoria, all three areas forming the twenty-first congressional district from which he was elected.

Also, during the recent Attica prison outbreak he was appointed an "observer" by Governor Rockefeller to study the prison situation. The governor disregarded the recommendation by four "observers" that he come to Attica in person.

What Badillo will be able to achieve in Congress cannot be foretold. But it can be assumed on the basis of existing evidence that he will make a strong effort to implement the program with which he has become identified.

BIBLIOGRAPHY

This bibliography is limited to the volumes the author has found most useful for gathering background material. Many more books and magazine articles were consulted as can be seen from a perusal of the Notes.

Harry Barnard, *Eagle Forgotten* (Indianapolis, 1938).

Robert L. Beisner, *Twelve Against Empire* (New York, 1938).

J. Boorstin, *The Americans: The Colonial Mind* (New York, 1958).

J. Boorstin, *The Americans: The National Experience* (New York, 1965).

Alfred Connable and Edward Silverfarb, *Tigers of Tammany* (New York, 1967).

Louis Filler, *Crusaders for American Liberalism* (Yellow Springs, Ohio, 1961).

Ray Ginger, *Altgeld's America* (New York, 1958).

Nathan Glazer and Daniel Patrick Moynihan, *Beyond the Melting Pot* (Cambridge, Mass., 1963).

Eric F. Goldman, *Rendezvous with Destiny* (New York, 1950).

Earl Parker Hanson, *Ally for Progress* (Princeton, N. J., 1962).

Earl Parker Hanson, *Transformation* (New York, 1955).

Willard A. Heaps, *Riots* (New York, 1956).

Stephen Hess, *American Political Dynasties* (New York, 1966).

Richard Hofstadter, *Social Darwinism in American Thought* (Boston, 1955).

Richard Hofstadter, *The Progressive Movement* (Englewood Cliffs, N. J., 1963).

Richard Hofstadter, *The Age of Reform* (New York, 1965).

James Joll, *The Anarchists* (Boston, 1964).

Maldwyn Allen Jones, *American Immigration* (Chicago, 1960).

Lewis Mumford, *The Brown Decades* (New York, 1931).

Gunther Nollau, *International Communism and World Revolution* (New York, 1961).

Richard O'Connor, *The German-Americans* (Boston, 1968).

John J. O'Neill, *Prodigal Genius* (New York, 1944).

Patrick Renshaw, *The Wobblies* (New York, 1967).

Patricia Cayo Sexton, *Spanish Harlem* (New York, 1965).

Lincoln Steffens, *The Autobiography of Lincoln Steffens* (New York, 1931).

D. B. Steinman, *Builders of the Bridge* (New York, 1945).
Eleanor Tilton, *Amiable Autocrat* (New York, 1947).
Rhoda Truax, *The Doctors Jacobi* (Boston, 1952).
Rhoda Truax, *The Doctors Warren of Boston* (Boston, 1968).
Rexford Guy Tugwell, *The Stricken Land* (New York, 1947).
Oswald Garrison Villard, *Fighting Years* (New York, 1939).
Oswald Garrison Villard, *The Disappearing Daily* (New York, 1944).
Dan Wakefield, *Island in the City* (Boston, 1957).
Raymond Walters, *Albert Gallatin* (New York, 1957).
Carl F. Wittke, *We Who Built America* (New York, 1939).
Carl F. Wittke, *Refugees of the Revolution* (Philadelphia, 1952).
Michael Wreszyn, *Oswald Garrison Villard* (Bloomington, Ind., 1965).

FICTION:

Ole Edvart Rölvaag, *Giants in the Earth* (New York, 1929).
Vilhelm Moberg, *The Emigrants* (New York, 1951).
Vilhelm Moberg, *Unto a Good Land* (New York, 1954).
Vilhelm Moberg, *The Last Letter Home* (New York, 1961).

REFERENCES

Chapter on ALBERT GALLATIN

1. Henry Adams, *The Life of Albert Gallatin* (Philadelphia, 1879), p. 3.

2. Raymond Walters, *Albert Gallatin* (New York, 1957).

3. Henry Adams, *op. cit.*

4. Raymond Walters, *op. cit.*, p. 4.

5. James Joll, *The Anarchists* (Boston, 1964), p. 98.

6. Switzerland has remained a country which despite its small size contributes a high ratio of trained personnel to America. The annual average between 1956 and 1961 was 10.6 percent. See Walter Adams, ed., *The Brain Drain* (New York, 1965), p. 157.

7. James Joll, *op. cit.*, *passim.*

8. In New York State in 1821, in Connecticut in 1818, in Massachusetts in 1820, and even later in the southern states.

9. One who did was James Fenimore Cooper, who produced several novels in which he presented pioneers and Indians as possessing superior moral stature.

10. Carl Schurz, *The Reminiscences of Carl Schurz* (New York, 1907), I, pp. 399-400.

11. Henry Adams, *The Formative Years*, ed. Henry Agar (London, 1948), I, p. 103.

12. *Ibid.*, p. 967.

13. A meeting in 1814 of several New England states opposed to the War of 1812. They pressed for revision of the Constitution and considered secession from the Union or a separate peace with England.

14. Johann August Roebling, *Diary of My Journey* (Trenton, N. J., 1931).

15. Raymond Walters, *op. cit.*, p. 346.

16. *Ibid.*, p. 36.

17. Pennsylvania did not adopt a system of public education until 1834.

18. Henry Adams, *The Life of Albert Gallatin, op. cit.*, p. 299.

19. *The Life of Albert Gallatin* contains some of Gallatin's correspondence.

20. Henry Adams, *The Life of Henry Gallatin, op. cit.*, p. 167.

21. Raymond Walters, *op. cit.*, p. 89.

22. *Ibid.*, p. 90.

23. *Ibid.*, p. 91.

24. *Ibid.*, p. 146.

25. *Ibid.*, p. 154.

26. Henry Adams, *History of the United States* (New York, 1962), I, p. 163.

27. Henry Adams, *The Life of Albert Gallatin, op. cit.*, p. 269.

28. *Ibid.*, p. 470.

29. Raymond Walters, *op. cit.*, p. 231.

30. Henry Adams, *The Life of Albert Gallatin, op. cit.*, p. 392.

31. Henry Adams, *The Formative Years, op. cit.*, p. 535.

32. *Ibid.*, p. 641.

33. Raymond Walters, *op. cit.*, p. 324.

Chapter on JOHANN AUGUST ROEBLING

1. The ten new states were: Kentucky, Tennessee, Ohio, Louisiana, Indiana, Mississippi, Illinois, Alabama, Maine, and Missouri.

2. Ralph Waldo Emerson, "The Young American," in Frederick I. Carpenter, *Ralph Waldo Emerson* (Boston, 1934), p. 153.

3. Cecyle S. Neidle, *The New Americans* (New York, 1967), pp. 93-95.

4. Johann August Roebling, *Diary of My Journey* (Trenton, N. J., 1931).

5. Cecyle S. Neidle, *op. cit.*, pp. 94-95.

6. D. B. Steinman, *Builders of the Bridge* (New York, 1945), p. 33.

7. *Ibid.*, p. 140.

8. *Ibid.*, p. 29.

9. This is the estimate of Lewis Mumford in *The Brown Decades* (New York, 1931).

10. D. B. Steinman, *op. cit.*, p. 275.

11. *Ibid.*, p. 97.

12. *Ibid.*, p. 165.

13. *Ibid.*, p. 179.

14. *Ibid.*, pp. 168, 175, 265.

15. Charles B. Stuart, *Lives and Works of Civil and Military Engineers of America* (Princeton, N. J., 1871), p. 309.

16. D. B. Steinman, *op. cit.*, p. 248.

17. *Ibid.*, p. 397.

18. C. Hall Sipe, *History of Butler County, Pennsylvania* (Topeka, Ind., 1927), p. 409.

19. Lewis Mumford, *op. cit.*, pp. 104-5.

20. D. B. Steinman, *op. cit.*, p. 387.

21. *Ibid.*, p. 364.

Chapter on JOHN PETER ALTGELD

1. Edward McNall Burns, *Western Civilizations* (New York, 1958), p. 654.

2. Samuel D. Orth, *Our Foreigners* (New Haven, Conn., 1920), pp. 129-30.

3. Gustav Koerner, *Memoirs of Gustav Koerner* (Cedar Rapids, Iowa, 1909).

4. Oscar Ameringer, *If You Don't Weaken* (New York, 1940).

5. These states were: Iowa, Wisconsin, California, Minnesota, Oregon, and Kansas.

6. *Encyclopedia of American History*, ed. Richard B. Morris (New York, 1953), p. 632.

7. Richard O'Connor, *The German Americans* (Boston, 1968).

8. Howard Fast, *The American: A Middle Western Legend* (New York, 1946), p. 172.

9. *Ibid.*, p. 283.

10. Harry Barnard, *Eagle Forgotten* (Indianapolis, 1938), p. 19.

11. Stephen Hess, *American Political Dynasties* (Garden City, N. Y., 1966), pp. 123-42.

12. Harry Barnard, *op. cit.*, p. 27.

13. Ray Ginger, *Altgeld's America* (New York, 1958) p. 61.

14. *Ibid.*, p. 8.

15. Edgar Lee Masters, "John Peter Altgeld," *American Mercury*, IV (February, 1929).

16. Harry Barnard, *op. cit.*, p. 415.

17. *Ibid.*, p. 421.

18. John Peter Altgeld, *Our Penal Machinery and Its Victims* (Chicago, 1884), p. 37.

19. Alexander Berkman, *Prison Memoirs of an Anarchist* (New York, 1912).

20. McAlister Colman, *Eugene V. Debs* (New York, 1930), p. 129.

21. Harry Barnard, *op. cit.*, p. 134.

22. Ray Ginger, *Six Days or Forever* (Boston, 1958).

23. *Ibid.*, p. 77.

24. Harry Barnard, *op. cit.*, p. 237.

25. *Ibid.*, pp. 248-49.

26. *Ibid.*, p. 240.

27. Edgar Lee Masters, *op. cit.*, pp. 163-64.

28. Waldo R. Browne, *Altgeld of Illinois* (New York, 1924), p. 135.

29. *Ibid.*, p. 172.

30. Harry Barnard, *op. cit.*, p. 361.

31. Edgar Lee Masters, *op. cit.*

Chapter on ABRAHAM JACOBI

1. Maldwyn Allen Jones, *American Immigration* (Chicago, 1960), p. 129.

2. Bernard Jaffe, *Men of Science* (New York, 1958), p. 17.

3. William Bradford, *History of Plymouth Plantation* (New York, 1958).

4. Bernard Jaffe, *op. cit.*, p. 17.

5. Daniel J. Boorstin, *The Americans* (New York, 1958).

6. *Ibid.*

7. Francis R. Packard, *History of Medicine in the United States* (New York, 1963), II, 952.

8. Daniel J. Boorstin, *op. cit.*

9. Francis R. Packard, *op. cit.*, I, 737-821, *passim*.

10. *Encyclopedia of American History*, ed. Richard B. Morris (New York, 1953), p. 544.

11. Eleanor M. Tilton, *Amiable Autocrat* (New York, 1947), pp. 72-73.

12. Gay Wilson Allen, *William James* (New York, 1967), p. 158.

13. John Allen Wyeth, *With Sabre and Scalpel* (New York, 1914), pp. 327-28.

14. Eleanor M. Tilton, *op. cit.*

15. Quoted by F. H. Garrison, "Abraham Jacobi," *Annals of Medical History* (1919), II, 199.

16. Willard A. Heaps, *Riots, U.S.A.* (New York, 1956), p. 29.

17. Eleanor M. Tilton, *op. cit.*, p. 107.

18. Willard A. Heaps, *op. cit.*, p. 29.

19. Rhoda Truax, *The Doctors Jacobi* (Boston, 1952), p. 213.

20. F. H. Garrison, *op. cit.*, p. 198.

21. Oswald Garrison Villard, *Nation,* CIX (July, 1919).

22. F. H. Garrison, *op. cit.*, p. 201.

23. Such an experience is described by Samuel Gompers in *Seventy Years of Life and Labor*. Gompers relates he had to threaten violence before the physician would come to attend his wife who was in labor. *Seventy Years of Life and Labor* (New York, 1925).

24. Arpad Charles Gerster, *Recollections of a New York Surgeon* (New York, 1917), p. 198.

25. Hans Zinsser, *As I Remember Him* (Boston, 1940).

26. Rhoda Truax, *op. cit.*

27. It seems to have been only five years since Dr. Jacobi arrived in America in 1853.

28. Rhoda Truax, *op. cit.*, p. 268.

29. *Ibid.*, p. 246.

30. This article is included in *Care and Treatment of Children and Their Diseases* (Boston, 1881).

31. Rhoda Truax, *op. cit.*, p. 213.

32. *Ibid.*, p. 132.

33. Cecilia C. Mettler, *History of Medicine* (Philadelphia, 1947), p. 764.

34. Abraham Jacobi, *In Memory of Ernst Krackowizer* (New York, 1875).

35. F. H. Garrison, *op. cit.*, p. 195.

36. W. A. Swanberg, *Joseph Pulitzer* (New York, 1967), p. 26.

37. F. H. Garrison, *op. cit.*, p. 198.

38. Walter Damrosch, *My Musical Life* (New York, 1926), p. 260.

39. F. H. Garrison, *op. cit.*

40. *Ibid.*, p. 195.

Chapter on EDWIN LAWRENCE GODKIN

1. Carl Schurz, *The Reminiscences of Carl Schurz* (New York, 1907), II, 37.

2. Cecyle S. Neidle, *The New Americans* (New York, 1967), pp. 101-3.

3. Frances Trollope, *Domestic Manners of the Americans* (New York, 1960), p. 311.

4. Rollo Ogden, *Life and Letters of Edwin Lawrence Godkin* (New York, 1907), I, 140.

5. Oswald Garrison Villard, *The Disappearing Daily* (New York, 1944).

6. James Ford Rhodes, "Edwin Lawrence Godkin," *Atlantic Monthly*, CII, 1908.

7. Rollo Ogden, *op. cit.*, I, 129-30.

8. *Ibid.*, pp. 153-54.

9. *Ibid.*, p. 73.

10. *Ibid.*, pp. 210-11.

11. Oswald Garrison Villard, *op. cit.*, p. 75.

12. Robert L. Beisner, *Twelve Against Empire* (New York, 1968), p. 56.

13. Oswald Garrison Villard, *Fighting Years* (New York, 1939), p. 139.

14. Harold W. Stoke, "Edwin Lawrence Godkin," *South Atlantic Quarterly*, XXX (October, 1931).

15. David Donald, *Charles Sumner and the Rights of Man* (New York, 1970), pp. 228, 234.

16. *Ibid.*, p. 228.

17. Rollo Ogden, *op. cit.*, I, 302.

18. Oswald Garrison Villard, *Fighting Years, op. cit.*, p. 120.

19. Harry Barnard, *Eagle Forgotten* (Indianapolis, 1938), p. 247.

20. W. A. Swanberg, *Pulitzer* (New York, 1967), p. 103.

21. *Ibid.*, p. 292.

22. Andrew J. Carnegie, *The Autobiography of Andrew Carnegie* (Boston, 1920), p. 132.

23. Henry Villard, *The Memoirs of Henry Villard* (Boston, 1916).

24. Harold W. Stoke, *op. cit.*, p. 340.

25. The facts about Tammany Hall were taken from: Alfred Connable and Edward Silverfarb, *Tigers of Tammany* (New York, 1967), p. 170, *passim.*

26. Rollo Ogden, *op. cit.*, II, 237.

27. *Ibid.*, I, 221.

Chapter on JOHANN MOST

1. Ferdinand Schevill, *A History of Europe* (New York, 1925), pp. 563-64.

2. Günther Nollau, *International Communism and World Revolution* (New York, 1961), p. 17.

3. Hector St. John de Crèvecoeur, *Letters From an American Farmer* (London, 1912).

4. W.E.B. Du Bois, *The Autobiography of W.E.B. Du Bois* (New York, 1968).

5. Andrew Carnegie, *The Autobiography of Andrew Carnegie* (Boston, 1920).

6. Andrew Carnegie, "The Gospel of Wealth," *North American Review*, 1889, p. 12.

7. *Commonwealth versus Hunt.*

8. Lewis Mumford, *The Brown Decades* (New York, 1931).

9. The law was repealed in 1885 through the pressure of organized labor.

10. Carman, Syrett and Wishy, *A History of the American People* (New York, 1961).

11. Illegitimacy seems to have been a factor that predisposed young people towards anarchism, for several prominent anarchists were of illegitimate birth.

12. Emma Goldman, "Johann Most," *American Mercury* (June, 1926), VIII.

13. Johann Most, *Memoiren* (New York, 1903), I.

14. Berkman received a sentence of twenty-two years for the attempted murder of Henry Clay Frick, which was commuted for good behavior to twelve years and ten months and one additional year in the workhouse. See Cecyle S. Neidle, *The New Americans* (New York, 1967), pp. 197-201.

15. Emma Goldman, *op. cit.*, p. 162.

16. Max Nomad, *Apostles of the Revolution* (London, 1939).

17. Isaiah Berlin, *New York Review of Books*, March 14, 1968, p. 13.

18. Emma Goldman, *Living My Life* (New York, 1931).

19. Johann Most, *op. cit.*

20. Max Nomad, *op. cit.*

21. Rudolf Rocker, *Das Leben eines Rebellen* (Berlin, 1924).

22. Emma Goldman, *American Mercury, op. cit.*

23. Henry David, *History of the Haymarket Affair* (New York, 1936), p. 93.

24. Louis Adamic, *Dynamite* (New York, 1931), p. 46.

25. See W. A. Swanberg, *Pulitzer* (New York, 1967).

26. Max Nomad, *op. cit.*, p. 286.

27. Henry David, *op. cit.*, p. 522.

28. Max Nomad, *op. cit.*, p. 289.

29. *Chicago Tribune*, May 8, 1886. I am obliged to Professor Arlow Andersen of Michigan State University for this quotation.

30. Three of nine verses printed in the *Washington Star*. Reprinted in the *Chicago Tribune*. Sent to the author by Professor Arlow Andersen of Michigan State University.

31. Rudolf Rocker, *op. cit.*, Introduction.

32. Emma Goldman, *Living My Life, op. cit.*

33. Max Nomad, *op. cit.*, p. 297.

34. W. A. Swanberg, *op. cit.*, pp. 281-82.

35. Morris Hillquit, *Loose Leaves From A Busy Life* (New York, 1934).

36. Rudolf Rocker, *op. cit.*

37. Morris Hillquit, *op. cit.*, p. 121.

38. *Ibid.*, p. 127.

39. Patrick Renshaw, *The Wobblies* (Garden City, N. Y., 1967), *passim.*

Chapter on NIKOLA TESLA

1. Ferdinand Schevill, *A History of Europe* (New York, 1925), p. 629.

2. Louis Adamic, *Laughing in the Jungle* (New York, 1932).

3. *Ibid.*

4. Carl Van Doren, *Benjamin Franklin* (New York, 1935).

5. Michael Pupin, *From Immigrant to Inventor* (New York, 1923), p. 272.

6. Bernard Jaffe, *Men of Science in America* (New York, 1958), p. 190.

7. *Ibid.*, pp. 185-89.

8. *Ibid.*, p. 197.

9. *Ibid.*, p. 195.

10. *Ibid.*, pp. 588-89.

11. Ishbel Ross, *Crusades and Crinolines* (New York, 1963), p. 201.

12. Kenneth O. Bjork, *In the Trek of Immigrants* (Rock Island, Ill., 1964), p. 128.

13. Michael Pupin, *op. cit.*, p. 339.

14. Inez Hunt and Wanetta W. Draper, *Lightning in His Hand* (Denver, 1940), p. 74.

15. John J. O'Neill, *Prodigal Genius* (New York, 1944), pp. 164-65.

16. Inez Hunt and Wanetta W. Draper, *op. cit.*, p. 88.

17. Nikola Tesla, "My Inventions," *Electrical Engineering*, April, 1919, p. 907.

18. Inez Hunt and Wanetta W. Draper, *op. cit.*, p. 88.

19. Nikola Tesla, *op. cit.*, February, 1919, p. 143.

20. Inez Hunt and Wanetta W. Draper, *op. cit.*, p. 39.

21. Matthew Josephson, *Edison* (New York, 1950), p. 233.

22. John J. O'Neill, *op. cit.*, p. 208.

23. *Ibid.*, p. 64.

24. Inez Hunt and Wanetta W. Draper, *op. cit.*, p. 44.

25. Andrew Carnegie, *The Autobiography of Andrew Carnegie* (Boston, 1920).

26. John J. O'Neill, *op. cit.*, p. 68.

27. The phrase is used by Inez Hunt and Wanetta W. Draper, *op. cit.*

28. *Ibid.*, p. 48.

29. *Ibid.*, p. 49.

30. The phrase is used by Arthur J. Beckhard, *Electrical Genius* (New York, 1959).

31. John J. O'Neill, *op. cit.*, p. 81.

32. Nikola Tesla, *op. cit.*, May, 1919, p. 64.

33. Ray Ginger, *Altgeld's America* (New York, 1958), p. 20.

34. John J. O'Neill, *op. cit.*, p. 103.

35. *Ibid.*, p. 105.

36. *Ibid.*, p. 108.

37. *Ibid.*, p. 107.

38. Robert Underwood Johnson, *Remembered Yesterdays* (New York, 1923).

39. John J. O'Neill, *op. cit.*, p. 123.

40. *Ibid.*, p. 165.

41. *Ibid.*, p. 175.

42. The whole experiment is reported by John J. O'Neill, *op. cit.*, pp. 170-75.

43. Nikola Tesla, "The Problem of Increasing Human Energy," *Century Magazine*, June, 1900, pp. 175-211.

44. John J. O'Neill, *op. cit.*, p. 198.

45. Inez Hunt and Wanetta W. Draper, *op. cit.*, p. 146.

46. John J. O'Neill, *op. cit.*, p. 211.

47. Inez Hunt and Wanetta W. Draper, *op. cit.*, p. 150.

48. *Ibid.*, p. 154.

49. John J. O'Neill, *op. cit.*, p. 214.

50. *Ibid.*, p. 226.

51. *Ibid.*, p. 228.

52. Inez Hunt and Wanetta W. Draper, *op. cit.*, p. 229.

53. B. A. Behrend frequently came to his rescue by redeeming his possessions which were being held as security against unpaid rent.

54. *Ibid.*, pp. 316-17. Tesla's feelings about the pigeon were similar to those of the English writer, T. H. White, about whom Walter Allen remarked: "He was only once . . . able to unleash his capacity for love—for Brownie, his red setter bitch. She died in his absence. He sat up with her corpse for two days and then went to Dublin where he kept himself as drunk as possible for nine days." Walter Allen, *New York Times Book Review*, April 21, 1968, p. 1.

55. Nikola Tesla, "My Inventions," *op. cit.*, February, 1919.

56. Inez Hunt and Wanetta W. Draper, *op. cit.*, p. 107.

57. John J. O'Neill, *op. cit.*, p. 239.

58. Inez Hunt and Wanetta W. Draper, *op. cit.*, p. 239.

Chapter on ANTON JULIUS CARLSON

1. See Vilhelm Moberg, *The Emigrants* (New York, 1951).

2. Carl F. Wittke, *We Who Built America* (New York, 1964).

3. See Cecyle S. Neidle, *The New Americans* (New York, 1967), p. 75.

4. Carl F. Wittke, *op. cit.*, p. 272.

5. See Cecyle S. Neidle, *op. cit.*, p. 28.

6. An example is Laurence M. Larson, *The Log Book of a Young Immigrant* (Northfield, Minn., 1939).

7. Carl F. Wittke, *op. cit.*

8. Michael Pupin, *From Immigrant to Inventor* (New York, 1923).

9. M. Cunningham, Jr., and Greer Williams, "The Man Who Understands Your Stomach," *Saturday Evening Post*, September 13, 1947.

10. Letter from Dr. A. C. Ivy, dated June 14, 1967.

11. Lester R. Dragstedt, *Biographical Memoirs*, The National Academy of Sciences, XXXV.

12. Lester R. Dragstedt, "An American by Choice," *Perspectives in Biology and Medicine*, VII (Winter, 1964).

13. Excerpt supplied by Dr. Dragstedt, Research Professor of Surgery, the University of Florida, Gainesville, Florida.

14. Lester R. Dragstedt, "An American by Choice, *op. cit.*

15. *Ibid.*

16. M. Cunningham, Jr., and Greer Williams, *op. cit.*

17. Ray Ginger, *Six Days or Forever* (Boston, 1958), p. 56.

18. Letter from Dr. Dragstedt, dated January 31, 1967.

19. A German custom intended to honor the recipient by means of a presentation of testimonials from colleagues, giving evidence of the esteem in which the recipient is held. The *Festschrift* given to Dr. Carlson was made available to the author by Dr. Joseph Hirsh, Professor of Community Medicine, Temple University School of Medicine, Philadelphia, Pennsylvania.

20. A. C. Ivy, "Anton Julius Carlson," *The Physiologist,* II (May, 1959).

21. *Ibid.*

22. *Ibid.*

23. Hans Zinsser, *As I Remember Him* (Boston, 1940), p. 203.

24. A. C. Ivy, "Anton Julius Carlson," *op. cit.*

25. University of Chicago Magazine (March, 1942).

26. Daniel J. Boorstin, *The Americans* (New York, 1958), p. 58.

27. Lester R. Dragstedt, "An American by Choice," *op. cit.*

28. The facts on alcoholism were supplied by Dr. Joseph Hirsh.

29. *Chicago Daily Tribune,* June 9, 1953.

30. *Ibid.*

31. Letter from Dr. Ivy, dated June 5, 1967.

32. Letter from Dr. Ivy, dated June 14, 1967.

33. Letter from A. Baird Hastings, Department of Biological Chemistry, Harvard University, dated January 29, 1950.

Chapter on OLE EDVART RÖLVAAG

1. Ole Rynning, *A True Account of America for the Information and Help of Peasant and Commoner* (Christiania, 1838). See also Cecyle S. Neidle, *The New Americans* (New York, 1967), pp. 101-3.

2. See Laurence M. Larson, *The Log Book of a Young Immigrant* (Northfield, Minn., 1939).

3. *Ibid.*

4. Francis J. Brown and Joseph S. Roucek, *One America* (New York, 1952), p. 67.

5. Johann Bojer, *The Emigrants* (New York, 1925).

6. Vilhelm Moberg, *The Emigrants* (New York, 1951); *Unto a Good Land* (New York, 1954); *The Last Letter Home* (New York, 1961).

7. Later ambassador to Iceland.

8. Theodor Jorgenson and Nora O. Solum, *Ole Edvart Rölvaag* (New York, 1939), p. 94.

9. Ole Edvart Rölvaag, *Giants in the Earth* (New York, 1927), p. xiv.

10. *Ibid.*

11. Michael Pupin, *From Immigrant to Inventor* (New York, 1923).

12. Henry Villard, *The Memoirs of Henry Villard* (Boston, 1916).

13. Theodor Jorgenson, quoted, *op. cit.*, pp. 45-46.

14. *Ibid.*, p. 49.

15. Einar I. Haugen, *Ole Edvart Rölvaag*, Norwegian-American Studies and Records, VII, 1933.

16. Theodor Jorgenson, *op. cit.*, p. 90.

17. *Ibid.*, p. 100.

18. Johan Bojer, *The Emigrants*, *op. cit.*, p. 351.

19. Leonard Covello, *The Heart is the Teacher* (New York, 1958), p. 167.

20. Theodor Jorgenson, quoted, *op. cit.*, p. 115.

21. Suggested by Theodor Jorgenson.

22. *Ibid.*, quoted, p. 163.

23. Einar I. Haugen, *op. cit.*

24. Ole Edvart Rölvaag, *Their Fathers' God* (New York, 1931).

25. Theodor Jorgenson, *op. cit.*, p. 230.

26. *Ibid.*, p. 330.

27. Marcus L. Hansen, *The Immigrant in American History* (Cambridge, Mass., 1948).

28. Einar I. Haugen, *op. cit.*, pp. 53-73.

29. *Genesis.* "There were giants in the earth in those days."

30. I am indebted for this information to Professor Kenneth O. Bjork, Saint Olaf College, Northfield, Minnesota.

31. Hector St. John de Crèvecoeur, *Letters From an American Farmer* (London, 1912), p. 43.

32. Ole Edvart Rölvaag, *Their Fathers' God, op. cit.*, p. 207.

33. Theodor Jorgenson, quoted, *op. cit.*

Chapter on SELMAN ABRAHAM WAKSMAN

1. Marie Waife-Goldberg, *My Father, Sholom Aleichem* (New York, 1968), p. 126.

2. Selman A. Waksman, *My Life with the Microbes* (New York, 1954), p. 52.

3. Selman A. Waksman, Autobiographical Sketch, *Perspectives in Biology and Medicine*, VII (Summer, 1964), 38.

4. Bernard Jaffe, *Men of Science in America* (New York, 1958).

5. Geraldine Joncigh, "Scientists and the Schools of the Nineteenth Century," *American Quarterly*, XVIII (Winter, 1966).

6. Isaac Babel, "The Story of My Dovecote," *Great Jewish Short Stories*, ed. Saul Bellows (New York, 1963).

7. Selman A. Waksman, *My Life with the Microbes, op. cit.*, p. 74.

8. *Ibid.*, p. 201.

9. *Ibid.*, p. 162.

10. *Ibid.*, p. 201.

11. *Ibid.*, p. 201.

12. *Ibid.*, p. 202.

13. *Ibid.*, p. 231.

14. Selman A. Waksman, Autobiographical Sketch, *op. cit.*

15. Selman A. Waksman, *My Life with the Microbes, op. cit.*, pp. 282-83.

16. *Ibid.*, p. 284.

17. *Ibid.*, p. 284.

18. *Ibid.*, p. 356.

Chapter on DAVID DUBINSKY

1. Max D. Danish, *The World of David Dubinsky* (Cleveland, 1957), p. 26.

2. Marie Waife-Goldberg, *My Father, Sholom Aleichem* (New York, 1968), p. 167.

3. Marcus E. Ravage, *An American in the Making* (New York, 1917).

4. Mary Antin, *The Promised Land* (Boston, 1912).

5. Harold Frederic, *The New Exodus, A Study of Israel in Russia* (London, 1892).

6. Lincoln Steffens, *The Autobiography of Lincoln Steffens* (New York, 1931), p. 244.

7. Marie Waife-Goldberg, *op. cit.*, p. 158.

8. Harold Frederic, *op. cit.*, p. 296.

9. Quoted by Samuel Chotzinoff, *A Little Night Music* (New York, 1962), p. 39.

10. Richard Hofstadter, *Social Darwinism in American Thought* (Boston, 1955), p. 44.

11. Benjamin Stolberg, *Tailor's Progress* (New York, 1944), p. 4.

12. *Ibid.*, p. 10.

13. *Ibid.*, p. 9.

14. See Morris Hillquit, *Loose Leaves From a Busy Life* (New York, 1934).

15. Lincoln Steffens, *op. cit.*, p. 208.

16. Sol Liptzin, *The Jew in American Literature* (New York, 1960), p. 121.

17. Benjamin Stolberg, *op. cit.*, p. 67.

18. Interview with Mr. Dubinsky.

19. *Ibid.*

20. *Ibid.*

21. Leon Stein, *The Triangle Fire* (Philadelphia, 1960).

22. Benjamin Antin, *The Man From 22nd* (New York, 1927).

23. Benjamin Stolberg, *op. cit.,* pp. 207-8.

24. Nathan Glazer and Danial Patrick Moynihan, *Beyond the Melting Pot* (Cambridge, Mass., 1963), pp. 155-58.

25. Morris Hillquit, *op. cit.*

26. Benjamin Stolberg, *op. cit.,* p. 85.

27. Interview with Mr. Dubinsky.

28. *Ibid.*

29. Samuel Gompers, *Seventy Years of Life and Labor* (New York, 1925).

30. *Ibid.,* II, 37.

31. Interview with Mr. Dubinsky.

32. John Dewey, *David Dubinsky* (New York, 1951), p. 24.

33. Interview with Mr. Dubinsky.

34. *Ibid.*

35. Max D. Danish, *op. cit.,* pp. 54-55.

36. Benjamin Stolberg, *op. cit.,* p. 137.

37. Max D. Danish, *op. cit.,* p. 51.

38. Benjamin Stolberg, *op. cit.,* p. 148.

39. *Ibid.,* p. 151.

40. Interview with Mr. Dubinsky.

41. Benjamin Stolberg, *op. cit.,* p. 152.

42. Interview with Mr. Dubinsky.

43. *Ibid.*

44. Benjamin Stolberg, *op. cit.,* p. 213.

45. *Ibid.,* p. 339.

46. *Ibid.,* p. 207.

47. Max D. Danish, *op. cit.,* p. 121.

48. *Ibid.,* p. 166.

49. Benjamin Stolberg, *op. cit.,* p. 344.

50. Interview with Mr. Dubinsky.

51. Max D. Danish, *op. cit.,* p. 211.

52. William Weinstone, *The Case against David Dubinsky* (New York, 1946).

53. *Justice,* XXXIX (June 15, 1957).

54. Max D. Danish, *op. cit.,* pp. 298-301, *passim.*

55. *Justice, op. cit.*

56. Max D. Danish, *op. cit.,* p. 217.

57. *Ibid.,* p. 221.

58. Interview with Leon Stein, editor of *Justice.*

59. Max D. Danish, *op. cit.,* p. 216.

60. *Ibid.*, p. 307.
61. Benjamin Stolberg, *op. cit.*, p. 239.

Chapter on HERMAN BADILLO

1. Earl Parker Hanson, *Puerto Rico: Ally for Progress* (Princeton, N. J., 1962), p. 11.
2. The term is Earle Parker Hanson's.
3. Ruth Gruber, *Puerto Rico: Island of Promise* (New York, 1960), p. 139.
4. *Ibid.*, p. 123.
5. Earl Parker Hanson, *op. cit.*, p. 61.
6. *Ibid.*, p. 14.
7. *Ibid.*
8. Rexford Guy Tugwell, *The Stricken Land* (Garden City, N. Y., 1947), p. 362.
9. Earl Parker Hanson, *op. cit.*, pp. 61-62.
10. Rexford G. Tugwell, *op. cit.*, p. 10.
11. Earl Parker Hanson, *op. cit.*, p. 247.
12. Homer Page, *The Quiet Revolution* (New York, 1963), p. 165.
13. Ralph Hancock, *Puerto Rico: A Success Story* (Princeton, N. J., 1960), p. 143.
14. Ruth Gruber, *op. cit.*, p. 68.
15. Earl Parker Hanson, *Transformation* (New York, 1955), p. 402.
16. Earl Parker Hanson, *Ally for Progress, op. cit.*, p. 92.
17. Rexford G. Tugwell, *op. cit.*, p. 126.
18. Homer Page, *op. cit.*, p. 123.
19. Theodore Brameld, *The Remaking of a Culture* (New York, 1959), p. 12.
20. Rexford G. Tugwell, *op. cit.*
21. Ruth Gruber, *op. cit.*, p. 13.
22. Interview with Joseph Monserrat.
23. Patricia Cayo Sexton, *Spanish Harlem* (New York, 1965), p. 15.
24. Joseph Monserrat, pamphlet.
25. Dan Wakefield, *Island in the City* (Boston, 1957), p. 38.
26. C. Wright Mills, Clarence Senior, Rose Kohn Goldsen (New York, 1950), p. 25.
27. *Ibid.*, p. 32.
28. Patricia Cayo Sexton, *op. cit.*, p. 35.
26. C. Wright Mills, Clarence Senior, and Rose Kohn Goldsen (New *op. cit.*, p. 27.
30. The phrase is Ralph Hancock's in *A Success Story*.
31. Joseph Monserrat, pamphlet.
32. C. Wright Mills, Clarence Senior, and Rose Kohn Goldsen, *op. cit.*, p. 87.

33. Piri Thomas, *Down These Mean Streets* (New York, 1967).

34. Woody Klein, *Let In The Sun* (New York, 1963), p. 40.

35. Patricia Cayo Sexton, *op. cit.*, pp. 29-31.

36. Piri Thomas, *op. cit.*, p. 14.

37. Patricia Cayo Sexton, *op. cit.*, p. 180.

38. Woody Klein, *op. cit.*

39. Joseph Monserrat, pamphlet.

40. Patricia Cayo Sexton, *op. cit.*, p. 51.

41. Dan Wakefield, *op. cit.*, pp. 195-96.

42. Piri Thomas, *op. cit.*, p. 42.

43. Joseph Monserrat, pamphlet, "Integration in the Urban School."

44. Martin Gumpert, *First Papers* (New York, 1941).

45. C. Wright Mills, Clarence Senior, and Rose Kohn Goldsen, *op. cit.*, p. 167.

46. *New York Times,* December 6, 1970, p. 51.

47. *Ibid.*, August 11, 1971, p. 19.

48. *New York Post,* June 17, 1970.

49. Personal interview.

50. *New York Times,* October 4, 1970.

51. *Ibid.*, February 7, 1971.

Index

Adamic, Louis, 35, 141
Adams, Henry, 7, 9, 13, 16, 18, 19, 20
Adams, John Quincy, 7, 25, 26
Alexander I, 24
Alexander II, 12, 223
ALTGELD, JOHN PETER, 43-65, 101, 229
Arthur, Chester A., 41
Astor, John Jacob, 20, 21, 46, 154

Babel, Isaac, 209
BADILLO, HERMAN, 245-74
Bakunin, Mikhail, 120, 121, 229
Barondess, Joseph, 226
Beaumont, William, 178
Bebel, August, 109
Behrend, B. A., 157
Bell, Alexander Graham, 139
Berkman, Alexander, 110, 118, 122, 126
Berle, Adolph A., 238
Bismarck, Otto von, 108, 109, 119
Bland, Richard, "Silver Dick," 63
Bojer, Johann, 186, 190, 192, 196, 197
Bok, Edward, 93
Boylston, Zabdiel, 70, 82
Brandeis, Louis Dembitz, 227
Bryan, William Jennings, 63, 64
"Bund," 233

Calvin, Jean, 1, 2, 3
Carnegie, Andrew, 112, 147, 259
CARLSON, ANTON JULIUS, 163-80
Childs, George L., 238
Clay, Henry, 26
Cleveland, Grover S., 48, 59, 61, 62, 63, 101, 103, 206
Colcord, Lincoln, 188, 198
Colt, Samuel, 138

Cooke, Jay, 166
Counts, George, 238
Covello, Leonard, 193
Czolgozs, Leon, 129

Darrow, Clarence, 57, 59, 64, 65, 173
Debs, Eugene V., 55, 61
De Sapio, 268
Dewey, John, 233
Dragstedt, Charles, 172
Dragstedt, Dr. Lester, 174, 176
DUBINSKY, DAVID, 221-43
Dubos, Rene, 215

Edison, Thomas Alva, 138, 145, 146, 147, 151, 157
Ellet, Charles, 33, 35
Emerson, Ralph Waldo, 26, 98

Fermi, Enrico, 139, 140
Five Hundred Acre Law, 250, 251
Flexner, Abraham, 72
Franklin, Benjamin, 138
Frederic, Harold, 22, 224
Fuller, Margaret, 68

GALLATIN, ALBERT, 2-22
Garrison, William Lloyd, 101
Germanic Confederation, 24, 108, 223
Girard, Stephen, 20, 21
GODKIN, EDWIN LAWRENCE, 61, 89-106
Goldman, Emma, 114, 118, 123, 126, 128, 130
Gompers, Samuel, 232, 233, 238, 246
Goodyear, Charles, 138
Granger Revolt, 51

Halstead, Byron, 212

[293]